TWO MILES TO TYNECASTLE

TWO MILES TO TYNECASTLE

ANDREW-HENRY BOWIE

APEX PUBLISHING LTD

First published in 2008 by
Apex Publishing Ltd
PO Box 7086, Clacton on Sea, Essex, CO15 5WN

www.apexpublishing.co.uk

British Library Cataloguing-in-Publication Data
A catalogue record for this book
is available from the British Library

ISBN 1-906358-18-4   978-1-906358-18-1

Typeset in 10pt Times New Roman

Production Manager: Chris Cowlin

Cover Design: Andrew Macey

Printed and bound in Great Britain
By Biddles Ltd., Kings Lynn

The author has his own website: www.AndrewHenryBowie.co.uk

In memory of Allan, 1974-2003

Preface

28th June 2006

Opens new Word document

So, today is a hot Wednesday and I'm at home in Edinburgh; not long in from work. A short while ago, my wife Lesley walked through the front door with two pregnancy-testing kits. Within about two minutes, the first one was flashing 'pregnant'. The second test said pretty much the same as the first and that was an hour ago now. I thought about heading to Tesco to buy a third kit, and maybe this time I'd pee on it myself. Otherwise, the first gift I have for my unborn child is this book.

This is the book of my life, and man has my life just changed! Whoever pops out in a little under nine months, I promise to love him or her forever. This book is dedicated and written for you (although I'll be making you wait a few years before you can read it). I would also like to devote these pages to my brother, Robert James Bowie, and my dear friends Lewis Thompson and Kevin English; all of whom encouraged me to write in the first place. Indeed, it was Kevin who suggested that Brian Blessed do the audio version of the book; perhaps hinting at his expectation of what sort of story lies ahead. But most of all, I'd like to offer this humble publication to my beautiful wife Lesley, who has put up with me typing away like Jack Nicholson in The Shining. Without her, I'd be nothing but a bum.

Acknowledgements

Before I started writing this book, I knew I had to try encapsulate the passion and the deep-rooted love that I have for Heart of Midlothian FC. I hope I succeeded. I tried to balance the Hearts content with the non-Hearts content; after discovering that there really are only so many ways to describe celebrating a goal! It was quite emotional remembering the old games, but I think it was the memories surrounding them, and the feelings involving them that gave each story its soul. Sometimes, I'd lie awake at night (as a hopeless insomniac) and think of an idea. Usually things were written on my hand, or on ripped pieces of paper. I also wanted to share my experiences with people, in order to feel comfortable writing about them. I feel bad for all the times I left Les sitting on the sofa, as I'd be hammering away at my lap-top, writing about stuff that happened twenty-five years ago. I'm lucky to have one of those anorak memories for dates, and Borthers was always on hand for grammatical assistance.

To find the photograph, I went round to my mum's house, and spent hours in the attic, just as I had done all those years ago holding the Argos punch bag steady for Bobby. It's like the Museum of Childhood up there, but I never did find that bastard 1982 World Cup sticker book!

There were places I'd go for inspiration for the book. I went back to the States via Toronto in the summer of 2006, and there I met up with Gary 'Hereward' and Ron 'Maple Leaf' from JambosKickback, and they gave me the encouragement and counsel that I needed at a difficult stage in the book. Sometimes I'd walk along the Water of Leith, bouncing ideas off (poor) Les. It's not an attractive river, but it has a sort of intrinsic charm. It takes about three hours to get to Leith from my house in Corstorphine. Similarly, we'd sometimes go to Almondell; where again, I'd think about the book, and ask Les her opinion, as the bridges criss-cross the river. I love the walk too, that runs along Braidburn Valley, from Greenbank to Liberton.

All these places gave me time to think and time to angst. I'm writing this sentence in my favourite seat, at the top of the stairs by the Paolozzi picture, at Starbucks in Stockbridge.

The walk here, by the river gave me more time to think. Whether I wandered alone, or talked to Les, the entire process involved me worrying over every last detail of the book's content, which inadvertently turned Les into a counsellor and a psychologist. For that I am grateful and the therapy is now over. From Roseburn to Dean Village, from Stockbridge to Cannonmills and onto Powderhall, where I'd imagine the Hearts and Hibs fans of the 1896 Scottish Cup Final; to Newhaven and finally to Leith, and the old restaurant boat where I washed dishes for two miserable nights all those years ago. It's good talking to Les, and there the river ends, all gone out to sea.

The following people provided me with help, advice and encouragement during the writing of my book. I would also like to thank people for being such good friends to me over the years, and putting up with me!

Callum Eadie, Mableann Fraser, Alison Mitchell, Ray French @movingstills, Nelson & Pricilla Fernandes, Ross Brown, Scott Moore, Bertha Molet, Jamie 'Borthers' Borthwick, Nigel Smith, Ron Butlin, Paul Hartman, Rennie and Maria Robertson, Steve Jones, Mike Smith, Gary 'Hereward', Ron 'Maple Leaf', Anne Sutherland, Murray Lyons, Colin Roe, Shona & SJ, Lewis Thompson, Kevin English, Scotty Forsyth, Dale 'the laugh' Irvine, David Gilbert, Paul Aylott, Jonny Yeoman, Scott Reilly, Kieran McLachlan, Stuart Connelly, Gavin Teesdale, Laura Johnson, Melvin Hart, Jackie Murphy, Tricia Lamb, Damien Burakowski, Paddy and Joe Barry, Jamie Stobie, Chris Moffat, Paul Jamieson, Michael Burns, Panda, Paul Laird, Bob Laird, Simon Laird, Mark Fairbairn, Will Page, Tom Page, Graeme Baxter (big time thanks), Sean Japp, Cat Young, 'Auld Jock', Pete Therapist, Andy 'Ahmed', Ian Porterfield, Sir James, Barbara Young, Jonny Marshall, Mr Cunningham, Gail Stevenson, Helen Garton, 'Boris', 'Portobello Jambo', Colin J.M Barrett, all @ The Diggers Bar, Scott Hughes, DD, Derek Hook, Franco, Nicky Cull, Craig Campbell, Catriona Peat and Sinead Healy. Also, Brian, Penny, Joanna, Morag and Claudia Barron (two of whom made the Commonwealth Games opening ceremony, much to my disgust), Frank & Cheryl Taylor (hope to see you soon), Fran & Simon, Gary & Elly, Gordon & Diane, Alan McNaught, Yolanda Wringe, John and Pam, Estelle Liebenberg, Ian Bowie, 'Das Root', 'Lovecraft', 'Tynecastle Terrace', Robert James, Denise & Rebecca Bowie, Stuart, Louise, Emily, Cameron, Kayleigh & the entire Wallace family, Paul Taylor, Pat, Donald Henderson and Andrew Henderson, Sarah Gardiner, Kerrin, Fiona & Joe Lumsden, my mum, JambosKickback.co.uk; boysinmaroon.co.uk; ATB; The splendid londonhearts.com website; and not least, Apex Publishing.

...and to Lesley, Jude-Lauren and Heart of Midlothian Football Club.

Contents

Foreword

When I was asked to write the foreword for this book, I thought I was introducing a simple story of an ordinary guy supporting a football team. But this is much more than that. It is a story, but one written with passion and comedy, not only about the Hearts, but growing up in the housing schemes of Edinburgh too. This story is an affectionate account of the highs and lows of following Edinburgh's oldest and greatest football club, but in a way I've never read before. There is real life in this book; real sadness and real laughter. I've known the author's brother, Bobby for years and you'll laugh out loud when you read about these two brothers being forced into sharing the same post code! I grew up not far from Tynecastle, and I recognised the places and streets, as well as some of the people that Andrew writes about in his book. Those of us who know and love Heart of Midlothian FC; and what the club means to the supporters; and who have lived their lives in the outlying areas from Gorgie will be in for a real treat. But no matter where you're from, and no matter what team you support, if any at all; you'll find this book to be a moving and humorous journey through life in the 80s, 90s and beyond. This is a story of an ordinary Hearts supporter, but whose talent for telling his story is anything but ordinary.

Gary Mackay
Heart of Midlothian Football Club (1980-1997)

Introduction

Thank you for choosing to read this, whoever you are. There is one rather perceptible question to ask as to why I've decided to write about my life, and the love I have for Heart of Midlothian FC. "So, why are you writing about your life and the love you have for Heart of Midlothian FC?" I hear you ask. It's not as if I'm famous; not even in my own house. I'm not a celebrity. If I was I'd say "get me out of here". I've never appeared on X-Factor or any of those other performing seal shows. I haven't climbed K2 or overcome a fascist dictator (apart from living with my big brother, which reminds me of another TV show I've never appeared on). So why am I writing my story? Well, hopefully because it will provide you with a compelling read, and that some passages will make you laugh and cry in places, and sometimes all at once.

This composition should also bestow you with the opportunity to get to know me a little better, if that is, you already know me. If you don't know me from Adam (Stephane, or otherwise), then congratulations: you've just saved the bother of growing up with me, buying me drinks, carrying me home; and not to mention trying to figure me out.

So, my autobiographical raison d'être can be explained on two levels. One, I have this story to tell, as you'll have sensed by the thickness of the book. And secondly, I see this project as a bookmark for a long running course of therapy I'm conducting. Don't worry, I'm not depressed or anything like that! Therapy comes in all sorts of shapes and forms, and this book is my therapy. Within, I will try to explain my life so far and how I've come to reach this point of self-analysis. This book is quite simply, my 'right of passage'; the defining document of a journey that began way back in the early 1970s.

"So what the Charles Dickens is this book all about?" Well it's about my life, the challenges that I've faced and my love for a Scottish Premier League football team called Heart of Midlothian. I've written about my time supporting Hearts and the memories it left me with.

To paraphrase one of those naff work-place stickers: you don't have to be a Hearts fan to read this book, but (I guess) it helps. Hearts are my team and I make no apology for referring to 'them' as 'we'. In this book there are tales of comedy, and anecdotes of tragedy. There are politics: but only really with myself. If politics equals power, then I convey how I fought to gain power over myself, and the life I was leading. I also explain the power others had over me; how I felt about it, dealt with it and tried to change it.

The impression I hope to leave with you though, is no matter what life threw at me, I faced it with heart, humour and observation; but you can make up your own mind. My story isn't the most famous that's ever been told, but it's the only life I've ever had. You might have been to the football matches I've been to, suffered similar heartaches, and dreamed the same dreams (though I doubt that very much). Judge me not on my right to write, but the way I told my story.

The ancient Greeks never wrote obituaries. They would only ask one question: "Did he have passion?" By the time you finish reading my book, all I wish for is that you sensed my passion for life, for Hearts and how I dealt with all the other crap!

The final question you might wish to ask is "just who in their right mind would want to read the life story of some waffling romantic?" Well…you, I guess…

I have this image of a bird's eye view, high above Tynecastle Stadium on match day. The stadium is still and brooding, but all around, like scurrying ants, are thousands of people making their way to the game. Some are locals, downing their last pint at ten minutes to three. Some are keen, and already in their seats. Others might carry the weight of the world on their shoulders, just glad to get out of the house for a few hours. Many have travelled from far and wide, and with great effort. Yet somehow, they all get there to make just one collective body of noise. Each person has their own route, their own routine and their own story to tell.

Ladies and Gentlemen, my name is Andrew-Henry Bowie. I was born on August 26th 1973, in Edinburgh, and I've lived there ever since. I'm an optimistic, yet somewhat fatigued Hearts supporter and hopeless insomniac. Are you sitting comfortably? Then so it begins. This, is my story…

Enjoy!

AHB '08

Andrew-Henry Bowie

Chapter 1
All roads lead to Saughton Mains Bank

Having been singled out by the Romani people, I felt somewhat compelled to get the fuck out of Eastern Europe and fast. It wasn't just the men of the small village that I had vexed. Women, children, the elderly and even their animals were in pursuit of me in a plethora of spluttering and manually drawn vehicles. I knew of no reason why they had to target me, but what I did know was that they were people not to be crossed, so I hastily made my attempt to flee them. Sometimes I managed to hitch a lift, or jumped aboard the open carriage of a slow moving freight train. But many times, like through Magyarország's great Carpathian Basin, I just ran as fast as I could. Yet no matter how hard I tried, my antagonists kept pace with me. Even when I got closer to home, I just couldn't elude the Roma. Sometimes it appeared as though they were out of sight, like in Northern France and near to the Scottish border. However, as I scrambled my way back to Edinburgh, and indeed to Saughton Mains Bank on the west side of the city, I became aware that my strength was sapped, and by the time I staggered up the cul-de-sac my level of defiance was deteriorating. As I finally reached the shielding sanctuary of my house, I was left horrified to discover that the maroon coloured front door was locked. My family, and indeed the entire neighbourhood, had seemingly vanished. There was nothing, nobody, not even a sound. 'How could it be?' I thought to myself, in desperate turmoil.

There I was, breathless. I had reached the periphery of the fenced-in grassy field that lay next to my house. And it was then that I'd finally stopped running. I gave up. I had to. Instead, I turned to look back, awaiting my fate. I just couldn't go on any longer. Now that I'd reached home, there was simply nowhere else to run. I sank to my knees. I was exhausted and defeated. They had me now.

And so the deafening hush that had greeted my journey's end began to dissolve against a growing rumbling of traffic. It was them alright. As I knelt there, my eyes were fixed back to the road, and slowly, inexorably, they came. Emerging from behind the Saughton Mains Bank lock-up garages, the Roma appeared. First came a man with a horse, and then another. A third man, sitting on a wagon drawn by a single horse, followed.

Next there was an old woman on a horse, and then a truck towing a trailer. Hundreds came, edging relentlessly into the cul-de-sac and towards me. Trucks, trailers, carts, wagons, horses and dogs; the massive convoy snaked its way up and circled me, but gave me a wide berth like a Boa constrictor preparing to envelop and crush its prey with sickening inevitability. But, as the huge procession reached within yards of where I stood, it abruptly ground to a halt. Eerie silence returned and no one spoke: least of all me. Everyone was now still; still like the dead, leaden atmosphere before a furious thunderstorm. But then the man at the front left his horse and moved towards me; his dark curly hair spilling out from underneath a worn black fedora hat and onto his black waistcoat. His stature wasn't remarkable, but his dark blue shirt matched the colour of the doomed sky. As he drew close, I realised he was not much older than me, but seemed more world-weary; his dark eyes and square jaw compensating for an unflattering moustache. He stared down, and blinked slowly before tilting his head up to look me straight in the eye. He spoke.

"Why did you run from us?" he asked in a rasping voice.

"I was running for my life," I replied.

"But what did you think we were going to do to you?" posed the man.

"Well I thought you were going to fucking kill me?" I said, with my heart pounding.

"NO!" snapped the man in a riled voice. He slapped his hands together. There was a long pause. He gave what seemed like a long, deep sigh before walking a few steps away, turning his back on me, only for him to swivel his head back round sharply. He glared at me again, only this time it was as though he was able to see deep into my soul, and said:

"We didn't come here to kill you…we came here…to warn you."

"Warn me?!" What the fuck?!

Without breaking eye contact, he signalled to his left and a brightly painted red wagon drew up next to us. On its near side was a wooden hatch, which the man lowered to reveal an old cinematic projector screen. An elderly woman fed the reel into the machine and I stood, frozen, as the Romani people gave me a glimpse into the future. There I saw wars, explosions, death and natural disasters. But worst of all, I saw a vision of me and it sent a shiver through my body. When the spool ran out, the only sound to be heard was the superfluous cine film flapping wildly against the rattling, spinning reel. The man then stared back toward me, and told me without speaking, that unless I changed the way I lived, my future would be as bleak as the images that I had just observed. He then approached me, and stood only a foot or so from my face.

"It was wrong of you to run. Never, ever run from me."

It almost seemed as if he wanted to smile, or acknowledge me: but he didn't. And so with that, he walked back to his horse, and the massive procession began to slip away, back down the field, slowly making its way out of Saughton Mains Bank. Although I knew they were at last going to leave me alone, I was left feeling overwhelmingly disturbed at what had happened. Like the Roma, I drifted away and it was maybe just as well that the dream ended there; for once, I didn't curse the alarm clock as it awoke me for another rainy, puffy-eyed and parched Monday morning. That was a couple of years back now, yet it still haunts me to this day. I will never forget it. It was an epic, and the disquieting Saughton Mains Bank finale was only the tip of the iceberg (although I never saw an iceberg on the cine film).

My dreams are downright odd: weirder than the most extreme surreal horror films, Eraserhaed; or weirder than the bloke that mimed in those Howard Jones videos; or weirder even, than Rent-a-ghost spook and all round camp cavorter, Timothy Claypole. Even though I've never been 'on the couch', I think it is my past that has had a significant bearing on these frightful visions. And all of these hallucinations come under an umbrella I call 'SND', or to give it its full name: 'Sunday Night Dread'. These forbidding episodes are exclusively sandwiched between a weekend 'on the piss' and a foreboding Monday morning at work. My close-to-death 'SND' dreams allow me to envisage images, like the time I had a special map of the British Isles that would reveal the location of surrounding shipwrecks and corpses if I stared at it long enough. Or the time when I nursed my best mate, Adam Ant, back to health as he lay on his deathbed. Or the night I realised the Pet Shop Boys were in fact a serious rival to both Hearts and Hibs; with their smart all-seater stadium accessed from a secret entrance inside the Balgreen Road tunnel. It is all very outlandish, often utterly terrifying and very much part of my disposition; and no, Adam Ant is not a mate of mine (imagine going down the pub with him in full costume?!).

More often than not I dream about three recurring scenarios. One is a football match that I'm running late for at Saughton Park, yet I can never quite make a dash diagonally across the large playing field to get onto the pitch. I suppose it's one of those 'running through glue' type dreams that are quite common. Another is that I'm back working at my old job delivering parcels, where I am faced with a hellish amount of work to do and I'm always running late (and there is usually the bonus of some kind of apocalyptical storm brewing). And finally, the most common occurrence is the setting of Saughton Mains Bank. I left home in 1995; aged twenty-one years old, but to this day, I live there in my dreams. The Romani chase dream, of course, led me to Saughton Mains Bank.

The reason I wrote about that dream has little to do with the good Romani people per se: but it's everything to do with the cul-de-sac where I grew up and of course there is that warning 'the man' gave me. It was both amusing and entertaining (if not more than a little disturbing at the time!) for me to actually write about the 'dream of dreams'. I've told it to friends a few times over the last couple of years, but writing it down gave the dream new life, new impetus. The dream's twist is always the best bit, but what I'm really concerned with writing about on these subsequent pages is my life, starting at Saughton Mains Bank.

Chapter 2
Away up in Gorgie
at Tynecastle Park

Heart of Midlothian, the most romantically named football club in the world is an absorbing Edinburgh institution. Scotland's capital city has a brilliant and colourful past and its history reads almost like a black comedy. Great tales of murder, witches and pestilence are as much part of the city's fabric as is medicine, philosophy, politics and law. It was on the cobbled streets of the famous Royal Mile, with Edinburgh Castle as the smouldering backdrop, that Heart of Midlothian Football Club was formed in 1874. A simple bus journey round the Old Town now, captures the imagination of what it must have been like back then. Edinburgh, with its great buildings and 'Enlightenment' make the heritage of The Hearts a beautiful one. The club is sown into the very fabric of the city. The young men who used to kick a ball about (no doubt to the annoyance to everyone else) were accosted by a policeman, who probably had a waxed moustache and sauntered up to them in a "well then well then, what do we have 'ere" kind of style. He then, more or less, told the lads to fuck off and go play football at 'The Meadows', the expansive open space to the south of the city centre that gave Edinburgh its 'lungs'.

'The Heart of Midlothian' was the familiar name of the Old Tolbooth Prison that stood outside St Giles' Cathedral on the Royal Mile, and it was the inspiration for Sir Walter Scott to write his book of same name. It is likely though, that the newly formed football team took its name from the 'Heart of Midlothian' dance hall that the young men frequented, when they weren't causing havoc on the Royal Mile. With Association football formed just a few years previously, Heart of Midlothian is the oldest football club in the east of Scotland (and indeed the thirteenth oldest professional football club in the world). 'Hearts' (to use their informal name), who soon started playing in the famous maroon and white colours, had several Southside homes in the early days, but eventually laid foundations in the west Edinburgh suburb of Gorgie, and settled into the present day site of Tynecastle in 1886.

In the early years of Hearts, the club became fairly successful, winning two League Championships and four Scottish Cups, as well as a host of local competitions. They were even crowned 'unofficial' World Champions after defeating Tottenham Hotspur over two legs in 1902. Heart of Midlothian had made a bright start and was one of the leading lights in football. Such standing was aided considerably by having the finest footballer on the planet starring every other week at Tynecastle. Midfield genius, Bobby Walker, was such a revered player that even the King of Norway came to Edinburgh especially to watch him play. Of course, anyone with any knowledge of Scottish football will know that the two big Glasgow clubs draw massive crowds. In the past, religious tensions were often manipulated to the maximum in order to sustain the 'Old Firm' of Celtic and Rangers. Both Rangers and Celtic (and the Edinburgh Hibernians) had strict signing policies, based on a player's religious background; indeed Rangers were still coy about signing Catholics right up until the late 1980s.

Neither Glasgow club though, could stop Hearts from producing great teams, and the 'Maroons' kicked off the 1914/15 season in sensational form, winning their first eight league matches. As Hearts looked unstoppable on the field, it became clear that it would take something extraordinary off it to prevent the Edinburgh team from bringing another championship back to Tynecastle. But something extraordinary did happen: and not only would it sap Hearts of its best players and cost them the league title, it would define the club for decades to come in an event history now calls 'The First World War'.

As society dealt with war, people became increasingly irritated with footballers continuing their careers as if *nothing* was happening on mainland Europe; there developed increased pressure for the nation's young sportsmen to take up Lord Kitchener's invitation to fight for 'King and Country'. It was then, in November 1914, that the majority of the Heart of Midlothian football team signed up to form what became known as 'McCrae's Own Battalion', The 16th Royal Scots. Hundreds of Hearts shareholders and supporters (as well as players from Hibernian, Dunfermline, Falkirk and Raith Rovers) were immediately inspired to join up as Edinburgh and its surrounding area put shame on their counterparts from the west. Indeed, as the Hearts players became sapped by intense military training, it was Celtic (with their players hiding behind their day to day jobs) who eventually overtook Hearts in the final weeks of the season, to win a hollow championship.

Seven of the Hearts team paid the ultimate sacrifice for their country, but their valour gained the club much admiration. For any Jambo, this above all else should make them proud to be a fan of Heart of Midlothian football club. In 1922, the clock which stands at Haymarket, Edinburgh, was unveiled as a memorial to all those who displayed heroism in the face of appalling carnage and sacrifice. In 2005, thanks to the endeavours of writer and historian Jack Alexander, a cairn was unveiled in the French village of Constalmaision and it became the national focal point for the 2006 Somme remembrance services. Although Hearts continued to play attractive football, with great players such as Barney Battles and Tommy Walker, in the period leading up to the Second World War, tangible success was not forthcoming. In the years following the war, it was local rivals, Hibernian, who dominated the Scottish scene with their talented 'Famous Five' line-up. However, by 1954, with a brilliant and patient youth policy, a new dawn of success was awakening at Tynecastle. And after a forty-eight year wait for silverware, it was not before time.

Chapter 3
In the beginning

Even with the most optimistic sense of perspective, the chances of my parents having a long and happy marriage were remote to say the least. Bob and Rosemary were products of Britain's post-war baby boom. Born just a year apart, they were from similar, yet fundamentally different backgrounds. Both had a working class upbringing in the Stenhouse area of Edinburgh. Both had two older sisters that made them the baby of their respective families. Both had a dominant mother. It is the respective fathers though, that had differing personas. My father's father (who I guess was my granddad) fought in the war and was quite a fiery, yet highly sociable man. My mother's father was, I believe, a more quiet and unassuming man who didn't fight the Nazis due to health reasons. My parents then, were from comparable backgrounds but for one rather significant difference: my mother was a Catholic and my father, a Protestant. Though neither of my parents had any issue with the other's religion, it would eventually represent a fundamental difference in culture and class as my parents' relationship bedded-in on sinking sand.

My father was the only male sibling, the youngest of the family and had an incredibly close bond with his mother. Both my father, and my father's father were proud of their association with the Masonic Lodge, and it became the focal point to both their social lives. As much as I'd like to, I can't tell you what role my grandfather played in World War II, as neither he nor my father ever told me. My grandmother was also very sociable and she was fiercely proud of her husband and her son, as the latter made his way up the Masonic ladder. It was a classic post-war, ration book, Scots-protestant setting, but although it may have been the 1950s and 60s, the values were purely Victorian: where words like 'trousers' were never spoken and the term 'hangover' was probably as taboo as seeing kissing on the telly (where legend has it my grandmother would leap off the chair to switch it off). My grandparents were married for fifty-five years. Sadly, I was never close to them.

The number three bus to Stenhouse Road was the setting for my parents' first ever meeting, sometime around 1968. My father asked Rosemary out straight away as she made her way home from work. Their courtship was brief and to the point. I suppose what helped was that Rosemary lived just a hundred yards or so along the road. What didn't help was that she was already a nineteen-year-old single mother; still taboo in John Knox's Edinburgh. The effect that would have on my father's mother would be the early catalyst that eventually drove them apart before they reached thirty years old. When Rosemary met my grandmother, the reception was frosty.

My mother's family were working-class Catholics who reproduced like there was *nothing* on the telly, never mind kissing! I have no idea about their early origins. Nor do I know much about them as people. My granddad on my father's side died in 1990 and my grandmother in 1999, so at least I knew who they were, despite not being close. However, on my mother's side, my grandmother died in 1968 and my grandfather in 1977, so I couldn't say what they were like. I don't even know what my grandmother's name was and I don't think my mum knows either! My mother, like my father had two older sisters. The oldest, Morticia, was (and probably still is) something of a 'free-spirit', and I imagine she'll be wandering around her garden right now in just a nightgown, talking to the geraniums. The other sister was Veronica. She was a religious woman, who would entertain old Catholic biddies whilst her husband, the amiable Uncle Bill, would do the shopping. Between Morticia, Veronica and my mother, they had eleven children but I wouldn't recognise some of them if they were sat in my living room wearing t-shirts that read "I'm yer cousin".

Before the disintegration of their marriage, I guess there must have been some optimistic times amid the early struggles for my parents. My father worked hard as an electrician, and my mum looked after Tommy. They got their first place together high up the Sighthill tower that overlooks Broomhouse Road. It was a real coup, with modern living and spacious rooms, long before the area became run down with drug addicts, 'Looking after JoJo'. I will say one thing for my father, he documented this period beautifully; I can view that period through the wonder of his cine film spools that I managed to get converted on to video some years ago. They only run for about forty minutes, but give a real nostalgic slant on the past. All my family are featured, as are glimpses of West Edinburgh in the late 60s and early 70s. From the thirteenth floor of the Sighthill flats, the camera pans round. But there is no Gyle, no Gogarloch, no bypass and no sound. The silence is golden when watching it, but the serenity back then wasn't to last long. Those cine films are unbelievably haunting, and they featured both sides of my family in a more innocent time. Many are now gone or out of touch. One ended up in jail, another got an MBE. One is away with the geraniums and another wrote a book about it all. The cine camera that captured all this eventually went under the hammer, but not the kind found at auctions. I was young and, I guess, destructive. I don't know why I did it.

Chapter 4
And then there were three

My parents became a sort of post-nuclear family when they were married on July 4th 1969, the same year as Woodstock and flower power. It was the year The Beatles made their last album before splitting up. Talking of 'families' and The Beatles, it was in 1969 that Charles Manson listened to another fab four album and thought the lyrics were for the benefit of his crazy gang of hippies. Oh, and a man walked on the moon, apparently.

The wedding was modest, taking place at the Haymarket Register Office. An afternoon lunch followed, and the honeymoon was a day trip to Dunfermline Abbey! My parents' first dwelling at Sighthill lasted three years. After a brief stay in Stenhouse, my family moved to a house in nearby Saughton Mains Bank. There goes the neighbourhood!

In 1970, my mother was expecting again, but tragically the baby (an unnamed girl) died, stillborn. It devastated my mother. I have only ever given the death of this baby brief thought over the years, and writing this has made me overturn a few stones that are maybe best left lying in the past where they belong. It must have been a dreadful experience to suffer and I'm sorry she went through it. Under the orders of the family doctor, my parents were advised not to have any more children for at least three years, so one can imagine his surprise when my mother became pregnant just a couple of months later. My brother, Robert James Bowie (Bobby) was born in March 1971, and his assignment for the early years of his life would be to make mine hell. I came along two and a half years later, at 11.26am on Sunday, August 26th 1973 at Simpson's Maternity Ward (no longer there), in the original Edinburgh Royal Infirmary. I weighed in at a cool seven pounds, eleven ounces and I had a full head of jet-black hair (which is more than I have these days in both colour and volume). When I was less than two years old, I unwittingly escaped from my garden. The incident sparked a major panic in my house and I was missing for about an hour. I showed up when the postman (who had discovered me) delivered me back to my mum (decent service for The Royal Mail). I had made it as far as Stenhouse Cross, about half a mile away. Not a bad effort: and maybe I was heading for Tynecastle?

My father used to talk about 'the old days'. He would tell me about the various trips I'd made to the Sick Kids Hospital (I was so accident-prone, that they should've named a ward after me). I remember one incident where I was sitting on the worktop between the cooker and the sink when a kettle of boiling hot water was knocked over and cascaded onto my arm. My Uncle Bill took me to the Sick Kids and I remember him making this four-year-old laugh because in the waiting room there was a giant cuddly bear with an arm bandage. My Uncle suggested it might have suffered the same fate as me: comedy champagne I say. Another favourite misfortune my dad told me about was the time when I fell off the back of a chair and cut the inside of my mouth, as I went crashing onto a nest of glass tables (most popular in the 70s). Even today, I can point the scar out to any interested party. A bad enough accident, it may have been, but as my dad ran over to get me, he stepped onto a cart that I'd been wheeling about. The cart went one way and my dad went the other, dislocating his thumb upon landing! It got worse for him as the doctor (who told my father he was merely examining the injury) suddenly crunched my father's thumb back into place. A few minutes later, as my father's tears began to subside, he asked the doctor,

"Why the fuck did you do that?"

To which the doctor replied, "If I told you what I was going to do, you wouldn't have let me do it". And he was right. The 70s were shit and the bin-men were on strike: but there was no messing about in the National Health Service in those days.

There were lots of things that made me go to hospital, but amazingly (touch wood) to this day, I've never spent a whole night in one. Whatever calamities I survived in my house, there were things that were simply impossible to mend. Many years later, my father told me that things seemed to change after I was born (so it's all my fault then, eh?). My parents were starting to argue as my dad blamed a change in my mum's moods, which seemed only to escalate my father's private social calendar. My arrival into the world may have been the beginning of my life, but it seemed to trigger the end of my parents' lives together. Arguments that were becoming more frequent would soon turn to violence, trashed furniture and visits from the police: and my earliest childhood memories were those of parents, lying on the floor, trying to throttle each other.

Chapter 5
The rise and fall

With heads caked in Brylcreem and shorts the size of parachutes, Hearts were plodding along nicely in the early 50s as their conveyer belt of local talent won admirers, if not trophies. Manager Davie McLean's premature death meant that Hearts and Scotland legend, Tommy Walker, was now in charge. His timing as a player was unfortunate, as World War II had somewhat curtailed his career. But as a manager, he couldn't have stepped into the hot-seat at a better time. Alfie Conn, Willie Bauld & Jimmy Wardhaugh were 'The Terrible Trio', scoring for fun. Between them, they racked-up a staggering tally of almost one thousand career goals. Goalkeepers all over Scotland must have had sleepless nights when this lot swaggered into town; but the fans loved it, and Hearts were always a popular draw, setting record attendances at many grounds over the years. Bauld was probably the most revered of all and he had film star good looks to go with his talent. Of course, it would be a huge injustice to the rest of the team to suggest that these players were the only stars of the side. They weren't. Dave Mackay and Alex Young were not only Hearts legends, they shined even brighter in England, where Tottenham Hotspur and Everton, respectively, enjoyed some of their best eras. Mackay named Hearts' 'Iron Man', John Cumming, the best player he'd ever played with and it remains something of a mystery as to why none of the big English teams came in for him. Cumming was the only player of his generation that Mackay was scared of, and he is still the most decorated player in the history of Hearts. The man is an absolute legend and for Hearts fans, it was a very rock-n-roll time to be standing on the terraces, as flat caps shielded rain and long raincoats protected flasks of scotch.

In 1954, Hearts swept Motherwell aside in the League Cup Final, with Willie Bauld, the 'King of Hearts', scoring a hat-trick. It opened the floodgates for eight years of unparalleled success for Hearts. Fewer than two years later and in front of a crowd of one hundred and thirty-three thousand people, Hearts won the Scottish Cup with a famous 3-1 victory over Celtic. The open-top bus street parties that followed these triumphs are to this day, something that Hearts do better than anyone else. Stuffy old Edinburgh, with her 'fur coat and nae kickers', seemed only too willing to let her hair down in a way that has been unsurpassed by any other city event. When the Hearts players brought the cup home, Edinburgh Castle was lit up to honour them. The League Championship was next on the agenda and during the 1957/58 season, and in a wave of invincibility barely witnessed on these shores before or since, Hearts annihilated the opposition, scoring an incredible and record-breaking one-hundred and thirty-two goals with just twenty-nine conceded. What was all the more remarkable in that this was achieved in just thirty-four league games, losing just once and with Rangers trailing in their wake. It was Hearts' defining moment in terms of sporting greatness. The club should've had three Championship wins in a row, but for a narrow loss in 1958/59. However, the title was secured again in 1959/60; add to that a smattering of League cups (four in nine seasons), it must have been an amazing time to be a Hearts fan, despite all that greasy hair lacquer and folk peeing in each other's pockets.

Although a couple of lean years ensued, Hearts looked well on course to win another League Championship in the Beatlemania days of 1964/65, with their next generation of players. The final day saw Hearts go head to head with title rivals Kilmarnock (interestingly, the Old Firm were nowhere to be seen in this Championship race). But, in what would become the start of a new Hearts trend of inexplicably snatching defeat from the jaws of victory, the Edinburgh side duly blew the match 0-2, losing the title by the slimmest of goal averages. Having felt this system was somewhat unfair and outdated, a wise man at the SFA decided to change the rule to 'goal difference', to stop teams like Hearts having agonising mathematical title losses. Hhmmm: cheers for that.

The horrible fall-out of the 1965 Championship loss was that Hearts entered a period of sustained decline that would last for over fifteen years. The men who ran Hearts prudently and conservatively were suddenly faced with an empty assembly line of marketable, cheap, local talent. Though the gents of the 50s and 60s oversaw some terrific triumphs, there was no development, no foresight and no building up of the club. In the 1930s, Hearts had planned to move out of Gorgie, to the edge of town in a project called 'The Sighthill Dream'. Now that was ambitious: a giant stadium, holding a hundred thousand people. Perhaps Hearts could have become one of the great superclubs we see now, such as Real Madrid or Manchester Utd. But 'the dream' never happened. Hearts became the big city club with the small-town mentality; run by the butcher, the baker, the candlestick maker. Everyone had a vested interest and the front door was locked shut. Hearts were neither a friendly nor open club. As the crowds dipped and the eminence of players plunged, the black and white era turned to colour. Hair got longer, side-burns grew and the pride of playing for Heart of

Midlothian was held in the same regard as the rubbish bags piling up on the streets.

The demise of Hearts coincided with The Sex Pistols, The Clash and the collapse of British industry. The Queen's Jubilee celebrations seemed comically ironic as the country (along with everything else) was going to the wall. In April 1977, for the first of three times in the club's history, Hearts were relegated from the top tier of Scottish football. Crowds dwindled and punk lasted just a hundred days. Debts spiralled out of control alongside post-punk and new wave. Performances plummeted to new depths, as did disco. Keith Moon, Ian Curtis and John Lennon died and Thatcherism was born. Interest waned as the Jam Tarts entered the 'yo-yo' years between the Premier League, the First Division and abysmal comedy records on Top of the Pops. There was anarchy in the UK, and on many occasions it was Hearts fans leading the charge in towns across Scotland. If ever an era was befitting to the fall of Hearts: it was this one. The club reached rock bottom and suffered some absolutely shocking results. In 1981, as Hearts were losing at home to East Stirlingshire, there was talk of the business closing, and Tynecastle was earmarked as a good place for a car park. This sparked a fire sale of club shares and a young, flamboyant (if slightly portly) Edinburgh businessman wrestled to gain control of the ailing club. In 1982, Hearts lost a Scottish Cup tie at home to bloody Forfar.

A once proud club lay in a pitiful state, and that was the condition Hearts were in when Wallace Mercer found them: as did I.

Chapter 6
Never eat on an empty stomach

In and around 1977 and 1978, as Hearts were relegated for the first time, and then promoted back to the Premier Division, I was a child living along the road at Saughton Mains Bank. As my domestic world dissolved into domestic arguments, I became quiet and withdrawn. My day would almost entirely consist of lying on the carpet, rolling my Matchbox cars around, and not saying very much at all. My father's career at the Freemasons meant that he had to invest money into hosting events that would see him spend much of his life being bundled in and out of taxi cabs. As my dad was a little guy, it didn't take enough booze to sink (or even float for that matter) a battleship to get him drunk. My mother said she received little money, and the best holiday we would ever have was a free stay in my uncle's caravan in Pettycur Bay, Fife. Shouting, swearing and food sliding down the wall were regular occurrences in my house, and my mum even has a scar above her eyebrow as a memento. They blamed each other.

One of the most harrowing incidents I remember was when my mother traipsed my two brothers and me to Stenhouse to my grandparent's house. The reason for her gripe was that my dad had failed to come home from work one Friday. My mother didn't have any money and she claimed that there was nothing to put on the table for us. As we approached the house at Stenhouse Crescent, there was my father and my grandfather, gleefully loading his van with crates of beer and clinking bottles of whisky. My father's proud, stoic mother looked on, as he worked his way up through the Masonic ranks. No doubt the sight of three boys in parka coats and one mad 'mutha' spoiled the party. What followed was bedlam, and my brothers and I witnessed a full-scale rammy. Certainly, I remember more than a couple of rumbles round at my Gran's house, as my mother reached the point of breakdown. To the rest of the family, my grandparents will always be revered as the golden couple who lived through the war (they were, and they did). But even after watching those old cine films again, I can't think of one thing to be nostalgic about. To me, they were players in a horrible set of memories.

Around this time, my father started to work for a soft drinks firm (he he), installing machines. His social life often ended up with him in the pub with his workmates after hours. After one last fight, my mother took my two older brothers round to her sister's house and fled with me to some sort of refuge. I have no recollection of this, but it signalled the end of the road for my parents. The fall-out from their separation was shattering. My father went back to the sanctuary of his mum. My mum was left a nervous wreck. Tommy began to misbehave at school and soon turned to a life of petty crime and Borstal. Bobby, despite sporting hilarious and unfeasibly curly hair, developed a tough exterior and cultivated a mean-n-moody persona that has never left him (although his hair is now long gone). As for me, well I don't know. I guess I was a sensitive child, and I became acutely aware of the terrible problems my family was experiencing. Just the grounding a boy needs when he's about to start primary school. With my father gone and as the youngest of the house, I was the archetypal mummy's boy; just like my dad. So although he was no longer around in my life, I guess I had become my father's son.

What certainly didn't improve the ambiance was that not long after my father had left, our house became the target of an intruder as we lay sleeping in our beds. It was in Tommy's room that this person first tried to gain entry, and despite my brother being no angel, it must have been a horrific ordeal to awake to find the prowler trying to climb through his window. My mum flew out of bed in pursuit. I ran through to my mum's room and stood in the corner facing the wall. Incredibly, the same guy came back just a few weeks later to smash our back door window in during the middle of the night. It turned out, that the person doing this had lived in the house before my mum and dad took up tenancy. What the hell he was wanting (or what his problem was) is beyond me; but if one was to assume that he'd left something behind all those years previous, then surely all the bastard had to do was chap the bloody door!

And so, on the back of the cat-burglar period, I began my education at Stenhouse Primary School, and I remember the first day well. It was really just a chance for the single mums (and I guess married one's too) to meet the teacher and let the kids encounter each other. We got our picture taken and it is still lying around my mum's house somewhere. I wore what was perhaps the most frightening 70s nylon print, polo-neck jumper known to man, or boy. The design was that of a red open-zipped jacket, with an inset of a large stadium crowd scene and check this: two bearded footballers! We were then all given a large sheet of paper with colour crayons to draw something. The fact that I chose to silently grind out a series of black crucifixes into the paper should have had Guidance Teachers running down the corridor, with the fire-alarm bells ringing at full volume.

Chapter 7
A concrete jungle

1950s prefabricated-built Saughton Mains isn't the worst place to live in Edinburgh, but Morningside it isn't. Muirhouse, West Pilton, Craigmillar, Niddrie and Wester Hailes all have far shoddier reputations; as does neighbouring Broomhouse. But Saughton Mains still had its fair share of gangs, warring families, drugs, theft and robbery when I grew up there. A lot of people looked like Yosser Hughes and some of them were blokes. In the hub of the scheme sits a pub called The Busy Bee, and going inside would often leave one identifying with Luke Skywalker's trepidation as he entered the bar in Star Wars. Many kids who grew up during my time there have been lost to drugs, lost to crime and just lost to life itself. Perhaps Saughton has a grim image because it shares its name with the prison (which is really between Stenhouse and Longstone). Saughton Mains is roughly divided into two parts: The northern half of the scheme is a collection of flats that look more like a prison than the prison itself. The southern part of the scheme mostly comprises houses that used to have flat roofs; this gave them a sort of giant concrete block look until the council did them up. Saughton Mains has Stenhouse to the east and Broomhouse to the west. Carrick Knowe lies to the north on the other side of the Edinburgh to Glasgow railway line, and Longstone is to the south, beyond the Calder Road dual carriageway.

Saughton Mains Bank is a cul-de-sac which was just off the through road of Stenhouse Street West (no longer a through road), near Carrick Vale Community Centre (no longer there). The access to my street passed a wonderful acre of wooded church ground (no longer there) as it snaked past the lock up garages (no longer there) to a large field (again, no longer there). Pedestrians to Saughton Mains Bank can pass through using three lanes; one to Stenhouse School, one towards The Busy Bee and the other past the church towards Carrick Vale. The street has a number of houses for old folk at the bottom, two four-story stairwells and a row of four houses at the top of the street. I lived at the top of the street.

My father's actual departure from the house is something I have no memory of. I remember him there and I remember the fighting. I remember him taking me to the newsagent at Chesser to buy me a new Matchbox car. I remember a trip to Pettycur Bay and sitting on the front seat on my mum's lap, and not a seatbelt in sight! I remember him taking me for my BCG jag when my grandfather (on my mother's side) died of TB. I remember watching The Rockford Files, the coolest show on TV ever. But I don't remember him leaving. Neither parent can recall the date, but it must have been sometime in 1978, the year Archie Gemmil scored that goal against Holland; the year Grease was the word; and the year of the Jonestown mass-suicide. It was the year of the three Popes, but The Bee Gees were Stayin' Alive. I'm glad someone was doing ok then.

One great thing did happen that year though. The summer Play Scheme, at Carrick Vale Community Centre, started after the locals were awarded a council grant. Suddenly the summer holidays had excitement and purpose. The large red-bricked building on Stenhouse Street West was now our playground. We had a gym hall to run (and cycle) around in, corridors to explore, organised games, and best of all, field trips. The memories are vague, but I remember the next few summers going to places like Aberdour, Burnt Island and North Berwick with Bobby and my friends, Allan, DD and 'Blue'. I recall one day, we had two mini buses booked and the kids had to decide if they wanted to visit Tynecastle or Easter Road. I must have been only five or six and I didn't get the choice. I was bundled into a mini bus and bound for Easter Road. I may now be a Hearts man through and through, but my first footsteps into any football arena were not that of Hearts: but of Hibs.

I probably only experienced about half a dozen summers at the Play Scheme, but Saughton and Stenhouse kids of my era will forever be grateful to a man called Dougie Bishop who ran the operation. I have no idea what he is doing now, but he gave 'the kids' something to look forward to during summer time in a housing scheme, where the heat would bounce off the concrete as much as the locals spilling out of The Busy Bee. At home, I remember watching a lot of TV including Top of the Pops, where Kate Bush gave me nightmares in between the battle of bands such as Showaddywaddy and Darts. Although I watched Children's TV, like Rainbow (as a wise-man once said, "the one with the seven foot bear that wears pyjamas to bed, but spends the rest of the day walking around naked"), I actually have better memories of blood-showers in the Hammer House of Horrors. There was also Tales of the Unexpected, where my mum and brother would be subjected to watching me dance to its famous theme-tune when standing in front of the telly! If someone can explain what subliminal message I was trying to convey there, please tell me. I loved the '01' of the General Lee, but I'd run into the kitchen when Dr David Banner turned into The Incredible Hulk. Add to that Arthur C Clarke, Blake's Seven and Richard Stilgoe's frightful jumpers then it's easy to understand how I developed a terrifying imagination.

Around this time, I had a near death experience at Longstone Burn, a little off-shoot from the Water of Leith. Bobby and I would go to the Prison Warders' Social Club for a Friday night cinema showing for the kids of the warders (although in our house, we had better connections to the inmate community). To get home we could either hike round the long way or cross the stream, which meant walking over the legendary metal pipe that graciously still spans its mighty width to this day. It was raining that night but Bobby managed to negotiate the greasy and unforgiving cylinder. We lost a lot of good men on that mission over the years, and on that occasion I slipped, and the high water level swept me away and towards the uninviting location of Edinburgh's premier penitentiary! As my short life flashed in front of me Bobby managed to pull me up and to safety, but I had a miserable walk home along Calder Road with my clothes saturated. Perhaps the worst thing about that episode though, was that my mum was hosting a 'Tupperware' party that night and I was unceremoniously stripped out of my sodden wares in front of at least a dozen neighbours and relatives!

Before the days of cuddly Frank Bough and Good Morning telly, my mum always had Radio Forth on in the background as Bobby and I got ready for school. I still have a vague memory of the morning of December 9th 1980, when my mum informed me that John Lennon had been shot dead. I may have been a mere seven years old, but I remember being quite upset by this (much more so than when JR Ewing took one in the chest that same year). What I couldn't understand was how he was getting number one hits after his death. I mean, he's dead, yeah? Was he singing them from heaven? A decade later, Lennon would become a hero to me, and boy was I in need of a hero! The radio was always blaring out in the morning which was nice. It kind of gave the house an energy, as if each day was a fresh start. There were good times and bad times, I guess.

Sometimes I'd do stuff to make my mum and Bobby laugh; like the time I pinched old Violet's bum at the fish van, or the Christmas when I ordered dozens of presents out of my neighbour's Freeman's catalogue. We kept the fish but the catalogue stuff was sent back, but that didn't stop Bobby spending hours staring at certain pages in the catalogue. Everyday before tea-time, I'd walk out of the house and over the road to my mum's neighbour's place. I'd bang on her door, walk in and demand my frothing pint; to which a fizzing tankard of Creamola Foam arrived. The neighbour would then watch in awe as I'd sink it in one go, slam the glass down and walk straight back out the door! This went on for months, finally she asked my unsuspecting mum why her youngest son was treating her house like

The Rovers Return! The radio reminds me of the time that I woke up to my birthday, and Stevie Wonder's 'Happy Birthday' was playing on Radio Forth. Birthdays were good, and often better than Christmas. Every year, I'd get a 'Domino' birthday cake from Crawford's baker at Stenhouse Cross. Retro.

As for Christmas, I remember when Bobby, Tommy and I got one big present each. Tommy got a Chopper, the most kitch of 70s bicycles. Bobby got a Grifter; a predecessor of the BMX, but for the fact that it weighed about half a ton. I couldn't find my bike, but the Wendy House waiting for me was a great place to shut the world out, especially when I thought of what had happened to me at the Hearts' Christmas Party at Palmerston Place the previous year. My grandfather had arranged the tickets, but for some inexplicable reason, Bobby's ticket said 'boy' and mine said 'girl'. Was somebody trying to tell me something? I remember it so well. Santa was completely pished and I just sat there, so sad and without a present. I remember being asked later as to where my present was, but it was too late. It sounds pathetic now, but that incident really pissed me off!

That same year, my devout Catholic Aunty Veronica arranged for some old priest to give all the young cousins a lecture on Christmas, and religion in general. His name was Mr Bird (but there will be no cheap jokes from me), and his chosen subjects were guilt and Pontius Pilate. Pilate, according to certain Christian gospels, presided over the trial of Jesus Christ and ordered his crucifixion. It's not really what a seven year old wants to hear and I recall being bored shitless listening to his endless yarn. My aunty never approved of my mum's apathetic approach to religion, and perhaps this was her attempt to bring Bobby and me into line with the rest of the family. Whatever her motives were for us attending that night, it just didn't work as Mr Bird's ramblings were completely lost on me and were way over the unfeasibly curly-haired head of Bobby. After a prolonged and loquacious sermon, Mr Bird finally wound up his talk by asking his puerile congregation if there was anything we'd like clarification on regarding the exploits of Pontius Pilate…anything at all…anything. After a long, vacant pause, my brother lifted his hand and piped up with what can only be described as the greatest religious-based faux pas up until The Satanic Verses. The floor was Bobby's.

"Yes my son", asked Mr Bird.

(Pause)

"Pontius Pilot", my brother posed, "Was he a pilot?"

Religion is something I've never concerned myself with, and only Bobby and Tommy were christened. I wasn't (although my mum has recently declared that a 'Father Pat' secretly dowsed me in some sort of tap water).

It was all such a confusing time, and it was in 1980 that I saw my father again, after what seemed like a long absence. I can't remember him picking me up in the car, but I do remember my granddad sitting in the front passenger seat, smoking. I felt sick, and after a longer drive than usual, we ended up at another strange cul-de-sac that looked a bit like Saughton Mains Bank, only newer, bleaker and even more of a concrete jungle. The street was called Forth Drive, and this was Livingston, not Edinburgh. It seemed my father had made plans to start his life all over again. But it wasn't going to be in the city where I grew up.

Chapter 8
Keep feeling fascination

In the summer of 1981, the Play Scheme decided to hold its very own mock-up of the big royal wedding. Britain surfed a heat-wave of nasty souvenir tea-towels and ugly looking coffee mugs displaying pictures of the happy couple. And talking of ugly mugs: as Charles reluctantly married Diana four hundred miles away, the Saughton Mains Play Scheme got busy making its very own fancy dress wedding parade; for which I landed the less than starring role as page-boy. My mum, who had played a keen part in the running of the Play Scheme, had for some reason taken the hump with someone that day. As I was sent on my way wearing a kilt, trainers and white shirt, my mum spent the afternoon sunbathing in the back garden, in the company of Martini Rosso. I always wondered why we had to have the parade at the same time as the real Royal Wedding. It meant we couldn't actually watch the bloody thing, but as the parade got under way, my mum must have had a change of heart and came lurching down the lane dressed as a drunk tennis player. From Martini to Martina, I cringed in horror when I saw the outfit she was wearing. Extremely high cut white shorts, a white t-shirt and a baseball cap; rounded off with a nasty looking wooden tennis racket. It was quite an entrance, and my mum was still in a terrible mood and looked ready and willing to smash the racket over Princess Anne's head at any given moment! 'Tennis player', like its 'footballer' counterpart, was the poor man's fancy dress option. I hated that charade: partly because I missed the wedding on TV; partly because of my mum's outfit; and not least because I looked like a complete tit myself.

I once watched a programme on STV about 1981 and it was fascinating to see what the country was like at that time. It seems like such a long time ago, although the 80s are considered part of the 'modern era' aren't they? But the decade (and especially the early 80s) is now a whole generation ago. Kids born in 1981 now have their own kids; and look at the state of Britney Spears! The world was a different place in terms of fashion, music, war, technology and political correctness. In photos my mum took with one of those nasty oblong cameras, everyone had a long wedge haircut and garden lawns too were overgrown, yet also bare in patches from all the football. In 1981, the first space shuttle, Columbia was launched. But for the privileged, the real technological advance was Pac-Man. Like Charles and Di's wedding, 'the nation' united once more as Bucks Fizz won the Eurovision Song Contest, but if my hazy memory serves, the sight of Cheryl Baker having her skirt ripped off might well have been the catalyst for the Brixton Riots.

It was also in this year, at the age of seven, that I discovered three new things: music, football and booze. There were three games of football in particular I remember watching and I reckon they were the first I ever saw. They were:

• Home International: England 0 Scotland 1
• 'Spurs are on their way to Wembley' – The Ricky Villa wonder goal
• Scottish Cup Final: Rangers 0 Dundee Utd 0

I was actually playing my new found hobby in the field at Saughton Mains Bank when my neighbour hurriedly shouted us inside:

"Scotland have a penalty!"

The permed West Brom player, Bryan Robson, had clipped scraggly Scots whipper-snapper, Steve Archibald just inside the box. John Robertson slotted home the penalty, and the living room erupted as cans of lager and piled ashtrays were sent flying. Two minutes later, we were back outside, re-enacting the goal, complete with high-pitched commentary. I had discovered football.

The Spurs game was a mid-week cup final replay and I was allowed to stay up and watch a breathless encounter. Spurs, with their white shirts and their little magician, Ossie Ardiles, looked so glamorous and talented. They won the match with Ricky Villa's wonderful solo effort in a game that I'll always remember. But it is with much scandal and shame that I confess that it is the dour 0-0 draw that Rangers played out with Dundee Utd in the Scottish Cup Final which had the most significant bearing on me. Because back in 1981, I was…a Rangers fan. Nobody gets a second chance to make a first impression in life, and likewise, I can never take that back. It is something that not many of my Hearts supporting friends know about, and I'd have preferred to have kept that one buried underneath a great big pile of rocks. But yes, Rangers were my first 'love' in football: 'whatever love means, eh Charles?'

It all came down to family dynamics. My father was gone and didn't introduce me to football at all. My two older brothers, Tommy and Bobby, were into their footy and as Bobby was my chief torturer and adversary, it was with Tommy that I bonded with the most. Despite his increasing disappearance from family life, all for the pleasure of Her Majesty (and I'm not talking Play Scheme weddings this time), his kind demeanour meant it was Rangers (at that time, his team), and not Hearts (Bobby's team) who I would swear my allegiance to. Not that there was any chance of me going to Ibrox of course, but looking back at a picture of school sports day at the ash-tracked Saughton Enclosure, there, with a can of Top Deck Shandy in one hand, and packet of Monster Munch in the other, is the embarrassing sight of a Rangers jersey. I imagine it was just a phase Tommy was going through, and within a year, both he and I were Hearts fans: without the bus fare.

My mum had a couple of male friends in the early 1980s and they were partial to a spot of anything containing alcohol. One looked a bit like John Travolta, but was gone quicker than I could say Greased Lightnin'. Another was in and out of my mum's life for nearly a decade, and I loved him dearly until he drunkenly attacked both my mother and me one night in a field near Stow. It was a camping trip straight out of Deliverance. Another was in my house for the New Year party my mum held. The neighbours were there and everyone was pretty pissed, naturally. The other kids and I were allowed to stay up too, which for me meant opportunistic quarterly-hour round trips to the kitchen to fetch myself another tumbler of QC sherry and lemonade! Now, as I loved The Banana Splits, I would often sing the bit in the show where one of them opened a window and two girls with a guitar sang (the Mexican), "la la la, la la la, lalalala, la la la, la la la, lalalala" (or such like). Well, there was an old guitar kicking around at our house party, and as I downed another sherry, I picked up the guitar and demanded the attention of everyone in the room. As I started to sing the "la la la, la la la, lalalala, la la la, la la la, lalala" bit, I began to giggle uncontrollably. I vaguely remember my mum's neighbour rising up from his seat and declaring: "that laddie's pished", as the room went dark and I slid down the wall into oblivion.

But the night wasn't over; I was later awakened to the sound of a smashing window. A drunken woman had pitched up at the house some time after the other guests had staggered home. As I made my way through to my mum's room, I could only wait there, hiding again, as the crazed banshee smashed her way through all of the panes of glass next to the front door. Fortunately, she was eventually led away by my mum's friend and we lived to fight another hangover. This scenario I remembered all too well from the two previous attempted break-ins. Although it seemed familiar, I could never get used to it. I don't feel any animosity towards anyone from back in those Lambrusco Nights. My circumstances were akin to a thousand lives across Edinburgh's housing schemes. My mum deserved happiness, and whatever friendship she could get was her business and her entitlement in those days. As far as I know, most of these guys are now dead.

Chapter 9
Haunted by Honduras,
falling for Hearts

When I said I discovered music in 1981, I didn't limit that thought just to pop music. In Saughton Mains, I knew the words to The Sash and Derry's Walls whilst still at Primary School. Sectarianism isn't a life or death issue in Edinburgh as it is in Belfast, or even the greater Glasgow area for that matter. But in housing schemes like mine, people back then took a passing interest; certainly enough to know the words of the 'party songs'. All sorts of songs were sung in front of the kids by adults at New Year parties. I admit that the repartees were often so impressive, that we would be laughing hysterically and begging for them to be done again and again. The people who sang and taught us these songs disappeared out of my life a long, long time ago. When I think back to those times, I wonder if people knew any better then, or indeed, do they now? I guess it was only an excuse for a sing-song at the New Year party: and who doesn't like singing at parties? Saughton Mains in the early 1980s wasn't exactly progressive; but then I only had to switch on the TV to see Love Thy Neighbour and Mind Your Language.

Although at eight-years-old I could rattle off a verse or two of 'traditional' UVF songs, I was much more into the words and music of Adam and the Ants. There was a record shop on Gorgie Road called Trax, and it was there that I bought my first ever single, 'Prince Charming'. I remember being thrilled seeing their new video, 'Ant Rap' on Tizwas; at the time I considered this to be the greatest song in the history of popular music (and I might still!). "Marco, Merrick, Terry-Lee - Gary Tibbs are your's tru-lee": inspired lyrics for Allan, 'Blue' and me. I had a couple of their albums and several records, with Goody Two Shoes being my latest favourite; even though I was blissfully unaware the band had actually split up by then. Adam Ant, of course, became something of a Fruit 'n' Nut case in his later years and perhaps it was the humanitarian side to my personality that impelled me to have the dream about helping him on his sick bed, wet towel to the head, etc (I guess Marco, Merrick, and Terry-Lee were busy pursuing solo projects that day).

I'm not sure if Bobby was ever into Adam and the Ants, but he did take great pleasure in being a horrible bastard bully. I remember when I brought a school friend, Keith (pronounced 'Keef') back home to stay for tea. My mum was out, so it was just Keith and me. I showed him the room I shared with Bobby (complete with Flash Gordon wallpaper), and my toys. Maybe we even did some homework? Things were going really well with my latest chum and I liked him. But then Bobby came home. And he proceeded to fuck everything up by being a complete bastard towards Keith; even forcing the poor sod to dance for him at one point. Keith could only take so much humiliation before he burst out crying and ran for the door. Fortunately my mum came in just as Keith made a bolt for it and she managed to calm the poor laddie down. Although he stayed for tea, I got the impression he walked back up the road a broken man! Bobby could be like that. Prince Charming one minute: no surrender the next.

On April 21st 1982, Bobby took me to my first ever professional football match. It was Hearts versus Ayr United in a First Division league tie at Tynecastle. Tommy had yet to change his allegiances to Hearts which left me with no choice but to grudgingly go to Tynecastle with Bobby. For months I heard talk of watching the games in 'The Shed'. A shed? I had this image of a few dozen Hearts fans crammed into some wooden shack left over from the Dodge City closing down sale. It was 80p to get in, and as I made my way through the McLeod Street turnstiles and onto the terracing, my breath was simply taken away. A real surge came over me, and I knew I'd never forget that moment. Although I was just a kid (and a bloody Rangers fan), I realised instantly what love at first sight meant. Right there and then, I was a Hearts fan. It just made sense. Hearts won the game 2-1, courtesy of a flying header from Derek Addison. A quick check of the excellent Londonhearts.com website tells me I was part of a crowd of just 5,299 hardy souls: although I actually spent most of the evening collecting bits of paper to throw in the air like the ticker-tape images shown from Argentina at the last World Cup. Ah, the World Cup…Hearts might have been my new love, but they would have to go on hold; just for the summer at least.

Spain '82. That's what I called it. To others, it was the all glitzy Panini FIFA 'Espania '82 Official World Cup Sticker Book for cool kids. With some change that I had saved up, my unofficial sticker collection began in earnest, and even slightly against my own will. Having a big brother like I did, Bobby was never in any doubt as how best to spend my money, and suddenly he turned on the charm. I didn't actually get pocket money in the form of a weekly allowance. My dad paid a basic allowance to my mum, but how can I state this clearly enough? We were fucking skint! We qualified for free school dinners, but the food was more Jimmy Boyle than

Jamie Oliver. When I was five or six, I did once receive money from my Dad. It was a pound note, and I ran all the way to the shops in Saughton Mains Gardens to buy a glass bottle of fizzy pineapple juice and about five chocolate bars. So excited was I by this reckless act of spending, that I actually stopped a young woman in the street and informed her of my recent good fortune; running her through my entire inventory! So when I did get money, I knew I had to enjoy it. Five packets of stickers and one unofficial sticker album later, I was ready to begin my summer project. There was no going back now, as Bobby had informed me.

Of course, I soon realised that I was up shit creek when all the other kids at school had the 'official' Panini collection. There was simply no one else around to swap a Hans Krankle for a Zibi Boniek. I also had four Mick Mills and a Spaniard called Lopez Ufarti. All the other kids (with packets coming out of their leg warmers) were quickly racking up full pages as they became familiar with the star players of Kuwait and Algeria. The only Scottish player I had was Dave Narey and to be frank, he wasn't the most exhilarating bloke to look at, despite his 'toe poke' v Brazil. And where was Socrates when I needed him? Or Zico? Or Maradona? No, the only team I had an almost full breast of was flippin' Honduras; and according to my pals, they were the scariest cast of characters since The Hills Have Eyes! To this day, I can still picture them as I struggle to sleep at night and the only reason the cool kids would look at my pathetic sticker album was to snigger at my Central Americans!

Despite plug players and no-swappers, I plodded on and faithfully tried to keep building the collection, only for the Saughton Mains shop to stop selling them as the tournament ended. I would go to the newsagent as a sort of pilgrimage, but the shop keeper merely shrugged his shoulders and my dream of completing the collection faded. I could now only look on in envy as the other kids finished their books in time for Paulo Rossi's goal spree and the sinking of the Belgrano. It was my one and only attempt at a sticker album. My brother soon found new ways of manipulating my loose change and my world moved on to supporting a struggling Edinburgh First Division football club. I loved the football at that World Cup, the first I became aware of. I loved it when the satellite image went a bit funny during the Scotland v New Zealand match which resulted in the pitch glowing a trippy shade of purple. Bobby and I were once more reunited with our Dad, and we spent a great week in the caravan at Pettycur Bay watching the crucial Scotland v Russia encounter, among others. To be fair, my dad only needed to buy chips or drop us off at the swimming pool in Kirkcaldy every now and then. The rest of our time was spent watching three games of footy a day in the caravan. I loved that holiday, and it was to be the best time I would ever spend with my father. The 1982 World Cup therefore holds a special place in my heart and on more than one level, but bloody hell: Brazil should've won it.

Somewhere, buried deep underneath the unfloored, thick loft insulation at my mum's house, rests a half finished, fully lost unofficial book of unsightly World Cup football players. Maybe one day I'll find it, whilst trying my best to avoid falling through the ceiling and into the spare room. Perhaps then, I can flick through the pages, and afford a laugh, not at the Honduras players, but at the eight-year-old boy who battled in vain (and in rain) for his mission, and ponder why I just didn't think to carry on using 'official' unwanted Panini stickers. But no, that would have been cheating, or perhaps boring or predictable. Maybe some symphonies are best left unfinished, and perhaps now writing this, I can put the disappointment to rest and at least be proud of my struggling perseverance, some twenty-five years ago. Some people think The Holy Grail is buried underneath Rosslyn Chapel. Not for me it isn't.

Chapter 10
Mother Nature's son

Despite knowing the words to every sectarian song this side of the Shankhill Road, my brother Bobby and I were about to go see The Pope, of all people, as he toured Scotland on religious duty, and just a year after taking a bullet himself in Rome. My mum chose a spot near Princes Street for us all to see the popular pontiff. Tommy wasn't there though, but then he was only to be a fleeting figure in my life, as his behaviour deteriorated. Bobby was there, with his incredible curly hair (and uncanny resemblance to Mickey Dolenz) but he wasn't in the best of form as he'd badly sunburnt his neck and shoulders during that long, hot summer. So I guess the last thing he wanted then was some drunk to stagger out of the Rutland Bar, slap both hands on his piping shoulders and shout "1690 ya fenian bastard" just as the Pope-mobile went whizzing past. Edinburgh folk only got a fleeting glimpse of Pope John Paul II, but Bobby didn't see a thing as the drunken bigot used my brother's shoulders as a sectarian step-ladder and the only thing I remember was seeing Bobby's contorted face. During the booing of the minute's silence at Hampden in 2005, I thought only of my brother's own pain and suffering.

Hearts were once again stuck in Scottish football's 2nd tier in 1982/83. I had seen my first two games the previous season (my second was a 2-0 win over mighty East Stirlingshire). My mum's friend took me to another mid-week game, only this time, the opposition was Rangers in the semi-final of the League Cup: my first big game. There wasn't a single bone in my body that didn't want Hearts to win as we went down 2-1; I still consider this match to be the night I finally put my Rangers shame to rest. I actually made a couple of away matches that season too and what is astonishing is that they were to be the only games of football my father ever took me to. One was a game against Raith Rovers which we lost 4-2, and the other a 2-1 defeat away to St Johnstone. I was at Tynecastle to see John Robertson make his debut when Heart of Midlothian played Queen of the South (I doubt if there's a grander named contest in world football than that); and Hearts finally managed to regain promotion by the end of the season. With Wallace Mercer at the helm, we were back in the top flight, but with attitude. The club had Alex Macdonald as player-manager and Sandy Jardine as his assistant. Experienced professionals were brought in, such as

Jimmy Bone and Donald Park. Macdonald talked about how, when he first arrived in 1980, the dressing room was 'like a disco', and players were turning up in bleached jeans, linen jackets and string vests! Now Hearts were back and it was 1983. Out went New Wave tossers and in came the New Romantics teens, complete with flicked wedges and streaked hair.

School too was about wedges, and friends; and we often got ourselves into mischief in a sort of Stand By Me kind of way. This was a time when Starburst were Opal Fruits and Mint Munchies were still Mintolas. Football was absolutely king, and by 1983 I had discarded my Fame leg-warmers and 'waffle' trousers to begin goalkeeping for both Stenhouse Primary School and Hutchison Vale Boys Club. I styled myself on the Spanish goalkeeper, Lois Arcanada, who famously spilled a harmless cross to allow Gerry Armstrong to score for Northern Ireland at the World Cup (great role model then). At school, there was Allan, Blue, Evan and a whole group of others. Bobby was the dominant force in my life and despite him often being a complete bastard to me, I now can't help but laugh at our relationship back then. As well as the football, our adventures were awesome. Sometimes we feared for our lives, and that was certainly the case when Allan banged on the back door of the Chinese takeaway at Chesser. I guess it was a mixture of mischief and escapade that took my friends and I round there, but as the door swung open, we were suddenly confronted with four mean looking chefs, all looking like they were going to kick our butts. Our only options for escape were wading through the rat-infested Water of Leith, or scrambling over the raised metal pipe bridge that spanned the filthy river. The pipe it was, and our panic-stricken getaway was concluded when we squeezed our bodies through a gap in the concrete tower on the other side of the river. When safety was reached, we reassessed our enemy, only to see them laughing at us hysterically, and enjoying what turned out to be a routine cigarette break. Despite our humiliation, it was amazing just how quickly we rediscovered our bravery and cockiness: apart that is, from the poor sod who selected the Water of Leith option!

We would be out for the day, passing through haunts such as 'The Lollies', a sinister looking little path behind Saughton Prison. There used to be a dog racing stadium next to it, and I think part of the scoreboard remains. The field next to the path used to be home to an old horse and across the river were allotments. The path back then was a means to reach the idyllic Craiglockhart Dell, which was both one and a million miles away from Saughton Mains Bank. Going from A to B there now would take me back twenty-five hazy years. There were other places we'd go; such as Crammond Island, the Tarzan at Saughton Park or a visit to Edinburgh Zoo (where we'd skive in, naturally; though with enough care as not to vault the wrong fence). Memories of zoo-skiving are more vivid than anything when I remember back. Allan, Blue, Bobby and I would walk down Saughton Mains Bank and along Saughton Mains Street. We'd cross the rickety metal Carrick Knowe Bridge (no longer rickety or metal) and down the long straight road that is Carrick Knowe Avenue. The weather is always hot in this memory and that's why I like it so much. I loved the summer holidays. We were housing scheme ancestors of Huckleberry Finn and Tom Sawyer.

Of all the memories I have as a child though, nothing compares with playing football in the field outside my house. Kids from nearby streets would make up the numbers like DD, Mikey, Martin, Andy, Colin, Steven, Vince, Gareth, John, Allan, Bobby, Blue and me.

The field at Saughton Mains Bank, just a jaggy shaped patch of grass in a working class estate, provided me with the happiest times of my childhood. We played in the summer and in the winter, in the sun and in the rain. We played in the snow and until it was dark. Sometimes we played in the dark with only the snow to provide the light. We played and we played. There was however, one slight problem. Our field was at the centre of a turf war between us kids and the old folk whose stairwell looked on to it. Led by an old guy we knew only as 'Grumpy', they waged a campaign against us for years. Broken glass, nails, paint and even fat (that's right: some sort of solidified animal fat) was strewn across the ground to stop us playing near to their houses. In fact, such were the extremities of Grumpy's tactics, that he even once feigned a heart attack by our road-side goal mouth! It was his *gros canons*. He actually quite liked me in later years, and I can now say I miss old Grumpy. He might have fought a bitter battle against us kids: but no one could accuse him of lacking passion for his cause. Our football field was magnificent, and I can still see it on my XYZ satellite picture of Edinburgh that hangs in my hallway. There, we were all equals. There, we had no family 'domestics' as life's entire quandary was put to one side. We had a football game to think about. At a time when I was just another long-haired kid from just another single parent family, football was my escape. From children to adolescents, we were superstars in our own back yard. Football was king. It's little wonder that we're so obsessed with it.

Whenever I see Gregory's Girl, I am reminded of alternate weekends spent with my dad in the West Lothian new town of Livingston. Entertainment was generally in short supply and at best, we got a trip to the baths, at aptly named Bathgate (though rather embarrassingly, I couldn't swim until I was fourteen). Sometimes we'd go round the 'trim track' which was great, or the cinema at the original version of the Almondvale Concrete Jungle Shopping Centre. No matter what we did, dad would join in for ten minutes, before having to go off, 'shopping'. An hour or so later, he'd pitch up refreshed from his shopping trip and sometimes he had even been shopping. I recall one Saturday when he got himself completely trousered; by 7pm we sat in his two-star Craigshill flat, Bobby perched on one of my dad's knees, and me on the other. All was quiet, apart from the ticking of a naff gold-plated carriage clock on the fireplace. It was light outside, but the curtains were shut. My father mumbled to us that he loved us, and I believed him. It's just that he was slumped in a chair completely pissed. Bobby and I didn't know what to do. I mean, who was going to make me my fucking dinner? But with a stroke of luck, my Uncle Ossie had been tipped off, and he came round to check up on us. A few minutes later, we were on our way down to Howden, to stay with a family unit that consisted of a mum, a dad, some kids and a dog that wore a lampshade over its head, having licked its balls red raw. I stayed the night in the same room as my adored cousin Stuart. I wore his black belt 'karate' pyjamas, and I watched him snore away for hours. I couldn't sleep. I think I drank too much coffee in those days.

At just nine years of age, I went to Rose Street with Bobby and Blue. As 'Karma Chameleon' was number one in the charts, we decided that getting our ears pierced was the best way to keep ourselves at the cutting-edge of housing scheme hip à la mode. How on earth the ladies in the shop allowed us to get this done, unaccompanied by an adult, at such a young age was perhaps a symbol of the times. Or there again, maybe Bobby's Magnum PI bum-fluff moustache and perm was enough to sway the age-barrier? My mum was fine about us getting our ears pierced and curly haired Bobby actually got both his lobes perforated, taking him from Magnum to Michael (as in George). But when my dad found out about this prancing caper, all of John Knox's fire and brimstone made its way along the A71 to Saughton Mains Bank for a high-noon. I hadn't seen my dad sit in my living room for years, but this wasn't Surprise Surprise with Cilla Black and Spit the Dog. After a long stand-off between my parents, my dad ended with a tirade before storming out of the house. It was a parting shot that has gone down in the annals of Bowie family history:

"Earrings in their ears and studs in their arses", he bellowed, and even Boy George wouldn't argue with that.

Chapter 11
The derby that
changed everything

Every so often, a football fan attends a game that reminds him, or her, why it really is worth all the hassle. For me, there was no hassle because I caught the Hearts bug when the club was rediscovering itself. For the fans that lived through seven years of humiliation and eighteen years of mediocrity, the first Edinburgh derby of the 1980s represented so much; on September 3rd 1983, Hearts and Hibs came head to head at Tynecastle. The match was a classic, and Hibs were heading for a win, when late goals from John Robertson and Jimmy Bone kept the two points at Tynecastle. It wasn't just any old derby win though. Hearts, it seemed, had sent out a powerful message to Hibs that day and history now shows that the Jam Tarts were to dominate the fixture for pretty much the rest of the twentieth century. So how did I feel at the final whistle after such a famous and important victory? I didn't feel anything. I had to go to FineFare with my mum to 'chum her with the messages'. But Bobby was there.

My mum had a partner called Charlie. He was a drinker and a little bit 'fly by night'. But I liked him because he was funny. He had bandy legs and crows feet and a face full of stubble. His relationship with my mother though, was volatile. Often they'd fight and that invariably meant damage to furniture and damage to themselves, which I'd witness. Sometimes he was around and sometimes he was gone for weeks. Charlie spent some years on the dole, but for me it was fantastic to have a father figure around to give me advice, encouragement and most of all: watch me play football. My dad only made it to a couple of games, and my football was an inconvenience to him. But Charlie would make his way to football fields all over Edinburgh and in all weather conditions to stand behind the goal, talking me through the game. I remember we once climbed up the rocky face of that hill next to the ski-slope. I got myself stuck in a gully near the top but Charlie talked me through it and I felt elated as we both reached the summit: not a bad effort in pouring rain and thick fog. All we had to do after that was walk back to Saughton Mains.

I would sometimes spend the entire day with Charlie and listen to his childhood stories of 60s brotherhood and gang-fighting. He was great to me, but a few years later, as the alcohol took its toll and the arguments got worse, my mother and I suffered that horrific attack on the overnight camping trip to Stow. The trip was already a strange set-up, but then he proceeded to fall out with my mum late on. Normally, if it had happened in Saughton Mains Bank, it would've resulted in Charlie retreating to the safety of The Busy Bee as my mum kicked him out of the house. But there in the wilds, the only thing getting kicked was my mum as Charlie's rage boiled over. As I tried to help her, Charlie pushed me hard to the ground and punched me, threatening me to the point where I actually feared for my life. It was fucking scary and we were all alone in the middle of runny-nosed, Blair Witch country. With Chick holding my mum captive in one tent, and me in the other, I didn't get a wink of sleep that night. This was in part due to the nasty physical attack on my mother and me, and also because there was a bloody hedgehog trying to get in my tent. Charlie died sometime around 2002. I never really forgave him after that night.

It wasn't just my mum who tried for new relationships. My dad started dating someone who was closer to Bobby's age than his own. 'Stepmom' was a twenty-year-old middle class girl from 'dan saff'. She was also a divorcee with a kid. What 'Stepmom' and my dad saw in each other is their business, but one thing is for sure, it had a monumental effect on life from that point on. As well as her infant daughter, 'Stepmom' brought discipline and order to my dad's life and my time spent there was no longer a lads' weekend. I was now participating in yet another post-nuclear family docu-soap called (Step) Sons and Daughters. I was slightly confused by this new world order, but I really liked 'Stepmom'. Pity my mum didn't. Her abhorrence of 'Stepmom' matched any football derby.

Chapter 12
When two tribes go to war

If 'Stepmom's' arrival on the scene meant stability for my dad, then the happy news didn't go down nearly as well at Saughton Mains Bank. My mum despised 'Stepmom' from the start and all her female venom was redirected from my dad, to his new flame. Why so? Well, my mum was stuck in Saughton Mains Bank, below the breadline, raising two boys and sometimes three, depending on whether the oldest happened to be incarcerated at the time. Suddenly she was witnessing my dad's life transforming while she was left with nothing but lawyer's letters and deep, emotional scars. Bobby and I weren't to be spared the abuse that would be fired back and forth between enemy camps. The first Christmas at that time was awkward as the nastiness began to set in, but I was more concerned with the concussion that I suffered after whacking my head from the black-ice slide that we'd created outside the house. Damn that Christmas. We didn't even have a TV. It was already on the blink when my mum sent it on its way by 'tapping' it with a bloody hammer!

Whilst playing in goal for Hutchison Vale one spring morning at Saughton Park, I had the unusual presence of my dad watching me, with his step-daughter by his side. Normally when my dad dropped me off (in the nick of time), he'd bolt back to Livingston, but I'm guessing he had an hour to kill that particular day. I was really pleased about that and I was determined to make the Old Man proud. I remember having a good start to the game and making a few saves, but I just sensed something wasn't right. Before leaving, I hadn't had time to phone my mum that morning which could spell bad news. The previous time Bobby and I had forgotten to phone, mum was pacing the pavement on Calder Road, waiting for us to come back. Bobby and I were then duly set upon by my mum with a four-iron 'Lee Trevino' golf club and as I got whacked on the head, Bobby escaped punishment by jumping out of a first floor window! It was, therefore, more than a little perturbing to see my mum making her way diagonally over the Saughton Park field in the same place and time as my dad and his surrogate daughter from his new, sanitised life. A minute or so later, a couple of dozen stunned parents and coaches, plus twenty-odd budding young footballers were treated to the sight of my mum chasing my dad out of Saughton Park, with his step-daughter on his shoulders. I think we lost in the end.

If that wasn't bad enough, Bobby and I were subjected to a mortifying aborted holiday send-off, as my dad and 'Stepmom' made an appalling custodial faux pas. Apart from our treasured week in Pettycur Bay, Bobby and I had never been away anywhere before. It was with some anticipation then, that as we prepared for our holiday, all our friends gathered outside the house to send us off on our way. Our glamour destination was to be a week long stay in the leafy surroundings of my dad's new in-law's house 'dan saff'. My mum had grudgingly agreed to the holiday. Bobby and I were ready, despite having the most appalling, matching, What Every Woman Wants, quilted pull-over jackets. Bobby's was burgundy and mine light blue. I can't even begin to describe how awful they were, but my mum also fashioned us both Hearts jerseys, patching the famous heart-shaped club crest onto maroon jumpers! It should have been a 4pm departure, but the clock was creeping towards five, when my dad's Nissan Sunny pulled into the street. Bobby and I leapt off our seats and a stir of excitement came over us and our friends who had been waiting outside, patiently. As we said our goodbyes, the car pulled up short, stopping at the lock-up garages about a hundred yards from the house. And instead of my dad being there to greet us, it was 'Stepmom': but not only that, she got out of the car and gave us a jolly and enthusiastic wave. To Bobby and me, it was a cheery wave hello. But to my mother, it was an insulting wave goodbye.

'Stepmom' would have been as well jumping out of the car holding up a big sign that read 'Fuck You'. Bobby and I were halfway out the gate, but we were summoned back to the house by my raging mum, who shouted to 'Stepmom' something along the lines of, "Get the fuck out of my street". 'Stepmom' did just that, and my brother and I were back in the silent living room. The dream holiday of a lifetime had been cruelly snatched away from us. Or so we thought. A phone call was made to my Gran's house by my mum, though it wasn't to discuss the poor weather we'd been having lately. About an hour later, the old Nissan, trundling in second gear, made its way along Saughton Mains Street to the back of the house. 'Stepmom' was driving again, and my father was sitting in the passenger seat, looking... 'tired'. As the car sped away, we had made it at last on our holiday, but I felt only numbness. As I left my little buddies behind, I realised that their motive for seeing us off might not have been in the name of friendship, but in the name of amusement; like the sort of kids that are into WWF pantomime wrestling. Entertainment was guaranteed - always. I didn't look back as the car left Saughton Mains and for the first time in my life, Scotland.

Bobby and I entered a strange new world 'dan saff'. The town itself was a fucking hole and I'd rather play leap-frog with a unicorn than live there.

However, 'Stepmom's' family came from the right side of the tracks. The house was large and the area 'leafy'. It had a big living room and a separate lounge and lots of bedrooms. There was a Commodore 64 computer, satellite TV and brand name soft drinks. It wasn't the house though, that interested me, it was the family; a traditional family unit and without conflict. 'Stepmom's' parents were fantastic: retired in their fifties, unbelievably kind, middle-class and welcoming to two Edinburgh schemies who had pitched up on their door-step. 'Stepmom's' younger brother also lived there. He was young, cocky, arrogant and in the Air Force cadets (or something). He saw me for what I was, but even he was ok, despite referring to me as the 'Little Jock'. I guess the guy suffered from high self-esteem. I loved it there, lived well and slept easily. It felt exciting and privileged. As much as I missed my mum, I didn't miss Saughton Mains Bank. This place was a long, long way from there.

The fallout from the holiday was depressing. There were more lawyers letters exchanged: one that included banning 'Stepmom' from my street. Holiday photos with 'Stepmom' in them were sent back through the post (complete with 'thank you' messages from my mum), and knitted jumpers given to Bobby and me were also returned (though that was actually a blessing in disguise). From a young age, I would accompany my mum to visit Tommy in various institutions for young offenders. I remember going to places like Polmont on a Saturday afternoon, while Bobby was watching Hearts. These journeys were usually made by train or on some smoke-filled bus. I was used to smoky bus journeys. From the age of nine, I would get a green SMT bus to Livingston with Bobby. This meant inhaling everyone's cheap brand second-hand cigarette smoke. At least when I visited Tommy in Saughton, it was only a short walk up the road. Seeing Tommy was a treat. I loved him as my brother and I'd sit there in the visitor's holding bay feeling excited that I was just minutes away from seeing him. When he came in, he always looked slightly embarrassed. Not because he felt guilty of the crimes he committed (usually theft), but more to do with the fact he had to make eye-contact with my mum and me, in a formal setting. For a young man in any situation, it had to be awkward. But if it was grave having to visit Tommy in the clink, it would feel like Butlins compared to his last months in the house. I'm afraid to say that Heart of Midlothian football club didn't feature too much in those very early days. Well, not in my life. But they would.

Chapter 13
When you have the big brother from 'Kes'

Bobby slept above me on the upper bunk. It shook a bit from time to time but I could never find an explanation. By our bunk-beds there was a lamp, and Bobby once asked me to put my finger in the bit where the light bulb went. So I did, and yes, I got an absolute bastard of an electric shock. When we were kids, sitting in the tub having our Sunday night wash, he made me drink Matey bubble bath. One night, several years later when my mum was out for the evening, he spent the entire night torturing me, both mentally and physically. At one point, he dragged me feet first down the stairs, cutting my back open, as blood oozed out onto my 1986/87 Hearts away top. Yup, he fairly shit himself after that happened. But hey, he's my brother. I forgave him. I fought a defensive war against him every day. Once, my mum wanted to get out of an evening with some old neighbours and asked Bobby to make the call. He refused, forcing me to do it. Unsure as to how to introduce myself, I sheepishly announced down the phone that it was "Mrs Bowie's little boy" calling, which caused Bobby and my mum to collapse on the floor in hysterics. I felt humiliated after that, but I have to admit it was fucking funny. Bobby was an outrageous character and he's a big bear of a man today. Thankfully we don't share a Sunday night bath anymore. The bastard always gave me the taps.

There was once a massive motor bike in our back garden, but I've no idea who it belonged to or what it was doing there. Out of curiosity, I tried to climb onto it when I was alone, but I knocked the monster contraption over. Fearing retribution, I fled. The bike had nothing to do with Bobby, but he took severe umbrage to my misdemeanour and waited for me to return home. As I approached the house, I spied him waiting for me and once more, I took flight. However, my big brother proceeded to hound me all over Saughton Mains like Keanu Reeves chasing Patrick Swayze in Point Break: only my brother didn't give in until I was caught. Now at the time, I fancied a really cute girl at school called Asha. I was running up the Saughton Mains alley, near her house when I saw her standing on the corner of the street. Trying to stay cool I said hello, but it was at that moment, and with no luck whatsoever, that Bobby finally caught his prey.

As Asha watched on, he proceeded to royally kick the shit out of me. I eventually made my way back to Saughton Mains Bank, my pride in tatters and tears rolling down my face. I hated Bobby that day and I tore down some of his Hearts posters when I got home: but not all of them. Not enough for him to really get angry. And besides: I needed some left for next time.

Bobby wasn't always bad and he was unbelievably funny at times. He used to buy things from jumble-sales we'd all visit and he once wore a ladies wig to school. Even after all these years, the sight of him playing football at Stenhouse Primary in the guise of Ann Widdecombe still makes me laugh.

During Wimbledon fortnight, the schemies of Saughton Mains made their own Centre Court by the lock-up garages of Saughton Mains Bank. When our friend John took umbrage at a disputed line-call, he pushed me to the ground in front of my brother. Bobby's response was as swift as it was severe. He took his wooden tennis racket and duly smashed it over John's head before doing a runner back to the house. I'm not sure if my mum was more upset at John trying to kick our front door in, or that 'tennis player' was no longer an option for her next fancy dress dilemma.

I won about half a dozen football medals with Hutchison Vale; most notably, the 1983/84 under-10s League Championship (shared with Glenpark). The title was decided on the last game of the season, and after we played out a tense 2-2 draw, our coach, a Mr Docherty, declared it a shared win. The game before that was won in fraught circumstances as I had a bit of a nightmare on the hard surface of Saughton Park's sloping pitch, near to the old bandstand (no longer there). We still won though, 5-3, as we also won the game before that. That was played out on a rainy afternoon at Fords Road. We beat Tynecastle Boys club 4-3 and the reason we won was nothing to do with great play, tactics or effort. We won the game because I spent the entire match pacing back and forth along my goal line, singing 'Uptown Girl'. If I hadn't done that, we'd have lost the match. My logic derived from superstition. I had to do it. Because in 1984, I'd become chronically superstitious. I don't blame my parents though, or for that matter, my brothers. I blame Colin Jack's mum.

Colin Jack wasn't the brightest lad in our class and he looked slightly dim-witted in his National Heath specs. His mum came into Stenhouse Primary to give us a talk on 'superstition in The Outer Hebrides': the place she was from. I sat there listening wide-eyed as she rattled off a long list of things 'never to do' such as putting shoes on a table, using the number 13, walking under ladders and standing on cracks in the pavement. It was a pity then, that the bloody path in Saughton Mains Bank was riddled with them.

Maybe I was vulnerable at the time, because I took on board everything that she said, and superstition became my way of stayin' alive. If I adhered to the rules of my superstition, I would live to see another day. I became unceasingly superstitious for about three years, and I wrestled with myself in almost everything I did. I never talked about it, but one day, as I was playing football by the lock-up garages in Saughton Mains Bank, I noticed Blue and Allan looking at me perplexed. Blue asked me why the fuck I had to tip-toe the entire kerb upon retrieving the ball. Although his observation left me feeling rather foolish, being 'outed' helped me start the process of getting over my superstitions. Besides, there was a lot of stupidity going around at the time. Like council authorities allowing crazed Hebridians to frighten the shit out of Edinburgh school kids.

Lots of strange things were happening at school. Our Primary Six teacher was one of those neck-scarf wearing new-age types who barred us from playing Dodge-Ball at gym time and 'British Bull Dogs' at break. Instead, she decided that what we schemies really needed was a lesson in 'donce-movement'. So using the theme tune to Hill Street Blues, she introduced us to the joys of "expressing one's self through the medium of donce". I still laugh when I think back to the outrageous shapes and movements we made, and the more we camped it up, the more we had each other in hysterics. The 'mothers' though, didn't find anything about this charade funny, and fuelled by the fear of rearing a generation of prancing fun-boys, they grabbed their pitchforks (or handbags) and lit their torches (or Regal King Size) before making their way to the gates of Stenhouse Primary School. Dodge-Ball resumed thereafter and the neck-scarf wearing teacher soon moved on; but the haunting gym-mat strains of the Hill Street Blues were never to be forgotten!

Tommy's latest domestic occurred on Christmas Eve, 1984. He was about to be ejected from the house when my mum went to my neighbour's house to get help. Bobby and I were left to sit through this misery. Tommy was alone with us, and said, "if am no getting a Christmas, then neither are you two". With that, he went upstairs, rummaged around for a bit and brought down a bin-bag stuffed with Christmas presents. It was blowing the myth of Santa Claus, Saughton style; the only thing that would ever come down our chimney was a trapped crow (as I sat by the fireplace). Bobby started to shout at Tommy to stop. I just sat there, a rabbit in the headlights. By the time my mum came back with the neighbour, Tommy was gone, taking Christmas with him. The police were called and Tommy was picked up a while later. For several hours though, we didn't know what was happening. I was distraught: but not for Tommy. All I wanted was my presents, and by late evening the bin bag of festive cheer had returned. The police took statements from everyone involved, including me and it was pretty harrowing. Some months later, I sat in the witness room of Edinburgh's Sheriff Court, eleven years old, waiting to give evidence against my own brother, who was waiting through another door. Fortunately, Tommy pleaded guilty and I wasn't called, but by then, the damage had been done.

Bobby, the enfant terrible and perpetual bully was never really the big brother from Kes. He was merely the big brother from The Goonies. As it turned out, it was Tommy who was the big brother from Kes. He didn't kill my kestrel, but he drank a few cans of it before taking my Christmas away. 'Feed the Schemies: let them know it's Christmas time.' That's what Bob Geldof and Midge Ure should've written. Bobby could be a bad bastard, but essentially, he wasn't bad. Old laws class foxes as bad and a menace, yet people protect their rights too. Bobby needed protection as much as me, but all the same he was a cunning and conniving fox. And as Mason Verger said in Hannibal: 'When the fox hears the rabbit scream, he comes a running...but not to help'.

Chapter 14
Hey you, the Rocksteady Crew

My heart sank when my coach at Hutchison Vale announced the exciting news that we were going to Holland to play in a prestigious tournament. As goalkeeper for the team, I had to be there with the rest of the boys, but I knew right away that I wouldn't make it. It would cost money: about £100. There was no way my mum had the cash and I didn't even bother asking my dad; my football was already a hindrance to my weekends with him, as was evident from the Friday he did an emergency stop in the car upon me telling him of an impending footy match the following morning. Missing that trip was one of my greatest regrets, but I still worked my ass off at our Corstorphine Church jumble sale to help my team-mates raise additional money. Despite winning many medals with Hutchison Vale, missing that trip signified the beginning of the end of my 'promising' football career. For the guy who replaced me in goal, it was just the start of his. Alan Combe was a nice guy to be fair. He made it. I made way.

If football was my top priority, then music was a close second. It was the 80s and all I wanted was a synthesiser. I had no qualms about begging my dad to buy me one, but all he would utter was that "there's a gift on its way". I held on and on and he kept saying that my "gift was getting closer". One Friday in March 1985, I went to my grandparents' house in Stenhouse and my dad said that my "gift had arrived". I was now just a short time away from my synthesiser; any make would do, just as long as it had loads of buttons to press like 'rumba' and 'harpsichord'. He wouldn't confirm what make it was or indeed if it actually was a synthesiser, but he did say that "I'd love it". A couple of hours and one more debate about the miners' strike later, we left my grandparents and headed for Livingston. I ran up the stairs to see my wondrous new present. But lying there wasn't a synthesiser: it was a baby. My step-brother Ian was born on March 1st 1985, and I was mesmerised by the sight of him. I didn't care about the family politics. I just knew right away that I'd love him forever as my brother: but I was gutted he wasn't a synthesiser. Ian arrived into my world that day, but the synthesiser never materialised.

In 1985, I was all set to leave primary school; but not before a scrape with authority. As a keen footballer, it wasn't my fault the odd window pane was broken with a stray shot. So it felt like rough-justice when the assistant-head, Miss Bailey, banned 'proper' footballs from the playground; a decree that prompted vigilante action. Mr Stewart, the janitor, approached me one morning to confiscate the ball trapped underneath my foot. As he drew nearer, I bamboozled him with a neat stepover before booting the ball away, leaving him red-faced and fizzing. Such insurgent behaviour was unlike me, so I merged into the crowd and hoped that I had gotten away with it. Mr Stewart wasn't a man to be messed with, and he had a bastard dog that nearly bit my ass off as I cut through the playground one summer. It was to my dismay then that Miss McArthur called out my name as I waited in line for the bus to Dalry Swimming Baths. She told me to go see the Headmaster. Oh shit!

I had barely spoken to Mr Davidson in my entire time at Stenhouse, but there I was, skulking outside the darkened shadows of the unlit hallway by his private quarters. We called him 'Bullet Face', as he had a rather impressive indent on his cheek. As I waited for him to appear, I considered if it really was true that he earned his nickname due to being shot in the face during World War II. One thing was for sure: I was scared. I was very scared. I was a quite a good boy, and not used to such dissension. I didn't go gang-fighting. I didn't want to end up like Tommy. The only previous trouble I had been in at school was when my friends and I contacted Adolf Hitler on my mum's Ouija Board. But even the dead leader of the Third Reich never prevented me from swimming with my inflated rubber wings. As Mr Davidson's clattering footsteps approached, I became very aware of his rank as Headmaster and his Regan-like appearance. He was carrying a wooden tray that held his lunch. He walked past, but he didn't see me lurking there in the dark. I stood frozen, watching him fiddle with his keys and he swore under his breath as he held his tray with one hand. He eventually jarred the door open, so it was then that I felt it was the right time to make my presence known.

"Mr Davidson!" I called out.

"Fucking shit!" was his reply.

And shit it was, because such was the fright I gave him, his tray catastrophically plummeted to the floor and with it, his lukewarm mince and piping hot custard, all oozing and intermingling over his black, polished shoes. It was to be a long dressing down. But as he lectured me on the rights and wrongs of pupil/janitorial degeneration, I couldn't help but drift off; imagining what custard and mince must have tasted like in one repugnant mouthful. Although, as someone reared on free school dinners, I'd probably tasted much worse.

There was something rather exciting about the summer of 1985. Not only were my friends and I looking forward to starting at Tynecastle High

School Annexe (no longer there), but we were discovering new cool things like fashion and breakdancing. Now I was a poor boy, but I witnessed the rise of the 'casual' movement. I wasn't really interested because I was never going to have designer clothes; nor was I in for the gang-fighting that became a right of passage for any self-respecting schemie. Saughton Mains kids would occasionally 'pavement dance' with kids from Carrick-Knowe, Broomhouse and beyond, but all I wanted to do was play football. Besides, getting into trouble would see me going down the same path as my brothers. I just didn't want my mum going crazy at me as I was shit scared of her. To be on the end of my mother's wrath still scares me to this day. I tried my best to ignore the 'casual' scene, but high school would make that difficult. And my scrapes with the notorious CCS were restricted to a couple of incidents with the 'Baby Crew'. One was being threatened at the top of the Scott Monument, (they propositioned Allan and me with an alternative route back down which boasted unparalleled views). The other event involved being chased across Saughton Park by about thirty of them in 1988 (and if Ben Johnson thought he ran fast that year...). The only other run-in I had with Hibs fans was when my friends and I were taunting them upon their return from their 1985 League Cup Final defeat. A couple of eggs were thrown at a supporters' coach, which didn't go down well with its passengers, or the car-load that screeched to a halt just after it. Thankfully, those Calder Road roundabouts always had a Tom, Dick and Harry escape-route feel to them.

Allan, Blue, Bobby and I went to the cinema to see Breakdance 2 one Saturday matinée. The last time I had gone to the cinema with Bobby was to see Jaws 3-D but there weren't any polarised glasses left and I ended up staring at a blurred screen for two hours. On this occasion, there was a much greater menace than a giant rubber shark. That's right: the cinema was full of schemies: schemies from other areas of the city. The rabble that ensued was enough for the lights to go up and for the manager to come out and tell everyone to shut the fuck up. I'd like to think that the lady that accompanied him was one of those iconic 1950s 'serving ice cream from a tray' beauties, but in reality she was a mullet-haired flat-top with a torch. The film eventually started which in turn sparked a mass outbreak of 'body-popping' up and down the aisles and even on the stage. It was a dark and scary, yet hilariously chaotic scene to witness. I have this picture in my head of the manager, who was probably left shaking his head at the rampage. He probably just thought "aw fuck it". Our football was put away for the summer as someone acquired a whopping piece of linoleum for us to practice our new hobby on. The only problem I had in all of this was that I couldn't breakdance. I just couldn't do it, and I wasn't that keen to learn, particularly as it made my friends look so incredibly stupid! But at least I had my saving grace, in that I could do some mean 'robotics'. 'Vietnam: n-n nineteen:' I wasn't really sure what was going on! And I really didn't know what the hell was going on as I stood there in the cinema, trying to fit in, performing crap robotics and looking like a complete trumpet! It was to be the last time I did that (apart from maybe when Patrick Swayze went up to heaven in Ghost).

To prepare for Tynecastle High School, my mum took me to What Every Woman Wants to buy me some shiny new clobber. On my first day, I walked through the gates wearing a truly horrific pair of grey leather slip-on shoes (complete with grey tassels), grey flecked trousers, a grey v-neck pullover, and a grey polyester jacket. We 'fade to grey' indeed, but looking like a tosser wasn't exclusive to me, as this was a time of Pod sandals and dungarees; sort of Stonewall chic. Sir Clive Sinclair enjoyed looking like a prat, as he got down, breakdancing with Britain's exhaust pipes in his doomed C5. In 1985, we were mesmerised by Back to the Future while Wham stuffed shuttlecocks down their shorts. Michael Jackson led the chorus in 'We are the world', looking like Michael Jackson should do; one glove, sunglasses, a nose! Tina Turner was pontificating too, with trademark big hair and bright lipstick; Bruce Springsteen hurled up all his flem; and Lionel Ritchie gave viewers the big thumbs up, which must have been a real comfort to the starving millions of Sudan. The rest just held on to their headphones as expressively as they could. 1985 was the year of Live Aid, and with fifteen years left of the century, the Rainbow Warrior was lost and the Titanic was found: but the only sinking ship that concerned me was the place I called home, at Saughton Mains Bank.

Chapter 15
A truly harsh lesson in breakdancing

My first year at Tynecastle High School coincided with possibly the most extraordinary footballing season in the history of Heart of Midlothian Football Club. It is perhaps worth remembering where Hearts were a couple of years previous: fighting for their very existence in the second tier of Scottish Football. The first game of the season was against Celtic. I was there with Bobby as we celebrated our debutant, John Colquhoun, firing us into an early lead, and we were sent flying by an enormous sway in The Shed. It took me about five minutes to find Bobby again but I loved the sensation; a human avalanche. So this was The Shed? Right, I get it now. Celtic though, got a sickening last-gasp equaliser and I'll never forget the sight of the packed away end erupting into bedlam. It was a horrible feeling, watching them as they must've watched us: but admittedly, it was an impressive sight. Bobby and I headed home together, talking as young brothers do about the game; me trying to keep up with his bigger strides, asking relentless questions, walking through quirky 'Puddle Lane', with its distinctive 'spirits' smell and imposing Communist Block-style blackened buildings (no longer there).

The next home match saw Allan and I get into big trouble for disappearing after the game, sparking off a search-n-rescue operation by Bobby and Allan's dad. They must have feared the worst for us, and it certainly showed in their displeasure when we eventually turned up. What we had been doing all that time was looking for (and finding some) money at the bottom of the children's ball-pit in the Brown Bear furniture store on Stevenson Road! We reckoned if we showed up every week, we could easily make a few quid. Despite the enterprising start to the season, 1985/86 began to pan out quite dismally. After the first quarter of the campaign, Hearts were second from bottom and the fans began preparing for a long, hard slog of a season. But the Jam Tarts' form was about to pick up, and spectacularly so...

If Hearts' season was to have a bit of drama, then so did my first day at Tynecastle High. Allan, Blue, Keith, myself and a couple of others went marching on to the playground armed with a ghetto-blaster, linoleum mat

46

and the best back-to-school fashion What Every Women Wants could offer. We were out to make our mark and the big boys of Tynecastle High Annexe had better take note: the new kids were here, and they were here to donce! As the music started, a crowd gathered instantaneously. Who the fuck were these little bastards with new trousers and abysmal slip-on shoes - though the tassels are quite nice? They were about to find out. Now our plan was straightforward enough. The lads would pull off a couple of 'caterpillars' and 'windmills', and ultimate cool status would be ours. Right? Wrong!

Things went badly from the start. The crowd was moving in on us and the guys just weren't performing to their usual standards. Even the basic moves, executed with ease at Saughton Mains throughout the summer, seemed hopelessly beyond them. The throng of second-year pupils began to smell blood: or was it the smell of fear? But either way, I couldn't just stand there and watch them go under. As part of the breakdance troupe, I had to act: and act I did. So I took a deep breath and threw myself right into the fray. Frantically, I began performing my robotics. My stomach may have been churning, but I grasped the mantle of leadership and tried my best to work the crowd. I remember shuffling round the edge of the lino in front of a now, quite bewildered audience. Older and bigger kids were doubled-up by my performance whilst many were left stunned, but I grimly kept going; craning my neck back round to my friends and growling at them through the side of my mouth:

"Keep it going lads: keep it tight at the back!" But it was all in vain. As the bell rang, the mob turned ugly, and they mercilessly piled in; abruptly and violently they brought the curtain down on our woeful performance. They may have spared us our ghetto-blaster, but the linoleum mat was never to be seen again. My own personal misfortune from the insurgence came in the form of a really hard punch to the ear. It was a truly sickening thud, and received in Dolby surround sound too. The bell had gone, but the ringing in my ear continued for quite some time. And as I went back to class, my tumultuous, summer-long love-affair with the robotic arm of breakdancing was over.

The Cold War between my mum and dad took another twist when my Old Man picked Bobby and me up one Friday in October 1985. It should have been just a normal, humdrum weekend, but my dad told us that we were going to a wedding: his, to be precise. We were under the impression that both he and 'Stepmom' were already married, but deception, bluff and smokescreen had prevented him from telling us why that wasn't the case, nor were we to utter so much as a word of this to our mum back home. My dad got married for the second time at the Howden Church of Muchos Concrete Jungleness. The reception was back in the new family home in

Eliburn. Their house was a bit bigger than my own at Saughton Mains Bank and it had lots of places to explore outside. I remember helping my dad lift some concrete blocks from the desolate wasteland (no longer there) over the road. This enabled him to build a rock garden and our midnight run at least gave us a chance to gain some much needed father and son time. I liked it there. Back then, it had a sort of rural feel to it, which was what I craved. I loved the woods and the stream, and going back to the house to be with my dad. But his wedding reception ended in disaster for me. A storm was gathering to the east, and my mum phoned up, going fucking crazy as to why I wasn't coming back for my Hutchison Vale football game. My sworn loyalty to my dad prevented me from explaining the real reason why I was in Livingston; but she just kept going on and on at me. I was in tears when she hung up the phone. All her paranoia, all her anger and all her lightening towards my dad was conducted through me that night; and being forced to miss football was just another nail in my Hutchison Vale coffin. I was the processed ham in the limp wedding buffet sandwich. When 'Stepmom' got the wedding photos developed, there on the sofa sits me, eyes red raw and puffed up. And the eyes never lie.

On Christmas Eve 1985, I suffered yet another traumatic Yuletide experience. For years, old Mrs Douglas (no longer there), a resident of Saughton Mains Bank, had a vicious little Jack Russell dog. My mum sent me to Bains the Butcher at Stenhouse Cross, to purchase some of their legendary pies. As I walked back to the house, by the old wall that ran adjacent to Stenhouse Nursery School (no longer there), the sadistic dog waddled past me. I was extremely wary of that dreaded mutt, and it was with dismal anticipation that I proceeded to watch it sink its rabid teeth deep into my left leg. I collapsed to the ground in an agonised and distressed heap, and what made the incident worse was not the sick inevitability about it all: nor was it the searing pain of my punctured flesh. No, the reason why I hate that dog was for the fact that as I dropped the bag which held the award winning pies, the little bastard started to eat my dinner off the pavement! A couple of hours later, I found myself in Sighthill Clinic with my mum, receiving a tetanus jag which the nurse duly dispatched into the right side of my arse. I was beginning to question the value of Christmas on all sorts of levels.

Chapter 16
Hearts beating stronger

Hutchison Vale is one of the top clubs in Scotland in terms of winning trophies and producing youngsters for the professional game, and I was the goalkeeper. For the first couple of years, I was considered to be one of "the best in the league" at school level, though my 'Edinburgh Select' trial was a non-event, as I hardly got a touch of the ball during a ninety-minute game in which my eleven won 4-1. Still, despite that and my lack of height, I was known for my bravery and spectacular saves; I must also admit that I came from the 'Bartez' school of mad-cap goalkeeping. In truth, I wouldn't have 'made it'. Perhaps if I had been a bit taller, I might have been 'spotted' and developed; or at least have made it to a reasonable level. However, there was one major weapon missing from my armoury, which would kill off any hope of making the Hutchison Vale position my own. 'The Dad Factor' at Hutchison Vale was a simple modus operandi. If the old man was in 'The Club', the kid was on the pitch. There were those in the team that were 'in', and the rest just made up the numbers. When the club captain (and his father) brought along the new goalkeeper, my tenure between the sticks was over, instantaneously. And as my place in goal was gone, with it went my confidence. I became little more than a gofer; the person who retrieved the ball from the river if we were losing a match: the 'Water Boy'. I put on a brave face and stuck it out for a couple of years, but eventually, I drifted out of the game and quit: aged thirteen.

Despite my football career dwindling to a dismal death, there was one other opportunity to obtain a level of sporting greatness. In 1985, Edinburgh school kids had the chance to audition for the upcoming 'Commonwealth Games', which would be held in the city the following summer. I was excited by this on two levels. One, because I had visions of me parading round Meadowbank Stadium, as the local boy made flag-bearer for the mighty USA (at this point, I hadn't realised that the USA weren't a commonwealth country: well at least not any more). Secondly, any kid lucky enough for selection for the opening ceremony would get to keep their complimentary tracksuit and perhaps best of all: Nike trainers. The 1986 Commonwealth Games Opening Ceremony then became my new route to glory; and all I had to do was pass an audition.

Now by my reckoning, Lud Romano (yes that really was his name) chose

Tynecastle High as one of the first schools in which to audition children for the opening ceremony. He was an English geezer with a moustache and a mullet, and his chunky framed glasses were as big as his hair. He looked like a frustrated Top of the Pops presenter. As my name was 'Bowie', I was in the first registration class of Tynecastle High. So it could therefore be that I was one of the first kids in Edinburgh to audition for the 1986 Games. So then by that calculation, it is entirely possible that I was also the first person to be eliminated from the entire process, despite having perhaps the loftiest ambitions of all! Looking back, it started well enough. All of the class were there, spread out in the gym hall facing Lud, another woman and a colossal ghetto-blaster (which evoked raw memories of breakdancing mob-violence).

Romano instructed us that when the music commenced, if tapped on the shoulder, it was time to go back to class, as we obviously couldn't dance. So when Chaka Khan's 'I feel for you' started up, the stale old gym hall burst into life as a variety of freestyles were undertaken by class 1E. The girl next to me immediately leaped high into the air before performing a stunning spin upon landing. I had considered my robotics, but that would've only worsened the memory of my throbbing ear and stolen lino. I then contemplated utilising my grounding in 'donce movement', but this was no time for Hill Street Blues or acting like a tit. So I decided to settle for a steady side-step movement which would see me through to Meadowbank; and by that time, the Canadian flag-bearing duty. But then like a bolt of lightning it happened; a hand came thumping down on my left shoulder. I had barely made it through the first verse of the song. Once more, my dreams lay in tatters. There was nothing I could do, but walk the trail of tears back to class, with the haunting echoes of the mouth-organ inspired rap blaring down the corridor, almost mockingly singing 'I feel for you'. My heart was broken; and now the 1986 Commonwealth Games would go on, but without me.

Hearts gave the fans a rare moment of cheer in October 1985 when they beat Celtic at Parkhead. I remember the day well, starting with the train at Haymarket. One of the windows in our carriage got smashed by some kids at Forrester Park, but about an hour or so later, I was in Polmont Young Offenders Institute, visiting Tommy. On the way home, I heard on someone's transistor radio that Hearts had won 1-0. It was the second week in a row we hadn't lost a game. Nobody realised it at the time, but it was to be the start of a staggering run of results that would keep going throughout the winter and beyond. By late December 1985, Hearts were top of the league as Shakin' Stevens was top of the charts. 'The Welsh Elvis' was smiling through gritted teeth wearing his appalling knitted jumper, for the video of 'Merry Christmas Everyone'. I too was smiling. I had fallen in love with Hearts nearly four years previous, but the feeling I had now was incredible. Hearts had captured my imagination, and the imagination of the British footballing public (well Saint & Greavsie at least). This was the real deal, and suddenly supporters were returning in their thousands. On Christmas Eve 1985, Hearts fans began to dare to dream of a League Championship: but in life, we were never far away from being bitten on the bum, or in my case: being bitten on the leg and jagged in the bum.

Chapter 17
The tragedy of the silver jersey

I was an average pupil at school, though school wasn't dull per se. At assembly, we'd often sing 'The Sound of Silence', which I thought was a bit odd. Strange too, was a rockin' version of 'The Lord's Prayer'. It was like one of those terrible 'Talk to God' TV shows. And it was quite bizarre that we didn't know if we'd be in at all from one day to the next. The school strikes of the mid-80s meant that we missed quite a lot of days and there were no extra-curriculum activities that I knew of, although Tommy's 1979 Tynecastle Yearbook showed basketball, rugby, golf and football teams. We didn't even have teachers some days. But when we did, I liked Mr Savage, who taught history, and Miss Simpson, who took English. I got by. Back at home it was a case of don't answer the phone and don't open the door to the insurance man. Like Edward from The League of Gentlemen, my mum didn't bother the outside world and didn't want it to bother her. School though, meant little to me and I had little appetite for that or the cardboard taste of processed economy burgers and lame chips that typified everyday life. I had been dispossessed at Hutchison Vale and defeated by The Commonwealth. Life and school was a struggle between mediocrity and endurance, but none of that mattered as Hearts, my team, were heading for the league title.

It wasn't just Tynecastle High assembly that was dabbling in musical psychedelia. Hearts too produced a new record that would've left The Velvet Underground scratching their heads. In the B-side to 'The Hearts Song' (the greatest and best known football club anthem in Scotland), and without the need to play the record backwards or at midnight, an abstract message was delivered to thousands of unsuspecting Jambos who had purchased the track. The message said "Marshalls: the Chunky Chicken Champions". They were the sort of extrasensory lyrics that might've rejuvenated a failing Warhol; or persuaded Roger Waters not to leave Pink Floyd. And what was the reason for this release? Well, Hearts were now good: very good, and breaking records as fast as they were recording them. The Jambos beat Rangers 3-1 at Tynecastle in March 1986 as football returned to TV screens after some awful dispute between men in suits. Archie McPherson said it felt great to be back, and that there had been something of a change in Scottish football since he'd last been on air! I used to love the footy highlights on the TV. Scotsport with Arthur Montford, Sportscene with Archie McPherson, and even midweek Sportsnight with Harry Carpenter; Nottingham Forest in Europe and a swift one-rounder from Frank Bruno. Next up was a Dundee Utd double-header in what could've been a defining moment in Hearts' history. I went to the Scottish Cup Semi-Final and when John Colquhoun scored a breathtaking volley, I leapt off the crush-barrier onto the back of a woman who happened to be standing in front of me! I was only little. Hearts looked fantastic in their v-neck maroon tops, white shorts and white socks. Craig Levein, Gary Mackay, John Robertson and Colquhoun all had the coolest wedge hairstyles; and the team played with incredible passion. It was as if they recognised that they were making history. For the fans, there was an excitement and freshness not seen for over twenty years. We won the game 1-0, and with it, a place in the final.

Next up was the head to head league game, but I was in Livingston. I so wished I had been at Tannadice though. It was possibly Hearts' finest hour of the decade. They took Utd apart, winning 3-0. Robbo scored one of the best goals I've ever seen (on TV). And for his second, he went one on one with the goalkeeper, rounded him and coolly slotted home. Tannadice became Tynecastle. We owned it and we owned them. And Utd were a great team back then, if a little dull individually. Players like Hegarty, Narey, Sturrock and Malpas made them a force in Scotland and in Europe. But they weren't cool. They were the beige trouser-wearing, Phil Collins-listening, middle-aged-before-their-time footballers. We had Robbo and Mackay with streaked hair, and when Utd did get us under pressure, we had Henry Smith in unbelievable form. With Hearts eliminating Dundee Utd from the title race, only Celtic could catch us now.

But then a couple of nervy performances followed as the finishing line approached. The first was a first-ever live TV league match in Scotland, as Aberdeen frustrated Hearts at Tynecastle. The Dons won a penalty with Willie Miller's obligatory escorting of the ref to the spot and there was silence as Aberdeen took the lead. Like a blubbering fool, I started to cry as time ran out. It seemed the dream was about to end, and I was that upset about it! But to the immense relief of all Hearts fans, John Colquhoun stabbed home an equaliser with just minutes to spare, and I leapt around in hysterical joy, still crying! The penultimate game of the season was a tense 1-0 win over Clydebank, with Gary Mackay scoring a brilliant individual goal. But Celtic won too, their seventh straight win and they were now hanging over us like the Chernobyl fallout. So we got to the last game of the season at Dens Park and I was desperate to be there. Bobby was going to Dens Park to see Hearts win the Championship: but he wasn't taking me with him. Bobby was different to me. He wasn't obligated to go to Livingston to stay with my dad, but legally, I was. Money also played a factor. Bobby, the oldest and more established Hearts fan got to go to the games; plus he was like a son to a friend's dad, who personally paid to take him to many matches. I got to the odd game, but Saturdays were spent in FineFare, Livingston or prison (a list written in no particular order). So my father had custody and I had to go to Livingston. I felt so annoyed by that, perhaps almost cheated. But there was only one thing that mattered above all else: Hearts had to win the league…

Many words have been written about the cruellest day in the life of a Hearts supporter. This is my story. My dad took me to his work place to play pool; a giant building in Kirkton Campus that made Britain's Giros (and in the 1980s, there were plenty of those churning out). It was the usual drill. We had to walk through the noisy machinery plant first, paying lip-service to some over-weight, roll-up smoking Rangers-supporting security guard with a Pirelli Calendar, before making our way up and along a labyrinth of corridors en-route to the canteen. My dad would often bring me here. Pool was a free activity that we could do together and it preceded our days at the more refined surroundings of Deans Snooker Club. But that day was different. I was nervous and quiet and my mind was only on events at Dens Park, and not least because I learned that a flu bug had swept through the Hearts squad leading up to the game. I thought of Bobby, and what a great and exciting adventure he was having. I couldn't wait to see him again. After half a dozen games of pool, we left the room and made our way back down to the plant. The guard was poker-faced as he told us Celtic were four goals up at St Mirren. It was chilling news and a feeling of deep discomfort came over me.

As we got back to Eliburn, my father seemed uninterested and that annoyed me even more. This was the biggest moment of my life and I was sitting in a living room with the man who should've taken me to Dundee. My dad began to potter elsewhere and I was now alone with only the radio for company. The commentator was becoming more and more animated. As the minutes ticked on, it seemed that Hearts were now hanging on for dear life. The tension was unbearable and I became gripped with fear, like I was going to be sick. I became frantic, and began ferociously pacing around, clutching my hair, pulling at it, begging for the end. And then came the moment that wrecked my world. The Dundee substitute, football journeyman and Bobby Ball look-a-like, Albert Kidd, came onto the park and scored. There were just seven minutes left. I sank to the floor and screamed; my young voice sending a shriek through the house.

And as my father raced back into the living room, Albert Kidd scored again. It was a quarter to five on May 3rd. We were undefeated since September 28th. But Heart of Midlothian, the Champions Elect – had just lost The Championship.

I sobbed uncontrollably, more than at any other time in my life, face down and sprawled on the carpet. I'd lived through some dire domestic situations and seen dreams dashed many times before and since. But this was the worst moment ever; worse than the time I slid on to a beached jellyfish at South Queensferry; worse than when I got kicked square in the nuts playing 5-a-side; and worse than the time I climbed a tree up Bonaly woods and ripped through every rotten branch on the way down, shredding skin off my body. I wasn't one of those fans like George Eggo, photographed crying on the Dens Park pitch, the scene of the catastrophe. Nor was I one of those thousands who bawled openly on the terraces in a massive outpouring of grief. I was stuck in my dad's house in Livingston and after half an hour of relentless weeping, my father could take no more and barked "enough!" In my darkest hour, he came up short. The least I deserved in that moment was for him to appreciate my pain. Instead he switched the TV on, and there was Kenny Dalglish celebrating on the Stamford Bridge pitch his first title win as Liverpool boss. Across the bottom of the screen ran a looped message:

Celtic are Scottish Champions. Celtic are Scottish Champions. Celtic are Scottish Champions.

Albert Kidd had changed everything, including time. My life was now defined as time that came before Albert Kidd and time that came after. For every Hearts fan that can recall that awful day, the images will haunt us forever. Hearts had worn a kitsch-looking silver coloured away jersey. Although it had actually been around for a few seasons, it became the defining icon of Hearts losing the league in the most crushing fashion imaginable. Bobby didn't react so well either in the wake of the devastation. He came home from Dundee and locked himself in his room for two whole days. All across Edinburgh and beyond there were rivers of tears, as one little moustached footballer destroyed our dreams to make himself an instant hero with Dundee, Celtic and even Hibernian fans. He broke my fucking heart. I try to imagine what my life would've been like if Hearts had won the league in 1986. It wouldn't have solved all my problems. But it would've meant everything, and I mean everything, to me. In 1986, it was the only thing I cared about. I was twelve years old when Albert Kidd crushed me.

Chapter 18
The children of The Commonwealth

One week after Hearts had blown the league title, I headed to Hampden to watch my fallen heroes in the Scottish Cup Final. Like the semi-final the previous month, I was taken to the game by my Hutchison Vale manager and a couple of the lads from single parent families. We walked onto the North Terrace and I remember that it was blustery, sunny and maybe even raining a bit. Like the seasons, I had all sorts of emotions. I was truly staggered by the size of the Hearts support; it was light years away from the crowd I had first witnessed way back in 1982. It was a wonderful sight and quite touching. Jambos stood together; defiant at the adversity thrust upon us from the previous week and twenty-four years. The teams lined up and once more, Hearts wore their ill-fated silver jerseys. I might have only been twelve years old, but I knew immediately from my first steps on to the crumbling, gusty terrace, that Hearts were going to lose this, and it took just five minutes for my fears to be realised.

It was a sad end to the season. The game comfortably finished 3-0 to Aberdeen and Hearts had now lost 'The Double'. In truth, we were still shattered from the week before, and although this cup final defeat was a huge disappointment in itself, it was the collective collapse of the season which really made it hurt so much. But as the dust settled on 1985/86, it became clear that this young team had given us something more than that which could be measured by trophies alone. In scenes never witnessed before or since in a Scottish Cup Final, it was the losing team and their supporters that stayed on long after the final whistle. Aberdeen fans were outnumbered by a ratio of 2:1 on the day. And most of the forty-two thousand Hearts fans stayed on way after the end. We stood, cheered and sang defiantly; and then we went home. Aberdeen had won their fourth Scottish Cup in five years and their second trophy of the season. In the early to mid-80s, they had what it took to be winners.

Celtic had won the Championship, as they had done many times before and many times since. Their final day mauling of St Mirren seemed as dubious as it was predictable, but then it could be argued that Hearts had blown the title not on the last day of the season, but on the first. Celtic (and

Rangers) fans I imagine, will probably be back at work on a Monday morning after a trophy win. For them, it's just another gong in a long line of gongs, and they're confined to their tit-for-tat goldfish bowl game of one-upmanship. But that goldfish bowl has a glass ceiling. And as much as I was gutted to see Hearts lose the league to Celtic in 1986, I don't envy them for one second because as a Hearts fan, I can still value the dream of winning a trophy. They must be bored out of their minds! For Hearts fans, we won only our pride back; no longer the forgotten team; no longer the dressing-room disco; no longer the perennial relegation fodder of just a few years previous. For me, I had six months of happiness that my home-life or school-life could never provide. When I look back at the team of '86, I smile at the fantastic memories, great goals, that haunting silver top and the streaked-wedge haircuts. That's worth more than year-on-year meaningless trophy wins. Football strips can be silver, and trophies usually are; we dream in black and white, and in shades of grey. But for a short, colourful time, Hearts made me dream and gave me hope. Hearts made my life good in 1985/86. For that, I will always be grateful. But I'd have sold both my kidneys on the black market for that Championship.

At 7pm on July 23rd 1986, BBC 1 cut to a lone piper standing on the ramparts of Edinburgh Castle, who played a poignant lament. David Coleman's opening address might have said something along the lines of:

"Although the Games have been a financial disaster, and they've had to be bailed out by a fat, dodgy media mogul, who'll probably one day, say five years from now, throw himself over the side of his yacht before he's allegedly caught ripping off his company's pension fund. Oh, and that half the countries have pulled out because of Thatcher's continued apathy towards Apartheid; and that the fastest man in the world who is here will probably get done for taking drugs in a couple of years; but fuck it. Let the 1986 Commonwealth Games begin without Andrew-Henry Bowie of Saughton Mains Bank, whose safety first, side-step audition dance wasn't quite good enough to get him to the second verse of Shaka Khan's 'I feel for you'. Uuuh, remarkable!"

I would have been outside playing football if it wasn't for the rain. But instead, I sat dissentingly in front of the TV to watch the opening ceremony of the 1986 Commonwealth Games, coming live from my home city. As the piper piped, we then heard the gentle introduction to a much more modern song; and the camera panned down from the ramparts to the esplanade; revealing the impressive sight of thousands of local school kids, jumping around in red, white and blue tracksuits. Then the beat of the music kicked in...

Do do do-do-do-do – doom doom do do do doom doom do do do doom doom do do do doooom (repeat!). . .

The kids went from random (yet cunningly organised) mingling into a spectacular choreographed dance display. Their flags waved in the air as they expertly performed their routine. After that incredible vista, the thousands of troopers began to pile their way down the esplanade and on to The Royal Mile. The song had motivational and sporty lyrics:

Now we're ready for the action, where all the people gather round...

take it to the bridge

...you're up against the best; all the eyes are watching you.

It was organised chaos but brilliantly executed. Stad de Meadowbank went from dull, council athletics stadium to Nou Camp-chic with teaming and towering temporary tiers. In all, around ten thousand kids took part and performed choreographed classics like Smile with us and Spirit of Youth. The former song seemed to be a two-fingered salute to all the countries that had bailed on the games (and perhaps the local audition cast-offs). The latter was a real stomper that ended with blonde haired, blued eyed salutes last seen fifty years previous in Nuremberg. Ambivalent attitudes towards Apartheid were every bit as evident as the athletes on show.

I was so gutted not to be part of it all. Even the free Nike trainers seemed futile as I watched my schoolmates play their part in something historical. This wasn't the Olympics or the World Cup; but it meant something to me (as it will mean something to those Glaswegians in 2014). To most folk, the 1986 Commonwealth Games is a forgotten memory, and there is barely a word written about the ceremony on the Internet. But missing out on it all remains a painful recollection. Meadowbank is still standing (just) as a crumbling relic to the old 'Empire' Games of 1970, as well as '86. Bob Maxwell's deed of saving the games won him a place on the bench, before he went for a dip. Liz Lynch won gold and became Liz McColgan; and Ben Johnson failed his drugs test in Seoul two years later. Maybe he realised life couldn't get better than the '86 Games. But many years from then I'd meet one of the participants of The Opening Ceremony, and despite having mercilessly slagged her off that summer's evening - she was alright.

Chapter 19
Round our way

I had lost my place at Hutchison Vale; seen my beloved Hearts blow the league and cup double and sat through a Commonwealth Games Opening Ceremony that I desperately wanted to be part of. There was a crap novelty record in the charts at the time called 'It's 'orrible being in love (when you're eight and a half)'. Fair enough for Clare & Friends, but it should have been me on Saturday Superstore, telling Mike Reid that 'It's 'orrible having life kick the shit out of you when you're just plain twelve'. But if the calendar year of 1986 hadn't been merciless enough, then there was to be one last, painful sporting memory which brings a more physical tear to the eye…

Saughton Mains and Broomhouse are collectively teeming with Hearts fans, but back then, one rarely ventured into the other's territory. Saughton Mains was a tough area, but Broomhouse had much more of a 'reputation'. So one evening in July or August 1986, it was with some trepidation that around twenty Saughton and Stenhouse kids went over the top towards the other side. The reason for this advance was to give our neighbours something resembling a 'take-on' at football. It was a gloriously warm night with a red sky and as we stood on the ridge that perched high over St Joseph's Primary School (no longer there), we looked down to the sunken pitch to find our opposition waiting for us. This wasn't going to be football as we knew it. This would be a village ruck, but without the village. In the Oasis song, 'Round Our Way', "the game is kicking off in around the park, it's twenty-five-a-side and before it's dark…" Well this was nearly twenty-five-a-side where the opposition included about eighteen lads, a couple of teenage mums, at least two dogs and one pissed adult with a can of Special Brew. I had never been so scared in my life (well, apart from contacting Hitler on my mum's Ouija Board). As I was just a small boy, I was going to have to keep the hell out of the midfield scrum; so I decided to play up front with an extremely optimistic view to maybe try and steal a goal. Besides, Bobby was there, so I was safe.

The 'take-on' took off and Saughton set out with a rigid 4-12-3 formation. It seemed that the game was going to be won or lost in a midfield battle that resembled the Ducky Boys v The Wanderers in terms of numbers and The Battle of Santiago in terms of competitive spirit. Time on the ball was precious to say the least, but I kept my concentration, and I revelled in my 'free' attacking role (despite having not yet touched the ball). As forty-odd youngsters, one staggering drunk, two bikes and a dog named 'Thor' chased the ball; there was little in the way of chances as the game raged towards the interval (but who on Earth was keeping time on this mêlée, I'll never know). And then came the bracing moment that still remains one of my most powerful and lasting footballing memories. As Broomhouse attacked, someone (possibly even Bobby) launched the ball up field and I latched onto it, and all of a sudden, I found myself bearing down on goal! I just needed one more touch and I'd be ready to shoot. But just as I was about to pull the trigger, my legs were ferociously taken from behind. I went sprawling to the ground, and a penalty was unanimously claimed by Saughton!

As the rest of my team were still some distance behind me, I immediately grabbed the ball to stake claim the spot-kick, but Bobby (and several of the older kids) demanded that they should be the one to take it. As the older boys argued with each other, I managed to hold onto the ball; despite my brother hissing at me. I doggedly placed the ball on the spot, signalling my intention that this was my penalty, that I had earned and that I was taking. But I made the mistake of looking around me. Broomhouse were frothing at the mouth (and not just the dog and the drunk), shouting a mixture of high-pitched and broken-voiced obscenities in my direction: but then half my own team were now snarling at me too, and threatening me to dare not miss. I turned to face goal, taking in a slow deep breath to steady my nerves. I then began my run-up, and struck the ball beautifully: but maybe just a foot wide of the post.

For a split second, time stood still as I sank to my knees. I had blown my big chance again. Through my fingers, I saw the face of jeering schemies, Lud Romano, his ghetto-blaster, Albert Kidd and the linoleum-stealing playground hate-mob. I saw my father, his head shaking with disappointment. And approximately four seconds after the penalty miss; although I didn't see Bobby's face, I certainly felt his boot, as he kicked me so hard up the arse, I actually bit my tongue as I squealed at the searing pain. But Bobby had merely dished out the retribution that half my Saughton team-mates were desperate to exercise themselves. There was cheering from all sides, as I momentarily united two great rival housing schemes; and then the game raged on. But for me, it was all over. I lay sprawled on the ground and in agony for about ten minutes; angry and confused at my brother; but no less so than at myself. My facial expression could not have been more contorted had I stuck three Astro Belts into my mouth simultaneously. Wiping the tears, I dragged myself up and limped away from the sanguineous fray of the football pitch; my dignity left lying by the penalty spot. As I departed the scene, I afforded myself one last glance back from the ridge to see the other kids play, and they were getting stuck in as I was left bloody-mouthed and humiliated. From the hill, the evening sky was now a deep scarlet, and as the sun set, I decided to head back to Saughton Mains Bank. It was what I knew best. It was a horrific evening, but tomorrow might well have turned out better. It always could in EH11. Final Score: Broomhouse 3 Saughton 2 (match abandoned after an hour).

Chapter 20
The bitter end

The 'casual' movement made school seem like a place where kids passed exams in fashion rather than maths or English, and I failed miserably. De rigueur in 1986 was a knitted v-neck jumper made by either Pringle or Lyall & Scott. Kagools were in, as were Adidas trainers, but not as much as those godawful dungarees and Pod sandals (pregnancy DIY meets Dexys Midnight Runners). If one was feeling particularly brave, a deerstalker hat, never seen before or since on the streets of Gorgie, might have been worn! But as fashion was evolving in 1986/87, Hearts went slightly backwards. The club probably suffered a massive Dens Park hangover, and although we weren't a bad team, all the attention shifted west, as Graeme Souness started a revolution at Rangers that brought their glory days back, and ended everyone else's.

After Bobby's shocking betrayal in the Broomhouse/Saughton take-on, it was fantastic to come home from school one day in August to find an old ally sitting in the living room. It was Tommy, my oldest brother. I couldn't believe he was back as my mum had given me no indication. Bobby, as far as I was concerned, could now go to hell - the big curly-haired bullying bastard. Simple and friendly Tommy was home and one of the first things he did was take me to Easter Road for the Edinburgh derby. The Hibs fans may have been taunting us about Albert Kidd, but this was the 80s, and Hearts dominated their city rivals throughout the decade. That day we won 3-1 and I was just able enough to join Tommy in the sways as the goals rained in (albeit, on my tip-toes). As Gary Mackay made it 1-0, a Hibs fan in the background stood up to vent his spleen. He was wearing a green, replica top and a light coloured, lightweight suit with the sleeves rolled up. I guess there was a bit of Miami Vice about Leith in those days. To be part of a ten-thousand strong away support on the Dunbar Terrace remains one of my most enduring memories as a Hearts fan. And in over a dozen or so occasions I stood there, we never lost once.

After the game, we walked to the top of Easter Road, and when I glanced back, all I could see were thousands of Hearts fans. It was a mesmerising sight, and there was an edge to football then. Tommy and I headed on to the East End of Princes Street to get the bus home to Saughton Mains, but by then, our numbers had become more sporadic. Around a dozen or so

Hearts fans were standing at the bus stop, when from across the road, a squad of Hibs casuals appeared. They made their way onto the central isle and the Jambos next to us were thinking about doing a bolt.

"Stay where you fucking are", demanded Tommy, "Nobody fucking move".

The Hibs casuals looked us up and down for a bit, but they moved on. Tommy's bottle had saved the day and I remember a couple of guys thanking him and chatting to us. Tommy was the hero of the hour. But that didn't last for long.

Social workers would often appear at the door. There was one woman, another neck-scarf wearing, tree-hugging type who would actually sit out on the grass field in Saughton Mains Bank as she waited for Tommy to appear. This was an astonishing sight, as no one ever just sat out on the grass at Saughton Mains Bank. What made this situation worse for me is that I had to take her out a drink of water, and in front of my highly baffled friends; who yet again gathered to see what the fuss was about. There were other social workers over the years and the name Bowie became well known in police circles. The reason for all this attention was simple: Tommy was a badly behaved young man. I don't know what was going through his mind but he just couldn't keep himself on the 'straight and narrow'. I never once judged him on his behaviour, and latterly, his petty crimes. I just loved him as my brother and it would have remained that way had he not started to take his frustrations out on me and my family. Tommy was fucked up in the head and he turned nasty; really nasty. He started to pick on me, becoming threatening and belittling me. He would steal clothes from Bobby and my mum would often chuck his stuff into a bin-bag and throw it out of the same window that our perennial burglar once tried to get in. One night, nearer Christmas, the police were called. He had hit me as well as taking out half the furniture. My statement was taken by a man with a beard, which I guess made him that year's link to Santa Claus.

The low point though, came in early 1987. I was off school with a horrible cold. Bobby was at school and my mum was out food shopping. Tommy, as he often did, would lie in his bed until well after mid-day, getting up only to head to the kitchen or in the general direction of The Busy Bee. Before my mum left, she ran me a bath. I eased my aching body into the warm water and lay still. But then I heard Tommy emerging from his room, trying the bathroom door. It was locked.

"Open the fucking door", he demanded.

"I'm not getting out. Fuck off", I replied.

"Open the fucking door now!"

Despite the pleasantries, it mattered not. Tommy forced the door open and I was thrown out of the bathroom quicker than you could say "pass the soap, New Fish". I went down to the kitchen; soaking, ill, shivering and seriously humiliated. He wasn't finished there though. He came downstairs and started shouting at me, telling me that "I'd never be as tough as he was". Yet a few years later, I'd be the same height and build as him. I guess that meant he could literally fit into my clothes if he chose to. For all the times that I defended him; for all the times I took a slagging off my friends about him; for all the times I was tarred by his brush; for all the times I visited him in Borstal institutions and even prison. Within a few weeks, Tommy was sent down for something. I never once felt compelled to find out what he got put away for; but whatever he did, he wasn't very good at getting away with it. The important thing was that my mum agreed that Tommy wasn't coming back to live in the house ever again. All I wanted to do was be his brother, but after the way he treated me that winter, I didn't love Tommy anymore.

Chapter 21
The Argos years

With Tommy gone, relative peace broke out in the house. Up until that point, Bobby and I still shared a room, although the bunk-beds were now laid side by side with a strip of no-man's land in between (though I'd often wish it was the Berlin Wall). Bobby controlled the TV, which faced towards his bed, meaning I had to watch it through a Hearts mirror. We may have shared the room, but Bobby called all the shots, decided what we watched on TV; what posters went on the wall; he chose when the light went out, apart from when trying to electrocute me. So it's easy to imagine how delighted I was, as a consequence of Tommy leaving, when Bobby marched towards his own *lebensraum* in the much smaller (and some say haunted) room at the front of the house. Within a few days, I had rid myself of not just one, but two horrible brothers, as my unitary house became a confederation.

This new found sense of personal space enabled me to develop my own ideas, discover new things and most of all, allow me the privacy to grow hair in places I never knew existed! One particularly prominent avenue for self-expression was consumerism. Only once had I ever had any real money in my pocket and the result was some garish Pony trainers and an oversized Diadora kagool that made me look like a kite. The previous Christmas saw Bobby and I make a cash request to Livingston when discussing the tricky subject of "what we want". My dad nearly choked on his single-malt at our £50-a-head starting bid. I was thirteen years old. I wanted things. So whatever spare change I managed to find and accumulate, went into a plastic bottle that once contained the cheapest of coin-cleaning Presto's cola. As the days turned to weeks, the bottle began to get heavy and Bobby knew nothing of its existence. My plan was to buy things that would make me happy and I didn't waste one penny. Despite life's setbacks, I still had my spirit, my determination. Now I had inspiration and the means to live the perfect, utopian lifestyle. I personally called it 'the promised land'. Others knew it as The Argos Catalogue.

After many weeks, I raised the £29.99 required to buy my first purchase; a small triangular two-man tent. The tent represented my new found love of property. I may have been lording it inside my own bedroom, but now I was spreading my empire as far as the back garden. In May 1987, the day

St Mirren won the Scottish Cup, the tent was purchased and I made my plan to spend that evening sleeping in my back garden with one or two selected friends. Spending the night outside one's house was often seen as a 'right of passage' for any young man, especially when it involved the luxury of a tent. But in Saughton Mains, an 'all-nighter' usually involved walking the streets, or looking for places to invent new back-garden-storming 'tourdies', affectionately naming them 'The Grand National' and such like. So when news got out about my tent: the whole fucking scheme and beyond descended on my garden. It was going to be a long, long night.

The chosen friends and I prepared for our night of camping (meant in the manliest sense of the word), by stocking up on essentials like Red Kola, sherbet dib-dabs, more sherbet products and a ten-year-old copy of Fiesta magazine. After we got rid of some hangers on, we got down to the business of staying awake. It was all going well: too well. But something felt wrong, like a bad presence was upon us. Sure enough, sometime after midnight, our tent was engulfed with punches, kicks and a whole lot of shouting. That's right folks: Bobby and his friends had arrived. And what should have been an innocuous teenage sleepover became the pile up from hell. Worse was to follow as a group of girls from Broomhouse were now on the scene. Chaos, screaming, chasing and talking went on all night and the neighbours were up in arms. Some of the guys got a snog from the Broomhouse girls and one bastard stole the bongo-mag. By the time the police were called, the tent was soaking with rain and condensation and it was ripped all the way down one side. To add to all that, my brother's knee was pressing right into my ribs and he was snoring. I was freezing cold, soaking wet and downright miserable. At 7am, I turned to Allan and said words to the effect of "I may be some time". Three minutes later, I was back in my bed, snug under the covers and trying to forget about my two mates and the three other gits in my ruined, two-man tent. Like St Mirren winning the Scottish Cup, there seemed no justice in the world, so it was Argos 0 Real Life 1.

If the tent proved to be a disaster, at least it didn't put me off the Argos 'promised land'. When I scraped the next pile of coins together, I decided to buy a punch-bag because I thought it would give my room and me a more macho image. When I arrived home with it, Bobby immediately offered his services to help stuff the flattened bag to its desired shape. As there was an old pile of sand lying in the garden, my brother set about the task with some gusto. Now I wasn't crazy on the idea of him helping me as I immediately suspected that he had some kind of hidden agenda. Plus, the problem with old piles of sand is that they tend to be wet, especially if left to stagnate in the garden for ten years. As Bobby dug deep into the sand, I began to sense a change in his optimism. He started to toil and became sullen. As the bag became three quarters full, I could see the panic etched on his face. As he stood the bag upright, his eyes became strained with the agony of his realisation: he'd fucked it up. So did he do the sensible thing and admit his mistake, empty the bag and start again properly? Did he bollocks.

Sweating profusely, Bobby barked at me to help him carry the heaving bag of wet sand up the stairs, to where he would attempt to mount it to the ceiling. We had only just managed to lift it to the top of the hallway landing, when Bobby looked up and struck upon the consolidating idea of dangling it from the attic with a metal pole bridging the hatch; not exactly in my room then! As I hoisted myself up and into the loft, I noticed that the damp sand was starting to seep through to the outside of my brand new punch-bag, but I didn't dare utter a word. I actually felt a temporary sense of relief as I made it up into the attic, as by that stage, Bobby was not a good person to be around. He gritted his teeth and strained his body to raise the punch-bag. I was able to quickly slide the pole through the rope noose for it to swing on, and the entire house creaked as the bag was allowed to rest upon its own weight. Now at this point, my punch-bag should have been a ready made vehicle for Bobby to take his growing rage out on. But that was to be very much not the case.

There was a silence, but for Bobby's heavy breathing; each pant ending with a desperate curse. After what seemed like an age, he threw his body forward and delivered a full-weighted haymaker into the solidified punch-bag. I cringed as I heard him wince upon his fist smashing against the unyielding pendulum. There was a long pause; maybe even a groan as the dull pain reverberated up the bones of his arm. Then, with his other fist, he sent an irresistible force crashing against the immoveable object. But the object won.

"Fuuuuuuuck", he bellowed, the pain becoming too much for him. Losing it completely, he then kicked the punch-bag, with me still grimly holding it steady from above. As the £14.99 sack lurched out of control, Bobby's next blow slapped the side of the bag, possibly taking the skin off his knuckles. And as his face turned to the deepest of all purples, he threw his entire body into one last agonising punch; but this time, he missed the bag completely, and battered his fist against the wall.

As my mum wasn't around for any of this, it seemed an entirely sensible idea for me to see out the next couple of hours just resting in the attic. Argos 1 Real Life 1.

Bobby's surreptitious ability to get his way spanned many years. As money was forever in short supply at Saughton Mains Bank, there was almost a natural self-destruction for anything deemed to be of value. As well as controlling the TV, my brother also ruled the waves. Our only source of music was a pitifully small one-tape stereo which was missing the cassette playing cover and only a twirling pen could rewind a tape. So when I bought myself, from Argos, a magnificent new double tape-recorder 'ghetto-blaster', it was the biggest event witnessed in my house since Dad left. Like a curly-haired version Dr David Banner, Bobby turned green with rage, as I went about my business of setting up my new music system (which was a dashing red in colour).

"Keep Your Fucking Hands Off!" was the cry from Andrew-Henry Bowie HQ. In the past, Bobby wouldn't think twice about throwing out my tape to replace it with one of his own. Now he could keep his pathetic little machine and could by all accounts feel welcome to shove it right up his hairy arse.

It was a Friday and I had just walked into the house and up into my room to find my new ghetto-blaster missing. It was strange, because I had padlocked it to the tie that bound my little sponge chair-bed at the far side wall. There was music coming from the direction of Bobby's room. I went in, and there was my brother, listening to his beloved Wet Wet Wet, and on my new machine. But this time, I was more impressed than angry at my Machiavellian brother.

"How did you manage that?" I laughed out. "That was padlocked."

"I know. Funny, eh?" Bobby said, trying to mirror my good mood.

"Well I'm impressed."

And I was. For a brief second, I pitied him. I mean, he was two and half years older than me, but had resorted to picking a lock to take my ghetto-blaster, just so he could listen to Wet Wet bloody Wet. I told him that I was going to get something to eat and that he could borrow it for now. But as I went downstairs to leave him with Marti Pellow, it suddenly dawned on me that I hadn't actually inspected the scene of the crime. So as I went back upstairs to my room, I looked down behind the sponge chair bed. Instead of discovering a crafty display of evidence-free lock picking, there was a giant gash down the side of my chair where he'd brutally torn the fabric to rip out the ghetto-blaster! The tosser! In the Scottish Cup draw for obtaining big brothers: I had come out of the hat with Rangers at Ibrox and then Celtic at Parkhead. I went berserk at my brother and I'm sure today he is now sorry for his callous act of theft and vandalism; just as I am for planting a pork-pie behind his wardrobe. Latest score: Argos 2 Real Life 1

Chapter 22
He puts the 'b' into 'subtle'

One of the reasons I was only an average school pupil was that I lacked concentration. I excelled at drama, and was decent at PE. English was at best, ok, as was history: but I'd spend my days in a hallucination, often longing for a better life somewhere far from the place I was in. Another cause for my day-dreaming was that I was in love with a girl in my class and it lasted for two years. But I never had the courage to tell her. Instead, I would just sit and gaze at her, hoping to catch her eye, and I'd sit beside her in class whenever I could. She was beautiful; but I just couldn't tell her that. Besides, why would she want to be my girlfriend? I was poor and skinny and wore cheap water-based hair gel that would run down my face on a rainy day, or on the number 33 bus window, if I fell asleep against it. Although I had dreams of a better world, I knew my place in the real one.

Throughout 1987, I continued helping my mum at FineFare or on any other shopping trip. Once, I watched her nearly get run over by a speeding car outside Goldbergs, and I shouted "MUUUUUUUUUM!" at the top of my voice, which might have caused seagulls to fly from the rooftops. One more step, and she would have been dead, of that I am sure. After that incident, I'd often think about how life would have been without her. I was so angry at her for that because one, she nearly left me standing there motherless; and two, because when I shouted her name, the whole street stopped to stare, leaving me feeling incredibly embarrassed. Sometimes I'd accompany my mum to Movie-Master in Slateford Road; the only shop in the west of Edinburgh to hire out our Phillips 2000 videos (and even then, the only films they had involved either Cannibals or Zombies). There was a period of stability in the house. Charlie was around from time to time, and Bobby spent more and more hours out, discovering his adolescence. He and I would still fight, like the brothers Babbitt, as he 'squeezed and pulled and hurt my neck in 1988'. I went to school, played football with my mates, supported Hearts and got into music.

As Bobby turned sixteen, he no longer had to spend weekends in Livingston. For some time, he'd been excused from this anyway as he simply didn't want to be there. He was more interested in booze, girls and adding to his compilation tape of winding up Radio Forth Agony Uncle, 'Father Andy'. He liked a joke did our Bobby, and despite him being a right curly-haired bastard to me, even I had to laugh at the time when he wrapped up a turkey's cock and gave it to a girl at her Christmas party. I had no such choice of lifestyle, and to be fair, there were many aspects of life in Livingston that I enjoyed; not least my dad's supreme Spaghetti Bolognese. I also liked spending time with the kids and 'Stepmom'. But it was often boring. Apart from the odd game of pool or snooker, we didn't do much. I'd entertain Ian but there were no fishing trips or football matches that a father should've shared with his son. He read his paper and drank his beer and whisky. His output was minimal and back in Saughton Mains, my mother pounced on this. Without me realising it, I became embroiled in a series of letters between lawyers that stated I was unhappy about the lack of activities. My dad went ballistic and grilled me about it. I told him I was happy with current arrangements. I said that to him because I didn't want to upset him. Thankfully, it was the last time I'd be the stick that my parents used to beat each other with.

Bobby would take me to watch Hearts from time to time. I was there when we beat Celtic in the Scottish Cup at Tynecastle in 1987. Robbo scored a late free-kick; there is wonderful footage of the Shed in a state of delirium and a couple of guys jumping up and down on top of the pie stand. But I also had another Hampden heartache; the semi-final of the Scottish Cup versus the despised St Mirren, who were trying that day. I stood once more, in the giant, swirling uncovered open terrace, to see Hearts lose a late goal and another brilliant chance to gain some silverware. Another season was gone. One year later, Hearts were just a couple of minutes from beating Celtic to reach another cup final. But it was at Hampden again, and Hampden meant heartache. Henry Smith, the legendary Hearts goalkeeper, must have accidentally spread low-fat margarine on his fingers as the game edged towards full-time. Once more we left the National Stadium with our tails between our legs. 'Henry Henry, drop the ball', sang the Celtic fans from then on. Between 1986 and 1988, Hearts should've won one league championship and three Scottish Cups.

Hearts were a decent team in 1987/88. The average crowds during that season were the biggest since the 'glory years' of Conn, Bauld and Wardhaugh. The team finished second, behind Celtic but above Rangers, despite the millions spent by player-manager, Graeme Souness (whose late, elderly father was someone I'd often chat to in The Busy Bee). I thought of Hearts a lot, but they wounded me many times in my still fledgling relationship with them. They charmed me at first, led me on; but then hurt and abused me: never enough to spurn me, but a constant stream of let-downs followed one after the other and it all got too much. In 1988, I didn't as much turn my back on them, I just played hard to get for a while and let

Hearts do the chasing. I still loved them; always did and always will, despite the bruises. With Hearts, I always dreamed that my time would come.

I did, however, become more interested in music at this time and my allegiances were more concerned with the Pet Shop Boys than 'The Gorgie Boys', as their third album, 'Actually', became the soundtrack to my 1987/88 season (surely every football fan lives his or her life in 'seasons', as opposed to actual 'years'?). I absolutely loved them, and although my sense of humour became dry and subtle, my love for the Pet Shop Boys wasn't; and the recently obtained blank canvas that was my bedroom became a shrine to Neil Tenant and Chris Lowe. I still had my burning passion for synthesiser based music. The shrine grew, and at its peak, all four walls and the ceiling were covered with some three hundred posters. What had my, what had my, what had my mum done to deserve that?

Chapter 23
A promising career in incontinence pads

The Pet Shop Boys posters didn't come free, so I got myself a part-time job after school. As Bobby worked for the local chemist delivering pharmaceutical prescriptions to customers, I'd occasionally work a Saturday for him. Now why the hell I didn't just get myself a paper round, I don't know. The chemist job was very demanding, and when Bobby simply couldn't be arsed anymore, he quit and the prestigious job was mine. It was 1988. A neighbour was kind enough to donate an old 'racer' bicycle for my cause. Unfortunately, she wasn't kind enough to inform me that pedalling round corners meant inescapably ending up arse over tit; as I was to find out on my first ever bend. The bike was a sort of hybrid: an adult 'racer' (and a bit too big for me) with pedals from another type of bike. So basically, the wheels would jam against the moving pedals, but only if the bike wasn't kept straight! So for six days a week and three hours a day, the manager asked me to sign on the dotted line; I was given a mega-bucks contract in which I'd bag a whopping £32…a month.

There were three of us who delivered for the chemist. At first, we used to deliver the drugs in bags that advertised the name of the business, but this was Edinburgh in the 1980s: Trainspotting country. After one or two incidents, it was decided best not to expose the nature of our freight, so from then on we cunningly used Edinburgh Evening News bags. I was pursued myself several times; I was chased through Kingsknowe Quarry by a gang on Mountain Bikes; a drunk swung at my two-wheeled contraption by The Busy Bee; and a man 'propositioned' me in Roseburn Park as I made my way back from the print shop. The dark, eerie lane behind Saughton Prison provided the backdrop for a young woman to inform me that she was about to have her baby; and it was at the same murky location where two local neds shot me in the ass with an airgun, as I found myself once more flying head first over the handle bars and into the field where the old horse used to live. I had to assume that the £32 per month incorporated danger money.

I was also in the business of delivering incontinence pads to the elderly (and I guess, 'infirm'). I would have two large packs stuffed into two

Evening News bags, one on either shoulder, bombing down the street like a German Luftwaffe. Whether it was inco-pads or prescriptions, I was usually greeted with a warm, appreciative smile by the people I delivered to. But frankly, I relied on the tips, and if that came in the form of an Orange or a Satsuma, then the good people of Stenhouse and Longstone could rest assured I would be launching their unwanted citrus fruit over the nearest hedge. £32 a month? Little wonder the manager drove a Mercedes. I worked there for over a year. I didn't particularly like my boss; he was a strict and serious businessman but at the same time, I didn't want to let him down. I felt loyalty to people, like my father, like Charlie and to some of my teachers. I didn't want them to be disappointed in me. Although he wasn't my cup of tea, I at least had some respect for the boss. So I stuck at it, even though I hated it. In the end, I was looking for a way out; and it was to take something special for me to quit. No pain: no gain, as the saying goes.

In March 1989, I was playing football in the field at Saughton Mains Bank when Allan tackled me fiercely. It hurt like hell, but it didn't prevent me from playing on. A day later and my leg was still throbbing, and maybe more so than the previous day. The day after that however, I was back in the grind of the prescription/inco-pad run and I was in agony. Whatever the hell was happening to my leg, it was causing me severe pain, and although I had to stop cycling, I didn't give up on those incontinence pads, as I felt a duty to the chemist, and I guess to those customers who were holding on for me! It was such a cold, bitter day and the rain was coming down too: but still I carried on. 7pm came and went, and I was on my last legs (well, leg really), but with just one more prescription to deliver in Longstone. My rickety old racer was being utilised as my crutch as I hobbled towards the last call. When I reached the path, a lady answered the door and cautiously asked,

"Are you alright, son?" Well, I could hold on no longer.

"Nooooooo - ho", I replied, bursting out crying. All the pain, all the elements of winter and all my efforts were too much to take. The woman, who I was supposed to be delivering medicine to, ended up having to drive me home. I left my bike lying there on the street, and thankfully, I never saw it again.

The next day, I shared a slow ambulance to hospital with an old lady who must have been a hundred-years-old. I wondered what her story was and how she ended up in with me. The terrible pain in my shin was only slightly relieved if I pressed my foot back up firmly towards my leg. It was too painful to let go, so I have to apologise here and now, for swearing at the nurse after she forced my hand away from my foot all those years ago.

I had a small chip in my shin bone that grated on a nerve, but as I was bandaged up and given crutches, I felt grateful that the pain had lessened from its most excruciating form. Besides, I was looking forward to going home and listening to The Innocents, the new album by Erasure that Evan had lent me. They were now my new favourite electro pop duo and much better than the Pet Shop Boys. Chased, assaulted, propositioned, injured and shot in the ass: those weren't Erasure lyrics, but the words to bring down the curtain on my first ever job; a job that ended with a trip in an ambulance and a fight with a nurse. I hoped never to see another incontinence pad again (now those should be Erasure lyrics).

Chapter 24
Watch out, the world's
behind you

On Christmas Day 1988, I was stunned to discover that a relative had given me a C.H.I.P.S police outfit. I was fifteen years old! What the hell was I supposed to do? Wear it down the park and handcuff my mates? Perhaps I should have swapped it for a size bigger and presented it to Tommy? Lost ironies were as much a part of life as incontinence pads, Eddie the Eagle and crap 'Loads-a-money' impressions. Hearts found a certain irony with their poor domestic season in 1988/89, because their European form was a complete paradox to dismal defeats by St Mirren and Motherwell. There was a stunning 0-1 away win at Austria Vienna (a game in which Walter Kidd announced his arrival on the European stage), and a 3-0 trouncing of talented Yugoslavs, Velez Mostar. Bayern Munich, one of the greatest names in world football, was drawn out of the hat for the quarter-final. Tynecastle was packed to the rafters for the home leg and a stunning goal from Ian Ferguson gave Hearts a precious 1-0 lead in the tie, leading to possibly the greatest Shed moment in history. Hearts went over to Munich for the away tie, but eventually lost out 2-0, despite a valiant effort. The Bayern game at Tynecastle remains to this day the zenith of Hearts' European exploits. The club though, has had a standoffish relationship with Europe over the years; certainly compared with some other Scottish teams. Celtic, Rangers and Aberdeen have picked up silverware. Dundee Utd reached a final, and a semi-final. Even Dundee and Dunfermline had some great runs in the 60s, and Hibs almost got to the first ever European Cup Final (on the strength of having floodlights mind!).

Life is as much about good timing as anything else. Hearts suffered from bad timing. When the Old Firm were floundering to varying degrees in the early 80s, it was Aberdeen and Dundee Utd that pounced, as they had the right men in place to do it. Rangers and Celtic, with players like Dave MacKinnon and Danny Crainie were no longer big hitters in Europe; nor were they paying huge wages to players to keep them out of reach of the chasing pack. And where were Hearts when all this was happening? Playing bloody Stirling Albion in the First Division, that's where. Europe too, happened just at the wrong time for Hearts. The 60s was the right time for the likes of Kilmarnock and Dunfermline to have extended continental adventures. But Hearts were already in decline because the people in charge were fucking useless! But I knew exactly what that felt like. Like Hearts in Europe, I had my odd moment of glory. But in the grander scheme of things, and compared to my peers, I was reduced to the role of also-ran because I was useless! At a time when I needed to do something about my life, there was no Jim McLean or Alex Ferguson around in my world. Computers, the internet, mobiles, Wikipedia: none of that existed for me and I was moping around like a fucking loser. Hearts missed the boat because they never had the foresight to pack their bags and arrange their passports. I missed the boat because the boat hadn't been built yet. And I was left in a quandary.

I was toiling in class, and even PE became an embarrassment. I didn't even have a school bag. I had a poly-pocket. That was fine for carrying my jotter and pens, but on a freezing cold day in February at Meggetland, it meant all I could fit in my plastic folder was a pair of white shorts and a 1983/84 Luton Town away top. My PE teacher, the late Mr Hanson, went crazy at me for turning up white and going away blue, but I didn't have a bloody clue. And when Kerry Shearsby hacked me down in the first minute at hockey, sending me sprawling head first into the Somme-like squalor of the Meggetland mud, I felt my life wasn't worth living. Most mortifying of all though, was my footwear. I didn't have a pair of running shoes or even basic trainers in 88/89. All I had was a £5 pair of beach shoes and my big toes pushed though the fabric on each foot as one tosser dubbed me 'The Little Tramp'. In PE, we would run out of the school gates, along Russell Road and take in the first mile of the urban tranquillity of the North Edinburgh Cycle Path. As my big toes were protruding from my flat-arched beach shoes, I was usually left lagging behind even the average runners in their designer wares. It wasn't until the end of term that I eventually got a new pair of trainers; as the beach shoes met a rather sticky ending.

Once a year, the hole which gapes the middle ground of the roundabout at Stenhouse Cross would be violated with a giant Christmas tree. Upon passing by one evening, I decided to impress my friends (and some girls) by putting the lower half of my body into the hole, as if to give the impression that the top half of my body had been completely severed. It seemed like a great idea at the time (and a chance to impress one or two of the laydeez). But unfortunately, as I got myself into position, my feet became entrenched in what was the most sickening, oily mire that has ever existed; even worse than Labyrinth's 'Bog of Eternal Stench'. My beach shoes were left to die horribly down the hole that night, and for all I know, they may well still be there, fermenting and marinating away, awaiting the next victim. I had to walk home in my socks and it took two days of disinfectant influenced bathing to lose the smell from my feet. I can still recall the agonising cold squelch as if it were yesterday; similar, I guess, to the sound of one spooning out the first serving of trifle. The result though, was a spanking new pair of arched-soled Hi-Techs, and I was never left behind in the Russell Road home straight again.

My small gains in footwear (and a £5 book prize for Drama) couldn't mask the slow death of my education. Apart from the chemistry teacher who had no chemistry, and the art teacher whose face was a picture, those who taught me were great. Some of my teachers looked like those cheerful Scottish County singers that stand by a roaring fire on TV, advertising CDs called 'Sounds of the Glens'. They were ok, but the end was near. I was severely in need of some guidance, so my guidance teacher arranged for me a job interview as a 'Painter and Decorator'. Great stuff, but for one slight problem: Why the fuck would I want to become that? It didn't make any sense to me at all, but my future as an 'apprentice' was now lined up. Bobby, the apprentice Joiner, and my dad, the Electrician, were keen for me to take it. My family had no concept or ambition of further education (or even higher education). My friends were looking to get into trades or just to get the hell out of school; so I went along to the interview wearing my chinos and a horrible patterned tie and was offered the apprenticeship there and then by a man who looked like David Dickinson. I walked into the interview a failed schoolboy and came out an apprentice Painter and Decorator on £29 a week. My exams came around and they didn't go well. My chemistry paper lasted as quickly as I could randomly select multiple choice answers, and my English poem was heavily influenced by Erasure. So in May 1989, I walked out of Tynecastle High for the last time and without so much as a 'cheerio then'. For all I know, the school might still have a 'missing persons' file on me, but somehow I doubt I was missed. I wasn't educated at Tynecastle. I was processed. And as I hadn't registered to go back to school, it was the Painter and Decorator job or bust. But I had no desire to be either a painter or a decorator: so I chose bust.

A few weeks later, my certificate arrived. I felt so down about it because I just knew it wasn't going to be good. I pulled back the flap to find my results on a yellow, laminated document. Until now, I've only ever grudgingly disclosed what was on it to one other person. My incredibly painful results were:

English – Standard Grade 3 – Who-hoo: General Pass!
Maths – Standard Grade 4 – Fail
Art & Design – 'O' Grade 4 – Fail

Craft and Design – 'O' Level 5 – Fail
Modern Studies – 'O' Level 4 – Fail
Chemistry – No freekin' mention – Teacher was a Jakey
Drama – Missing in Action!

My minimalist, yet perfectly functional coffee-table clearly didn't impress the craft and design adjudicators whose flowery tastes I wouldn't want to appeal to anyway. Maths, I suspected, and art was taught by a miserable bastard with a tit on his head. Modern Studies was a disappointment, but worst of all; my 'Drama' wasn't even mentioned on the certificate. To this day, I have no proof that I passed my GCSE in drama, my best subject. I put the certificate back in its envelope, and there it stayed for nearly ten years. I blanked it out. School was out forever, and the happiest time I had in four years there was snogging a girl behind the canteen and running from my thoughts along a cycling path in Roseburn. Pretty sad really, but at least I had my C.H.I.P.S uniform. Nobody could ever take that away from me.

Chapter 25
All washed up

As undignified as my last school days were, I still had pride in my ability to work. Having left the chemist job, my friend Evan got me into a tough early morning paper round that paid a staggering £80 a month! Not bad for 1989. It was based at Queensferry Street Lane; the sort of malodorous backstreet Starskey & Hutch could tear up, ploughing through an unwitting stack of empty boxes. I did two rounds: the beautiful but physically demanding Dean Village, and the plush foreign embassies of Melville Street; a world away from '10 Regal' Saughton Mains. The paper round was mammoth, but it got me some cash for my yuppie Argos habit. It was also a chance for me to obtain some delicious fruit juice, kindly left out on the doorsteps of the letterboxes I delivered to. If I wanted freshly squeezed fruit juice in Saughton Mains, someone would have to punch me in the face when eating an apple.

I delivered posh newspapers to Edinburgh's posh people, with Evan; I also distributed the working class Edinburgh Advertiser to the people of Whitson and Stenhouse, with Allan. Whitson Road is huge and has about ten other streets off it, in addition, our patch took in roughly a quarter of Stenhouse. We got paid a miserable £6 a week between us and for the first couple of times we actually delivered the papers in a laborious five hour operation. One house had a dog that would see me coming and would batter its meaty body on the front door upon tearing the paper from my hand. Allan made me deliver to that one as he was terrified of dogs (not much use being a paper boy then, if you ask me). The third week I spent the entire sweltering day delivering them by myself, as Allan had developed a mysterious five hour illness; the fourth, fifth and sixth weeks, we dumped the whole lot in a skip in Saughton Park.

The break-up of my Edinburgh Advertiser partnership with Allan symbolised a collapse of our friendship. When he started Stenhouse Primary School half a year after me, I showed him around and we became best friends. As adolescents we played football together, and went on adventures with Bobby, Blue, DD and whoever else. Pretty much every evening for about four years was spent kicking a ball about Saughton Park's Astroturf pitch, playing Subbuteo or waiting an age for his Spectrum computer to power up. But by the age of fifteen, we'd grown sick of the sight of each other. It was simply a case that we'd become so close that I annoyed him and he annoyed me. Like some married couples, we had just run out of things to say; and it became frustrating (as if being fifteen wasn't difficult enough). Alcohol and girls were just around the corner, but for Allan and me, it seemed we'd be heading towards them on different paths.

Evan popped round to see me one day and was highly amused at my unkempt appearance. After my paper round, I'd crawl back into bed and there I'd lie for as long as I felt like it. My mum kept saying that I'd have to go back to school if I didn't find myself a job, and my standard response was that 'I can't just go waltzing back to school'. It actually became something of a running joke; this image of me in a ballroom style top-hat and tails, fleet-footing my way down McLeod Street. Going back to Tynecastle High was never going to happen no matter what means of dance I used to get there. Evan knew my 'waltzing' predicament so he brought round a newspaper for me to look at the jobs. As I came from a house where the phone was never answered, the very thought of me picking up the receiver to call for an interview was way out of the question. If I had to get work, then it would have to come to me. I was badly in need of Biactol and my dandruff was head and shoulders above anyone else's at the time. I had no clue, no strategy and no answers; and I'd spend the majority of my time slouched in bed, self contesting, two or three times a day,

"I didn't know you had dandruff?"

"Well you do now, so fuck off."

Evan flicked through the paper for me and spotted the perfect job for a fifteen-year-old boy of my standing. As I refused to phone up for it, he gave me a pathetic look and dialled the number, pretending to be me. He was even kind enough to escort me to the interview, possibly just to make sure that I actually went inside. I stuttered and bumbled my way through half an hour like John Redwood attempting to sing the Welsh National Anthem. My skinny frame, gelled hair and terrifying tie gave me a distinctly adolescent and lost persona. After the interview, I was told that they'd 'let me know'. I didn't get the job, but the girl who did quit after the first day, so I received a call back to start at the petrol station at 06:45hrs. Thanks to Evan, I now had a job which meant I didn't have to waltz my way back to Tynecastle High. I was no longer a school boy. I was no longer a paper boy. I was no longer a painter. I was no longer a decorator. I was no longer a drop out. I became Andrew-Henry Bowie, Cleaner. Life might well be about luck and good timing. But most people make their own luck in life.

Chapter 26
Some dance to remember:
some dance to forget

My dad exploded when I told him. For him, choosing a trade was the only option. He left school early, became an apprentice, and ate pig trotters with tripe (and oxtail soup round my Gran's house meant exactly that). The fact that I didn't want to be a Painter and Decorator didn't register. Of course there is nothing at all wrong with the trade, or any other for that matter. It's just that it was wrong for me. The petrol station offered me a sensational £70 per-week. YTS painter and decorator wages amounted to just £29. Like my father, there was only one option for me too. I didn't choose the petrol station to piss my dad off. But had I taken the apprenticeship, he would've been able to tick the final parental box that said 'job done: son on his way'. By becoming a cleaner, I became a misfit to him and we had both failed.

Evan, Dean, Butch and I began frequenting a pub lounge for games of pool, and with soft drinks only. Butch was a nice, shy, ginger-haired chap but he was tighter than Lionel Ritchie's leather pants in the video for All Night Long. Butch never got a round in. Evan told me that Butch once went on a date with a girl, but said he couldn't think of anything to say to her the entire evening. By the end of a dismal night, when the poor lassie's bus eventually came into view, Butch finally racked his brains and thought of something to talk about. As the doors swung open, he flapped:

"What sort of records do you like?"

I think the bus left without Butch ever getting his answer, the poor sod. I guess that if she had replied, she might have said,

"Black round one's with a small hole in the middle."

I recall too when Lucozade Sport first hit the shops, Dean opened up his first can and confidently declared

"Yeah, you can really taste the isotonic." His amazing ability to instantaneously identify athletic liquid enhancements that help balance mineralised sugar levels mimicking the osmolality of blood matched his confidence with girls. But although I was never one to shy away from buying drinks, I was much more like Butch when it came to the opposite sex.

For me, girls were tremendously scarce. I didn't have the gift of the gab. I didn't have either a gift or a gab. I knew nothing about sex. I thought fellatio could be a Shakespearian character and that cunnilingus was an Irish airline. Evan got girls because he was gruff and treated them pretty mean. Dean got girls because he was pretty which kept them keen. Bobby got girls because he plied them with booze and told them he was a professional footballer. I didn't get girls. I liked girls, a lot, but probably too much. I was in awe of them. I actually had two very pretty girlfriends at Tynecastle High, but both dumped me without as much as a kiss or a cuddle. I mean, what was I to say to them?

"Do you like ma beach shoes?"

I didn't even manage to have one conversation with the first girl. I was too shy. Maybe I could have asked her what records she liked whilst swirling Lucozade Sport round my mouth, recognising the isotonic aromas. Rarely was I in a position to brush off a girl. There was a girl at school who liked me, and I liked her. But she left me petrified and I eventually ran away from her attentions. And I tried to shake another one off by giving her 'my phone number', which was in fact that of Azad video store on Dalry Road.

By the summer of 1989 and just fifteen years of age, Evan and I, almost grappling on to each other, crept our way through the doors which lead to the main bar at the pub. An attractive girl was getting served (but then most girls were incredibly attractive to me at that stage in my life). The two pint glasses that she received contained a foaming pink ale. Having never ordered a pint before, Evan and I looked at each other and we both knew right away what the other was thinking: this was the drink for us! The barmaid glared over at us, and I sheepishly asked,

"Two pints of those please", pointing to the other girl's drinks. She hesitated for a moment, giving us a stern look, but commenced pouring us our first ever bought alcoholic drinks in a pub. History was made at that moment. A right of passage, and the boy became a man. Well, sort of.

Evan and I had cracked it. By keeping our cool, we had found our way of becoming real men; big boys with our very own Kray-like drinking den. Now all we had to do was keep it quiet.

Within two or three weeks, there were around twenty underage drinkers, many as young as fifteen years old. For me, each 'Pink Panther' was an event in itself; the thrill of going up to the bar, asking for and being served a pint. It felt so accomplished (a word not too far away from being 'completely pished'). Downing the lager, like not choosing a trade, became the only option, and three or four pints later, I was smashed. My summer became an orgy of underage drinking binges. It was peer pressure, right of passage and living dangerously all rolled into one. Booze was consumed, (as Sir Edmund Hillary might have said) 'because it was there'. Maybe I was drinking to discard the past, or more likely, I was shutting out the present. The future was altogether more unthinkable. Drinking helped me celebrate with my friends and it blocked the bad stuff out.

Of course, it wasn't just that first ever bought pint in a pub that got me into boozing. Before that, on 8th April 1989, just a week before football suffered the tragic Hillsborough disaster, I went to Love Street to see Hearts take on St Mirren. I would be hard pushed to find a Hearts fan anywhere who could recall this game, which ended in a dire 1-1 draw. The significance for this fifteen-year-old boy though, was that I went to the match utterly trolleyed. It not only gave me a new angle on the game (being that I watched it with one hand over my eye), but I had renewed vigour to rediscover my relationship with Hearts. The pure football love-in experience had died after a short romance. But now, after a trial separation, the old flame was reignited; and fuelled very much by alcohol. I guess if I was going to be a proper Hearts supporter, it helped if I drank; drank to remember: drank to forget. And it was only some time much later that my friend Kev Littlejohn informed me, that a Pink Panther was, in his own graceful words: 'a poof's drink'.

Chapter 27
Old Bastard

I had to report for duty, outside, at 06:45hrs but I got there early and it was bloody freezing! The old petrol station (no longer there) represented the beginning of a new chapter in my life and I remember waiting there as if it was yesterday. A young man eventually arrived to open up the shop. He smiled, said hello and shook my hand. He told me Old Bastard would be along shortly, but in the meantime I could help him put the flowers and the fire extinguishers outside. When Old Bastard appeared, he walked right past me, gathered his keys and went on his way. Just as he was about to turn the corner, he twisted his head back toward me and barked,

"Come-oan then you". I sheepishly followed Old Bastard round the back of the building, not in the least bit sure as to what fate awaited me.

Upon reaching the rear end of the building, I discovered Old Bastard standing there, waiting for me with an impatient look. For sure, he was old, and a bastard. He wore an Old Bastard flat cap; had Old Bastard glasses; was dressed in a long Old Bastard overall and stood only about five Old feet and six Bastard inches tall. His mouth was small and pursed, and he scowled at me in a way that only a clandestine Old Bastard could. Standing between Old Bastard and me were fifty years, a World War, rationing and a stoic bitterness that made me feel like I was something he'd just trodden in. Lying between Old Bastard and me was a massive, dark, foaming puddle. The stinking pool, as I was about to discover, was resting on the spot where customers would jet wash their cars. And somewhere underneath the filthy body of water, lay a drain.

"Sweep that puddle down the street, empty the drain and dump all the shite that's left over by the hedge", growled Old Bastard. Puddle? I thought to myself. This was a fucking Lake Zurich. But I took a brush and started to shepherd the puddle off the forecourt and onto the road, where I assumed it would eventually find its way to a drain, or maybe even the sea. The puddle soaked my feet, but the worst part wasn't over. I looked at the thick, dark residue that had gathered underneath. It was the mud from a hundred cars and it looked like the same sort of shit that burst rivers leave behind in low-lying living rooms after a flood. It also reminded me of the mud at Meggetland, where Kerry Shearsby viciously scythed me down with her blunt hockey stick; or perhaps maybe the bog of eternal stench where I dunked my legs at Stenhouse Cross. Actually, no, nothing could be that bad! But the voluminous mire that awaited me there, was now my 'career' summed up in all its glorious hell.

I shovelled the shite into a pale.

The morning's cold and blowing a gale.

The man standing over me was shouting "go faster".

What a total and absolute right Old Bastard.

I then had to stick my finger into the rancid gloop to unhook the drain cover. When I finished shovelling the filth, I replaced the drain cover and dumped the sludge by the hedge, as instructed by Old Bastard. And that was what I'd face everyday, with Old Bastard always on hand to tell me where I was going wrong. Next up was forecourt and pavement litter pick-up and if I hurried, I could have a quick break before cleaning the new bogs of eternal stench. Afternoons were spent stacking shelves, as at last, an alluring glamour crept its way into my schedule. I met the big boss, who graciously employed me at the second time of asking. Then I met Lewis, the manager who ran the place on a day to day basis. He was only twenty-four when I met him, but he quickly became my friend, my mentor and my confidante.

Lewis was sharp and funny and came from a middle class background. I knew some middle class kids at school, but I wasn't really close with any of them (apart from the girl I snogged round the back of the canteen). What I liked about Lewis was his sense of humour, and he also had a great sense of style: but he didn't like mine. That's not to say he didn't like me. He did. Lewis thought I was funny and we'd make each other laugh. But what Lewis didn't like was my vernacular, my accent and my opinions. For Lewis, I was damaged goods; so he decided to help me. This meant picking up on everything I said and correcting me until I didn't do it again. I had a truly hideous gold watch and he banned me from wearing it. He taught me how to converse without the need for colloquialisms and opinions fostered into me, Saughton Mains style. I learned more from Lewis in four months than Tynecastle High could throw at me in four years. It was like finishing school, but for puddle sweepers and drain-scoopers.

I may have been improving my social and verbal skills, but I was embarrassed as hell as to what I did for a living. It was an appalling job. Erasure had a lyric at the time: 'your shame is never ending', as each mundane cleaning task became 'one psychological drama after another'. My job was my shame. My friends taunted me about it, my father went berserk about it and Erasure even sang about it. It turned out though, that there were two reasons why Old Bastard didn't like me. One, because he really was just a grumpy old bastard, and that he didn't actually like anyone; which was wrong of him. And secondly, he figured that I had somehow been employed to replace him, and therefore do him out of a job. Well to be fair to Old Bastard, he was right about that.

Chapter 28
Mark Chapman;
the newAlbert Kidd

John Lennon, as I discovered in 1989, was my new hero; and I always needed a hero. It struck me suddenly. I was into synthesiser-pop for years, and out of loyalty to Chris Lowe and Vince Clarke I resisted any kind of guitar-based music. But then I hired 'Imagine' from Azad Video and I became infatuated with John Winston Ono Lennon. I listened to The Beatles constantly on my walkman and in my bedroom. Lennon's political agenda didn't really interest me, nor did I share his attraction to Yoko Ono. It was his music that I loved. His amazing voice, his brilliant presence and his fabulous sense of humour had me struck; all of this coming some nine years after his assassination. Lennon was a hurt child and a tortured man. He was vulnerable. It didn't worry me that I was a sixteen-year-old boy, listening to music that was ten or twenty years old. In Lennon, I found what I'd been looking for at that time, and so what if I was backward looking in my musical taste? That's just the way it was. I missed out on Joy Division, The Smiths, The Fall and Acid House. I just loved The Beatles, and I still do.

David Hasselhoff, bless his hairy chest, claimed credit: but the Berlin Wall came down anyway as the 80s were drawing to a close. Evan and I would go to the cinema together most Fridays, as I never had a girlfriend, and Indiana Jones and The Last Crusade was the box office smash that year (with Mr Bronson playing Hitler!). The Stone Roses managed to debut in between countless Stock, Aitkin & Waterman pop-paps such as blow-dried turnips, Big Fun, and Scouse slappers, The Reynolds Girls. It had been a traumatic decade; one in which I suffered a lot of despair. Yet there was still nothing registering in my head to say that I could actually break free from the crap life I was trapped in. I saw no way out because I wasn't looking for one. I knew not of the concept. It was a decade of struggle at Saughton Mains Bank, and a decade of alternate weekends, getting on a smoked-filled green SMT bus to Livingston. I would walk past the wall at Stenhouse Primary School before waiting on Stenhouse Road, getting on the bus and inhaling a lot of smoke. From Calder Road, through Dalmahoy, Wilkieston, Camps, East Calder, the ugly square building on the bend, the bridge at Mid Calder, I smelled cigarettes, then Dedridge, and finally I was there, at the old concrete jungle bus station at Almondvale.

One evening in December 1989, Evan called me with a plea for help. The restaurant he worked in had lost their kitchen porter and he begged me to come down and assist. So I got a taxi from Saughton Mains Bank to Leith Docks, which cost me about £7. The restaurant was some kind of run down boat and incredibly (unlike many things from my past) it is still there. I washed dishes non-stop all night and by the end of it, the Chinese manager paid me the staggering sum of £10 and offered me the job. My £3 net-profit went towards my taxi home and by one in the morning, my evening's work was done with only a small financial loss. I was absolutely exhausted, but all the chefs praised my efforts and they, along with Evan, pretty much begged me to take the job and come back the next evening. I suppose being wanted was a boost and as I had a day off I reluctantly said I'd do it. But it was a decision I'd regret.

It was a hellish night. There was a bitterly cold wind and it was snowing. I felt like bloody Dr Zhivago as I battled my way to the bus stop. The ground was covered in slush from the previous day and it took me about an hour and a half to get there. Upon my arrival, the manager instructed me to clear the trash. A dozen burst bin-bags later and I was royally soaked before facing a mountain of dishes. The manager then asked if I was taking the job and I said yes. But I had lied to him. Something was wrong. It just didn't seem as much fun or heroic the second night and the greasy confines of my kitchen sink lost its appeal pretty abruptly. Suddenly, I felt really overcome and I told Evan I was leaving. Within minutes, I slipped out the door and into the snow, without asking for pay. It took nearly an hour for the number 1 bus to arrive. When it did show up, I was drenched, frozen and quite miserable. And to make a sorry situation worse, I got on at the wrong side of the road; meaning a long journey through North Edinburgh and Drumbrae before wading home through the slush of Saughton Mains Street, and finally, Saughton Mains Bank. All I wanted to do was go home to bed and be warm; away from the snow, away from the world. But by 05:45, the alarm went off and I was back up for work, the bike ride to the petrol station, the fire extinguishers, the flower stand and the sludge of the car wash drain. I was shattered.

I listened to John sing, and I bought all The Beatles' stuff on video and cassette tape I could get. But the only trouble I had with my hero John Lennon was that he was dead. By the end of 1989, I withdrew from public life somewhat. I still went out with Evan occasionally, but I began to immerse myself more and more into the world of Lennon. I would try to comprehend why anyone would want to shoot my hero. What motivated

Mark Chapman, the podgy twenty-five-year-old drop-out and minimal wage worker? Why was he reading The Catcher in the Rye? I just couldn't grasp it. I'd look at John Lennon, and feel grieved that he was living without knowing the horror of what would be his destiny; always drawing ever closer to his fate. The more I thought about it, the worse it seemed. His murder was way back at the start of a decade that I too had become unstuck in; and as the 1980s ended, I was only just beginning to understand that he really was gone. I was like one of the Dakota Building mourners, but nine years too late. At sixteen years old, I was discovering my independence, but the consequences brought me solitude. I think I was depressed.

Chapter 29
Beetroot and creosote

Hearts had a good start to the 1990s, beating Hibs 2-0 with John Robertson scoring twice. But no matter how hard I try, I have absolutely no memory of this game and I sometimes wonder if it was all just an elaborate hoax. I pride myself in my support of Hearts and my ability to remember things. But not only was I absent from this game, I can't even remember what I did that day or even hearing the result. The truth is, I was so miserable I probably didn't even bother getting out of bed. But I certainly got a New Year/New Decade jolt at work though. The boss told me I was losing my job!

The petrol station was to be demolished and rebuilt from scratch. That meant finding another occupation for four months, so I looked into the possibility of working part-time, just to recharge my batteries and chill out for a few months. I landed a job in Scotmid, at Chesser Avenue (no longer there), as a shelf-packer and I nervously turned up for the evening shift. I was led to a holding room, where inside a large group of teenage guys sat at one table and a group of older women at another. I sat alone at my own table. No one spoke to me. The teenage boys were toy fighting and swearing at each other at the very top of their broken voices. The older women were chain-smoking and drinking vending-machine coffee. When the hour struck, everyone bolted out the door and made their way downstairs to start packing the shelves. One of the chain-smoking women showed me how to work the price gun and gave me some stuff to get on with in the pickled food aisle. It was going reasonably well until after about twenty minutes, a massive jar of beetroot slipped out of my hands and smashed to smithereens all over the floor. I was wearing my Chinos (oh come on, it was 1990) with my white shirt and frightful tie. The accident created a scene like a cheap bloodbath video-nasty and the boss wasn't at all happy with my disastrous debut.

Perhaps he made his next plan for me after surveying the damage I caused. One thing was certain, after he revealed his proposal, I decided there and then that there was no way I was willing to stand behind the deli counter wearing a stupid straw hat! I had mates who would be using this store and the last thing I wanted to do was serve them sliced ham, looking like the lead singer of the fucking Bluebells. I was out of there, and walked home in all my Texas Chainsaw Massacre-chic. My next job was at a DIY store (no longer a DIY store) on Glasgow Road. With an hourly rate of £1.69 per-hour, I was expected to be an expert on plumbing, carpentry, electricity, gardening and my 'first love': painting and decorating. But how was I supposed to be 'Jack of all Trades' when I didn't even know how to shave. Indeed, it was my line manager at the DIY store who suggested I might want to lose the bum-fluff off my face before the wind blew it away. I had never comprehended the need to groom myself, such as learning how to use a razor. Like many things in my life, I simply stuck my head into the sand. So, at sixteen years of age and a full-time working man, I had my first proper wet shave: and thanks for doing that Mum!

The DIY store was the absolute fucking pits. I hated the job so much but yet again, I saw no way out; other than to hang on for a few months until the petrol station reopened. The customers couldn't grasp that I didn't know the answers to their highly technical questions. The managers were woeful and I ended up being talked into working eleven-hour days. I wished I had stuck it out at Scotmid and I even considered buying my own straw hat and walking up to the deli counter with a full rendition of 'Young at Heart'. The thought of serving old ladies and telling them that their corned beef weighs 'just a little bit over' didn't seem so bad after all. Why so bad? Well, one day in the DIY store, as I pulled a pallet of creosote onto the shop floor, I turned a corner too sharply, and the pallet brushed against a shelf. At that moment, two or three columns of the wood protection fluid fell 'just a little bit over' onto the ground with a sickening thud. Around six or seven of the tubs cracked open, which added up to around thirty-five litres of creosote oozing onto the shop floor. Whereas the beetroot incident spelt disaster for my Chinos, this latest catastrophe was on a different scale altogether. Like the baddie cop in Terminator 2, I became engulfed in liquid: liquid nitrogen for him – 'own brand' garden fence creosote for me. The Meggetland mud, the Stenhouse Cross mire, the petrol station sludge and now the creosote spillage of oil tanker proportions. It seemed that if shit was to fall from the sky: it was bound to land on me.

The new weather-proofed shade of floor tiles caused by my creosote catastrophe was nothing compared to the colour draining away from the face of my boss. Two days were spent cleaning it up and he growled at me constantly from that moment on. Meet the new boss: same as the old boss. Years later, before the store took on another purpose, I went back there with Bobby; and I took great delight in pointing out to him a large discolouration of one particular part of the shop floor. Spillages in beetroot and creosote in 1990 followed on from debacles in incontinence pad delivery and newspaper dumping. There were more than a few calamities in those days, and it set the scene for the many that would follow. The DIY store chapter is now a long time ago. It's strange, but 1990 sounds like a reasonably modern year, yet it is approaching two decades and half a lifetime ago now. Apart from one desperate fumble with a girl that I hardly knew, I was only sixteen and had never been kissed (well, almost).

Chapter 30
Rule No. 1: Never electrocute the boss

I thought then and still do to this day that the World Cup of 1990 was rubbish. I even missed the Scotland v Sweden game as I was flattened by food poisoning (sweet and sour revenge from those chasing Chesser Chinese takeaway chiefs). The football was as memorable as Craig McLachlan's follow up single to 'Hey Mona' and fashion was epitomised by dreadful West German moustache and mullet combos. Yet one of my favourite goals of all time was scored by Freddy Rincón of Columbia versus West Germany at Italia '90. It was a magnificent team goal, with superb passing and running. I think that one, plus the delightful chip scored by Newcastle's Philippe Albert over Peter Schmeichel are my favourite goals of all time. Football was still in my heart. The rebirth of my Hearts career (supporting that is) was completed on the back of a rather sensational event. In the summer of 1990, the saviour of Hearts, Wallace Mercer mounted an audacious takeover bid of city rivals, Hibernian FC. This event sparked off a desperate backlash by Hibs fans who feared (and with good reason) that they would see their team swallowed up by Hearts as Mercer dreamed of a 'united' Edinburgh team. What it meant for the great name of Heart of Midlothian remained unclear, but Hibs had spent the last ten years in dull mediocrity, and looked vulnerable under their current owners. But Mercer's bid galvanised the Hibs support, and they eventually staved off Waldo's advances as Sir Tom Farmer stepped in to be their sleeping overlord. I knew how the Hibs fans felt. Having spent much of the last few years merely paying lip-service to Hearts, it was time to give my heart and my soul back to my football club again. Mercer lost out on Hibs in 1990, but he had me back as consolation. Hearts were restored to the head of the queue and even John Lennon had to get back into line.

The petrol station reopened in early summer, 1990. I was relieved to be going back there when I compared it to my hellish, drawn-out existence at the DIY store and my ill-fated Scotmid bloodbath. Old Bastard had been given the brush and the old car wash drain had been awarded a permanent mud-burial. My new clean-up duties didn't last too long anyway, as I was promoted to serving customers on the night-shift. Without the need for an agent, I negotiated a wage-hike up to a hefty £100 per-week, and the extra money served to cushion an increase in digs money back at Saughton Mains Bank. The bulk of my wages were spent on booze and football and I just blew the rest! Life was simpler back in those George Best on Wogan days.

On Saturday 15th September 1990, Hearts played Hibs at Easter Road. It was the first derby game since Mercer's aborted takeover bid, and there was a venomous atmosphere in the ground. Some ten years after my first visit there with the Saughton Mains Play Scheme, I still loved going to Easter Road. In some ways, it gave me an even better sense of being a Hearts supporter than I felt at Tynecastle. I loved Tynecastle, and still do; but there's that pressure of 'play it this way/play it that way' from the fans. People often sit back and wait to be entertained. But back then at Easter Road, there was a feeling of solidarity. Like some medieval army, ten-thousand strong; all of us in it together, for one cause (though the woman standing on the fence in the purple shell suit was no sister of mine). We were ready for war. Hibs were baying for blood after nearly being killed-off by Wallace Mercer. But it was Hearts who put their great rivals to the sword, and we smashed them by three goals to nil by half-time.

I consider myself fortunate to have been able to watch football in a vertical stance. We may have been human-cattle; cash cow fodder for clubs to milk, but I loved it. At Easter Road that day, I stood with friends and became absorbed in the living, swearing, breathing, singing crowd. And when the goals flew in, magnificent chaos ensued, sways of biblical proportions swept us down steep embankments of crumbling concrete. It became a religious and addictive experience; one that can barely be described on paper to the uninitiated. Some people take drugs to get high; others do a bungee jump, a base jump or extreme ironing. I followed the Heart of Midlothian. There is nothing, and no words to really do justice when describing the feeling of a big goal sway. Football had its 'edge' to it. I didn't go in for the fighting though. I was in for the sways, like ex-football hooligans went in for Ecstasy. Mass delirium goal-celebrations at football matches were like trips to me; but unlike sweaty, eye-popping ravers stuck in a warehouse in the middle of nowhere, I didn't have to go ten hours without a pint.

We left the stadium and headed up Easter Road. And again, the massive away support allocation made for quite a sight. To see so many thousands of Hearts fans on their way out after a derby victory was both exhilarating for us and menacing for anyone else. And in the 80s and 90s, there was much to celebrate, and that's the real reason why I loved Easter Road. Going there gave me so many happy memories because we won so many times. Unfortunately, I couldn't go out to celebrate after that particular game, as I had to start my first ever night shift. Like a hapless Frank Spencer leaving the careers centre yet again, I thought this latest job might've been just the ticket, but I couldn't have been more wrong, again!

A bloody big gang descended on the petrol station after midnight. Around twenty of them were either drunk or high, or both, but certainly looking for trouble. Some of the tougher lads in the mob banged on the window, asking me for a 'square go'. But all they achieved was to make the Lion Bars cascade from the confectionery shelf. Some rattled the door, trying to break-in and in the coming weeks they would spit on the hatch, or smear Chicago Town pizza against the window. Eventually, I had to call the police. All I wanted to do was mop the floor as my roster dictated, as despite the 'promotion', I was still cleaning the bogs. The problems I faced wouldn't go away. Drunk after drunk would show up, most looking like they were auditioning for a three-legged race. Taxi drivers would pull up in their droves, and stand chatting for hours at a time. People walking the streets would turn up and ask me fetch them one item at a time, some looking like the sort of people that would wander about Calton Hill at midnight with a leash but no dog. Yet I was expected to restock the entire shop and clean it as well. By 06:00, the mop and bucket were still waiting for me to finish some five hours after I first started; the Sunday newspapers were piled up like Stonehenge with over a thousand inserts to be interleaved (The Sunday Times looking outstandingly daunting); the morning rolls were stacked eight crates high without a hope in hell of being bagged; and the shelves were as well stocked as a 1970s East German deli.

It was a pretty bad moment then, for the big boss to pull up in his Mercedes to spot-check me. I tried to explain the situation to him but he wasn't impressed. Instead he grumbled about my lack of work and set about showing me how to do my job. It was a humiliating experience on the back of the gang attack and the philosophising taxi drivers. But as I got on with mopping underneath the drinks cooler, I accidentally dropped the plug into the bucket of water. Now that was a problem. After the throng of thugs had tried to smash their way into the shop, and my boss had made me feel as stupid as a Pat McGinley own goal, there was no way I was going to finish off the shift by electrocuting myself! So, as we cleared up before unlocking the door, I 'happened' to drift off through to the storage room, leaving the big boss man to plug in the drinks cooler. For as long as I live; I will never forget the scream he made as he pushed the plug back into its socket. The electrocution of my boss was a defining moment in my life. I knew in that instant that it would be impossible to ever find a better tale to regale to my workmates on the Christmas night out and to be fair, the big boss man himself still loves hearing the story!

"Aaaaaarrrhhhhh!!! - Fuuucckk", he he.

For weeks, the gangs would come. They'd appear from nowhere, like a pack of wolves; howling and frothing at the mouth. There were about half a dozen who would try to make my life hell, but I always tried to keep my cool. Years later, I saw one of the worst perpetrators walking up the steps by the Telford Subway, at Dundee Street. He was wasted and so gaunt after years of nocturnal drug abuse that I had to look twice to be sure it was him, but it was. My skinny frame had filled out and I was about three stone and half a dozen steps up on him. Despite being all set to karate kick him into next week, I decided not to do or say a thing to him; other than to just stare him in the eye. And as I looked at his pathetic withdrawn face I just shook my head. He and his gang tried to coerce me; but it was his own life that was pitiful. I hated my job, and it really sucked like every other job I had taken before it. But I did it with courage under fire, and with the sort of dignity this person shuffling up the stairs towards me could never apprehend. If I had flattened him, I'd probably have done him a favour. I never had too much going for me in those days; except for my ability to get off my arse and work.

There was a lot of binge-drinking in my life back then. My friends and I would go out and I wouldn't return home until I was in a state of blacked-out oblivion. As I worked permanent night-shift, my image of 1990 was one of darkness. And those were dark days. I was stuck on the bottom rung of a functionalist society and the charts comprised terrible music from the likes of MC Hammer, Right Said Fred and Adamski. I fulfilled my position, but for what purpose, I couldn't comprehend. It was as if I accepted my fate and I rolled with it. The utilitarian side of my personality forever pushed towards creating a little happiness and avoiding a little pain. But it was a dark, dark year; the black-outs from teenage booze-binges, the blacked-out bedroom, the constant night-shifts, and the nightly attacks from gangs. By the time I left the petrol station that calm Sunday morning, the win at Easter Road seemed as far away then as it does now.

Chapter 31
Rubbish boyfriend

I have a theory that the early to mid-90s were so very non-descript. There was hardly anything in the way of good music and the fashion was terrible. What is there to remember? Pete bloody Sampras? Nigel Mansell? Arsenal? What were we: the sons and daughters of John Major? Jesus! After a chance meeting, Allan and I became great friends again and the time we spent apart had done us both good. We now had Hearts and pubs. We rediscovered a good football scene at Saughton Park as old school friends like Franco, Scott, Jimmy, Stu, Graham and Nicky organised full-size Sunday morning games. At home in Saughton Mains Bank, my mum came home with a friend while I was in the living-room with Allan and a few of the guys watching TV. I didn't mind too much when I heard them come in, but to my horror, both my mum and her friend were wearing matching, repugnant green and black shell-suits! I guess it was a sign of the times, and it wasn't even the first shell-suit crime committed in the house. The previous summer, Bobby had paraded round Saughton Mains with a 'Gazza-Rip' shell-suit and to the tune of 'Fog on the Tyne'. Yet typically for me, life back then was all about locking the door at midnight, mopping the floor, waiting for the gangs to appear, or a lone nutter, or worse still: a talkative taxi driver. Morning would eventually come. I'd make a coffee and stand outside in the quiet fresh air, before the rush hour. Then at eight in the morning, I'd walk back down the road, home to bed in Saughton Mains Bank.

On Saturday, August 17th 1991, I finished my nightshift and met Allan for a 09:00 beer and a game of pool. The high of the day was incredible. It was the first home game of the new season and having already won our opening fixtures, we went head to head with Rangers in what would be an epic, top of the table, battle. There was a new look about Hearts, captured beautifully by Burton in Princes Street which displayed giant images of Hearts' new look strip and the forward line wearing it. Robertson, Baird and Crabbe; the goal-scoring legend, the James Hewettesque Englishman and the scampish young gun, all set to raid goals in Joe Jordan's first complete season in charge. By noon, I was drunk, and without sleep for nearly twenty-four hours, it seemed once more, I was gearing up to press my self-destruct button. I completely blacked out. I was told later by the

Police, that at ten minutes to three o'clock I had attempted to gain access to the stadium, in breach of the Scotland Act (1980). The back of any old ticket-stub states that it is an offence to enter a football stadium (section iii): whilst completely trousered.

I was carted off to St Leonard's Street Police Station; photographed, thumb printed and banged up in a cell. I remember zilch. When I awoke, I was lying on top of a tattered sponge mat and confined to a small space. I felt horribly claustrophobic and I had a raging hangover to deal with. I had no idea what day it was, never mind the time. About half an hour later, the door opened and a policeman took me to a room to collect my things. There, I saw a mug-shot of a young man, grinning like a Cheshire cat into the camera, as he held up a number. I could hardly believe it. Bobby, Allan and Ally had been looking for me, but not before partaking in a giant pub-crawl. Despite his role as the great tormenter, Bobby always came up trumps. He got me out of 'jail', and back to Gorgie in time for last orders.

But I thought of only one thing: my mum. She still ruled the roost with a four-iron golf club, and if she had found out about my arrest then my life would be over quicker than you could say 'Lee Trevino'. I was due in court to face prosecution for my heinous crime, but I actually managed to convince my mum that I had a job interview! She fell for it and told me how proud she was when off I went to bag myself a middle-management role at a West End accountancy firm (not too bad an 'opportunity' for a teenage tosser who cleaned petrol stations). I was summonsed to court at 09:00, but the bastards had me waiting all day. My Legal Aid guy informed me that as it was my first offence, I'd only get a ticking off. So I was mightily unimpressed when the judge fined me £40. I thought it was way too steep, but in the end, I was just happy to pay it and get the fuck out of there. As I left the court, the Legal Aid guy saw me and tried to give me a stern lecture about how people 'in his day' were able to go to rugby matches without the need to cause trouble. 'What a complete stroker', I thought to myself.

Bobby may have got me out of the nick, but that didn't mean to say he didn't enjoy seeing me suffer.

"You're fucked", he hissed, tossing me the broad-sheeted Evening News. On page three, with the headline: "Young fan celebrates much too soon", was me. It must have been a slow news day on the North Bridge. Why they had to make a sensation out of a nothing story is beyond me (though I reserve my right to discuss it here!). It even said I was "shown the red card". Oh come on, spare me the naff football puns! The article went on to declare that I'd dipped into my "birthday carry-out". Well, to be fair, Allan met me that morning with a bottle of Becks. My surprise eighteenth birthday party was a purely Saughton Mains affair. Yet amazingly, it went off without anyone enlightening mum to my arrest, and it seemed that I had escaped her wrath after all. My coat was on a very shoogly peg at the time, and threats to throw me out began because I was "using the house like a hotel". There was though, an interesting footnote to my arrest. Upon being lifted at the turnstile, the young lassie working there, collecting the match-tickets, took note of this incident in her diary. Not only because a drunk, skinny young man had been apprehended at her gate: but that he was, in her own diarised words, "quite cute". Oh, and Hearts won the game 1-0 thanks to a Scott Crabbe wonder volley after just 80 seconds: Result after all! As for my mum, I almost got away with the whole thing. But a few weeks later, whilst backed into his own corner, Bobby told her what really happened, the whistle-blowing bugger.

Ally, Shane, Allan and I decided to go to a naff British holiday camp in the south of England. It was a ridiculous idea, but what the hell, we went anyway. We inhabited what can only be described as a concentration camp and I'm not so sure if the fence was to stop folk from coming in or to prohibit us from getting out. It did however, give Allan and me the bug for exotic travel. Next time, a classy package holiday to Spain would beckon. There were lots of drunk girls in Spain, and any port would do in a storm. Yet I really was just a bona fide romantic; forever seeking the affection of a good woman. I'd fall in love instantaneously with the girl on the bus, or in the street or in the petrol station. But as the song goes: "It's funny how the girls you fall in love with never fancy you", which is so true. In Spain I wasn't bothered about any of that and there were plenty of girls; even if many had the body from Baywatch but the face from Crimewatch. Spain suited me perfectly at the time because I couldn't get a bird in the real world! And besides, housing schemes were never the most romantic places for meeting young debutantes. As teenagers, there was no Dawson's Creek style exchange of feelings and mature debate:

"Ah love you man, but am pure angsting and verbalising man."

"Ah love you too man."

"Aye, man but ah need tae define masel first ken, eh? At Film College likesay or maybe Stevenson."

Cue angst-ridden music as the sun sets on the scheme cape, and romantic views of the harbour. Actually, no: it's a just a pallet.

I did eventually get a few girlfriends into my life. They were:
Girlfriend 1: Jan – March 1992
Girlfriend 2: February – April 1993

99

Now out of that list, all dumped me; bar Girlfriend IV – A New Hope. Five girlfriends isn't a lot, especially as three of them came in 1994 alone (though during the reign of two Hearts Managers). I don't bear any of these girls any ill feeling (especially after dumping GIV). I sincerely hope all are well, happily married and long over me. G1 was so beautiful. She was tall, skinny and had long dark hair and a model-like face. She was nineteen years old; twelve months older than me and I was madly in love with her. To this day, I can't believe I pulled G1 in the first place. Mind you, she was drunk at the time.

Up until G1, my success with the opposite sex was appalling. I was really skinny (not anymore), my face long and stretched (not like now) and my hair was long and lank (now it's sort of 'scalp' coloured). Lewis suggested I use the petrol station as a means to get girls.

"Maybe you could show them your collection of Focus magazines", the cheeky bastard said. I was intensely proud of my World in Focus magazine collection and they were an interesting and informative means to learn about space, science and technology. One night in the Laich Bar, my mate finished with a girl who was not exactly known for the preservation of her celibacy. As she sat on the step outside, drunk and downtrodden, I went to comfort her (in the vain hope that I might get a rebound snog). After an hour of consoling the wretched strumpet, my mate came staggering outside and, without uttering a word, led her round the back of the pub. I stayed on the step, gathering my thoughts when a short time later, a taxi pulled up. The meter was ticking as it was Saturday night rates. My friend and the girl then reappeared and got into the cab. I never got the chance to say goodbye to her as the taxi sped off. But I did notice that her lipstick was spread all over her face and the tights that were once on her legs were now hastily wrapped around her shoulders.

One of the greatest days of my life was 4th January 1992, when I went to Celtic Park. The 1-0 win over Rangers at the start of the season gave Hearts the initiative in the league and the confidence to mount a challenge for the championship. By the turn of the year, we were still top. Our allocation of six thousand sold out and Hearts attacked towards our end in the second half, with the score still locked at 0-0. Hearts started to play well: really well, and we sensed something was about to happen. The tension was building, and on the hour-mark, Tosh McKinley slid the ball in to Scott Crabbe and he clipped a magnificent curling shot past the keeper and into the net. The celebrations were mind-blowing. All of us together: bouncing, hugging, shouting, swaying; with a deafening roar, bodies flying through the air, paggering down the terrace in one massive outpouring of joy. This was big time. And just as I eventually turned to face the pitch, Robertson fed to Millar, and Hearts scored again!

There have been some breathtaking moments following Hearts over the years, and some truly atrocious medicine swallowed; but that day at Celtic Park takes some beating. We celebrated so much that when I turned to Scott and looked at him, I thought his skull had been fractured. But as it turned out, he just looked like that. I sat on the Saughton/Cross Keys Hearts bus and gave a nod to secretary, John Borthwick, as we listened to the goals being relayed over the radio coming home. The legend that is 'Fuzzy' was so pleased that his hair was literally standing on its grey, split ends. I'd not seen Hearts fans so giddy in a long time. As for me, I had a feeling of immense happiness, because not only had I just witnessed a momentous Hearts victory, but I was about to have my first proper date with the gorgeous G1. It's just a pity I dressed like an absolute plum in those days.

Oh the fashion. I can barely bring myself to describe my clothes. I had a thing for white jeans in the early 90s and I even had white baggy trousers like Peter Hooton, the singer in The Farm. White jeans and dodgy shirts: and when I asked for the white trousers, the guy in the shop thought I was a butcher! Whatever G1 and I talked about on our date, I had a great time at first. But things soon started to go wrong. As much as I was in love with her, I couldn't deny the fact that G1 was just too good for me. I was head-over-heels, but inexperienced and scrawny. I also worked in a flippin' petrol station. In the end, she must have realised I wasn't much of a catch. And as the Hearts season reached that magnificent summit at Celtic Park: just one week later, a disastrous 0-4 home defeat to Aberdeen followed. Like Hearts' championship challenge, my dream-like courtship with G1 came to a crushing and sudden end. My innocent heart was ripped out of my chest and squeezed to death as it still throbbed. G1 was gone. It was over. She picked me up from the petrol station, broke the bad news on Calder Road, and then drove me home to Saughton Mains Bank. As a token of consolation, she told me she hoped that we'd still be friends, which I think is always nice to hear after being dumped.

Chapter 32
The two gentlemen of
Saughton Mains Bank

Hearts' season died a slow death after the 0-4, Aberdeen game. However, the club did make it through to the semi-finals of the Scottish Cup. And luckily, we were to face little Airdrie which meant avoiding Rangers or Celtic at the penultimate stage. But two games, two trips to Hampden and two hundred and ten minutes of the most frustrating football imaginable, saw Hearts taken to penalties by Airdrie; and we lost. It was a humiliating and crushing defeat and a waste of a lot of money. And the long, late journey home started off a three year period of desolate mediocrity for Hearts. But the worst thing about that defeat was that I was already really miserable after G1 had dumped me. The defeat to Airdrie would rank as one of the most unpleasant I'd ever go through. I felt grief stricken, as well as being heartbroken. It was a shit time. This was 1992; just six years after Albert Kidd; who arrived six years after Mark Chapman. Six years...six years: if this was to be some kind of sick cycle, then I would be hoping for better luck...in 1998.

In the spring of 1992, the house at Saughton Mains Bank was broken into and the evidence all pointed to a person who I used to hold dear to me. A cheap hi-fi and video were taken from the living room. Small change. But in my room, new clothes were missing from my wardrobe: clothes that I had bought, with money that I had earned, for a holiday that I had paid for. To top it all, he put the clothes (and I guess, the video and hi-fi) into the large sports holdall that was mine too, and again, bought for my holiday. It was an appalling thing for him to do, and we all knew who had done it. As far as I was concerned, he and I were over; I never spoke to him again. He knows now not to bother me.

Despite the stolen clothes, my Spanish holiday got me over some of the pain of G1, but the monotony of life soon enveloped once more. Because for me, life is invariably judged upon how Hearts are performing at the time. The 92/93 season was as dull and insipid as Eammon Bannon's bald head and Ally Mauchlan's moustache. My social scene was pretty much the same: same people, same places, same attitudes. At home it was a case of one man in, one man out. Bobby, the big brother from hell, moved out.

He and his mate, Skinner, got themselves a flat at Forrester Park where one can only imagine what went on! My mum's new partner moved in, but he was a Hibby. For her, it was the first time in fourteen years she had a partner living with her under the same roof. And for me, it was the first time we had a Hibs scarf hanging in the hall. Talking of Hibs, my friend John cut his hand through a window on the day of a 0-0 derby match (because a 0-0 draw simply wasn't a good enough result for him). I got roped into taking him to hospital, but as we waited so long, I fell asleep on one of the big window sills at the A&E (no longer there). When I awoke, his hand was fixed but mine had gone to sleep. When I reached to get the taxi fare from my jeans pocket, my hand was flopping about, unable to take orders from my brain. I had only gone and damaged all the nerves in my wrist, and it took four months for it to come back. Only I could go to a hospital waiting room and come home more injured than the person I escorted!

Hearts had qualified for Europe by finishing second in the league. Our first round opponents, Slavia Prague, were beaten at Tynecastle on a night of high drama. I stood in the Gorgie Road End for the first time in years and we sealed it with a sensational late goal from Glyn Snodin. The next day, an old man stopped me at Stenhouse Cross to discuss the game. He said he was so delighted to have beaten "those filthy, cheating, diving foreign bastards", as if he'd just returned from Dunkirk. I guess the old chap must have fought in World War II: and so I suppose he therefore knew it was all about winning in Europe. Our next opponents were Standard Leige, of Belgium. The first leg 0-1 defeat was a big disappointment, but I was still looking forward to my coach trip for the return leg. The Cross Keys bus wasn't leaving until midnight, so there was plenty of drinking to be done in Senior's Bar beforehand. By the time 'Fuzzy' and John Borthwick got the troops on the coach, I was like a bag of washing! I didn't even see out the city bypass, and by the time I woke up in Dover, my eyebrows had vanished. Maybe I had left them behind? Magical Mystery Tour!

The first night was chaotic. There was trouble in the bar and I managed to get whacked on the head with a motorbike crash helmet. I wouldn't have minded, but for the fact I was snogging a female in our party at the time. She had a room, so naturally that would be my next port of call. What I didn't expect was her dad to knock at the door a minute after I had showed up. With little option available, I positioned myself behind the curtains with only the bottom of my legs showing. He was mumbling away about getting something out of his bag when suddenly, he fell silent. He then gently drew the curtains back to find me tapping the back of my left hand, as I glided it gently over the wall.

"Aye, you're right love," I said, "there is a bit of damp in here". And there was!

The next morning, I bought a carry-out for Allan and me to drink on the coach. We were having a great time and I felt myself becoming a little merrier with each downed-bottle. But as we approached our destination, Scott enquired as to why our bottles of lager had a different coloured label to everyone else's. Now I had no idea that I had bought the 0% alcohol beer: but all I'll say is that if they sold that stuff in UK bars, drink-driving offences would be snuffed out overnight. The coach dropped us off at the 'Welcome to Hell' (do me a favour) gates of the stadium. We looked around for a bit; it felt so strange being in a European-style ground. Things were different, like the shape of the stands, the seating, the language of advertisements and the thought of my team being 'foreign' opposition. I was a foreigner, like when Saughton played Broomhouse. It was then time to walk into town and towards the best pre-match party that I'd ever had.

We were the first coach load to arrive in the main pedestrian area of Leige, and we found a bar by a fountain (what is it about football fans and fountains?). It was only lunchtime, and over the next five hours or so, more and more fans arrived, maybe five bus loads in all. There were hundreds of us drinking, singing, laughing and taking the piss. With Grant, John, Derek, Scott, Nicky, Allan and me there, standing among my fellow Hearts fans on foreign land was as emotional as it gets. Somehow, we managed to sink more beers nearer to the ground. The pub got its windows smashed in, which only added to the feeling of escapade, and maybe danger. Hearts lost 1-0 on the night and that was that. But the Leige fans were so impressed, that they stayed behind just to watch us and we even got an ovation as we walked across the river, back to our coaches. I loved the experience of that trip. Despite a long, hellish journey home (where we were forced to watch the entire 'Rambo' back-catalogue), I felt so good about following Hearts, and for once, good about me. A day after leaving Belgium, the coach pulled into The Busy Bee car park. I said goodbye to the guys and headed through the path, back to Saughton Mains Bank and rehab.

G2 came on the scene and like G1, she dumped me after a couple of months. I got the impression that G2 preferred flashier guys anyway and so it ended up being just Allan and me, hanging with friends and going out at the weekend. We went to a nightclub in Manchester once with our friends Frank and Cheryl (big Manchester City fans), and as Allan forever had itchy feet, he insisted we leave to go somewhere else. So we left the club and went round the corner, stood queuing in the pissing rain, and paid £10…to get back into the same nightclub! Hearts too, had me going round in circles. Everyday, I'd hang on tight for the Evening News to give me some little scrap of information, something to take us away from the relegation zone, or perhaps word on the stadium rebuild. My obsession was unflinching. One morning, I got out of bed and walked down to the kitchen to tell my mum some random thought I had about Hearts. With a mop in one hand and a duster in the other, she looked at me with bewilderment and told me I "should go see a psychiatrist". But instead, I saw a bank clerk and took out a loan that bestowed the club with £500, which went towards building the new Wheatfield Stand. And when I awoke to discover the club had signed legendary striker, Mo Johnston, I immediately splashed out £80 for the Asics tracksuit he wore at the press conference; pastel shades almost, of the Saughton Mains shell-suit days, circa 1990/91.

Preposterous clothing wasn't uncommon. I hired a giant blue 'Deputy Dawg' outfit for The Busy Bee's fancy dress minibus trip to Ibrox in December 1993. The game was a 2-2 draw, and the hire shop let us all keep our outfits over the festive period. The prodigal son and big brother, Bobby, was coming back home for Christmas dinner. This meant (in his world) that we should all bow down before him and hail His Majesty's triumphant return. However, one can only envisage his distress, when upon arriving at the house, he saw me as the centre of attention, playing with the kids (getting punched and kicked, de facto), and looking resplendent in my seven foot tall 'Deputy Dawg' costume. 'The King' had been dethroned: long live the new King.

The two of us were now locked in a joust that he started, Mum. Bobby seethed and reviled at me all morning. Like the odium of an Old Firm match, my blue garb was matched only by the spitting green of his face. As time went on, the atmosphere reached a point so full of poison that something had to give. And give it did. Shortly before Christmas dinner, Mum was in the kitchen basting the turkey with her partner. Bobby hissed over to me:

"Well do you want your fucking Christmas present then?" I was deeply unimpressed by his offer. Turning impertinently to face him, I invited him to "shove it right up (his) fucking ass". However, just as I tilted my head back to the endearing comforts of Noel Edmunds' Christmas Presents, I caught sight of something from the corner of my eye. It was Bobby: and he was coming my way!

Jean and Hector, an elderly couple who lived across the way were coming up the path. Frankly, they both liked a good drink, and the amount of home-made vodka they threw down their throats could make a baby elephant collapse. Imagine then, the sight that greeted the old timers at our front window, as they made their way up our garden path. My six-foot-two brother trying to strangle a seven-foot blue coloured dog, as the real Alsatian dog jumped on both of us with the eight-foot tall Christmas tree crashing from one side of the room to the other. The poor couple must've thought they'd drunk one 'white Russian' too many before swiftly withdrawing back to The Busy Bee. My mum threw a tearful wobbly at us, and my brother was thrown out of the house. Apparently, as I learned later, he ate just a bag of crisps for his dinner and my mystery gift was subsequently launched over the Carrick Knowe Bridge. It was a white Christmas in Saughton Mains that year.

Chapter 33
The girlfriend years

With just three minutes left on the clock, Wayne Foster ran through on goal. The Scottish Cup tie was the first knock-out Edinburgh derby since the late 70s and the city was on full alert. Foster kept his head, duly slotting the ball through the bandy legs of Jim Leighton. We were positioned near the front and there were about twenty of us in all. When the ball went in, it was pandemonium. Hearts had done it, and how we celebrated in the Wheatsheaf that night. In the middle of winter, and during the bleakest of spells, this match has gone down in Hearts folklore. And after eight long years at Hearts, Wayne Foster became an instant hero. But the most profound aspect to that memory was the terracing. Mass terracing sways: the greatest thing ever in football. How I wish they'd bring it back, even a nice, sanitised version would do. The next day, I bought The Sun because of its iconic "Wayne's Whirl" back page. The picture's backdrop is the ecstatic Hearts crowd. I could've been in it, had I not been a few feet to the right and by then, at the bottom of a huge pile-up. At the top of the page, a girl's face can just about be made out.

G3, GIV & G5 all entered my life in 1994 (and disappeared as quickly as they arrived). G3 was pretty and posh. She was also pretty smart; too smart for me; very assured. She was a student, but on a gap-year. I was at school with G3. We even snogged a few times (the one behind the canteen) and I stood her up once back then. I was a bit scared of her at school, but by 1994? She was hot and I was no longer scared! At first, we both seemed very excited about the rekindling of our relationship. Or at least, I was. But before long, we fell into a trap. The trouble was that she lived at home with her mum in the poshest catchment area of Tynecastle High. And I too still lived at home, in Saughton Mains Bank. We didn't really have anywhere to go hang out. In our new relationship, five years on from school, G3 and I would go to the pub, and just sit there, chatting. Then one evening, we simply ran out of things to chat about. It was excruciating really, and as G3 was in a bad mood anyway that night, she dumped me.

At weekends, Allan and I were lager-drinking, football-loving, young lads, interested only in our next night out. However, our behaviour became slightly tempered when we both got girlfriends at the same time. For me, GIV represented an increase in velocity. For the first time, I had two girlfriends in the same calendar year (Callum Best, eat your heart out). I suppose it was flattering that she asked me out, but I was never in love with GIV, unlike G1. G2, I wasn't so bothered about losing, but G3 left me feeling sad, but only because she was so damn good looking, like G1. However, getting to G3's house was quite frankly, a pain in the arse and although I passed my driving test one week later, that was one week too late in the end.

With no brakes, no clutch and having had my first car catch fire the previous week (whilst sitting in it), I had been wheedled into not only driving GIV to Gateshead for a freekin' Bryan Adams concert, but I had to attend it too. I hated Bryan Adams, not least because of that godawful, flem-ridden summer-long yarn about Robin Hood. But what really compounded my melancholy was that the concert came on the same day as the 1994 World Cup final, and that I was going to have to give the footy a miss. GIV may have been happy at that decision, but I wasn't. In truth, GIV was making me miserable. Not because she was a bad person (she was a good person): it's just that she was deeply unhappy herself. And the more I discovered about GIV, the more I realised she needed someone who wasn't me. Luckily, Allan and I had another lad's holiday coming up, this time to Kos. It was a chance to get away and think, and I had plenty of that to do. So for the first time in my life, I thought. Like Rodin's 'Thinker', I thought long and hard.

When I returned from Greece, and I went to get my car at the airport, waiting there patiently for me were the new shoes I'd accidentally left sitting on the roof. With hearts in mouths, I somehow got my yellow Metro, without brakes, without a clutch, and with a slow puncture, back to Edinburgh. We made it in time for a 21st birthday party and a night up town. I crashed on the floor of GIV's house before racing to catch Kenny Taylor's 09:00 West End Hearts bus to Pittodrie for the first game of the 94/95 season; and still in the same gear from the flight home the day before: blink and I'll wake up dead! Transport, inevitably, played a huge part in away trips. I remember being part of the Hearts casuals' police escort on a 'football special' train to Dens Park. I had a trip to Easter Road in the back of Allan Redpath's transit van; shared with about fourteen other Hearts fans and a complete set of work tools. And near the start of the 1994/95 season, the entire West End bus was forced to reach Dumbarton's ground by rambling over someone's back garden! Back then, my dream away trip was actually to visit the exciting Estadio Santiago Bernabéu; home to Real Madrid. But in those days, Boghead would have to do.

I eventually finished things with GIV, but in truth, I was only mourning the loss of The Shed. It was my favourite place; celebrating goals and hugging friends as we went crashing down the terracing. I now looked onto the new stand. I had put money into it, and I drove there most days to watch it being built. I was dreaming of a new era, and in more ways than one. But the new stand opened with a game against Hibs, and Hearts not only lost it, but they also waved goodbye to their long, twenty-two game unbeaten run against their greatest rivals; and all on the night I celebrated my 21st birthday? (Cheers you bastards).

Whilst away on holiday, my Greek philosophy/lad's holiday 'thinking' spawned what I dubbed 'The Three Point Plan'. It reads as follows:

1.   Gently 'let go' of GIV.
2.   Find a new job.
3.   ...and...cue Eastenders end-credit drum roll...leave Saughton
Mains   Bank.

Point two and three were for another day, but number one was quickly mission accomplie and it led me to G5, who was old! Well she was about ten years older than me, depending on what her actual age was. She was quite good fun though for a couple of weeks, experienced but way too streetwise for me. I was just twenty-one, had long curtains in a middle parting and wore Caterpillar boots. I met G5 through a friend of Allan's and we went out for about six weeks in all up to Christmas Eve 1994. I bought her perfume for Christmas, but she never got it. I wasn't too bothered about losing her. She lived in Meadowbank, and in 1994, that was a long way from Saughton Mains Bank as my car had given up and was preparing for its new life as a vessel for dog meat. Like all the others (bar GIV), she got a bit bored and after she failed to call me back a couple of times, I took the hint. It actually ended with a phone call from her and me being 'apologised' to. I was ok about it because I knew the drill. Plus I was on a night shift that evening and she'd just woken me up to say her goodbyes. I don't think I even made it all the way through to the end of her explanation, because as I was given the news, I kinda drifted off back to sleep. Once more, the love train to Waverley had thrown me off at Haymarket.

Chapter 34
G6

Hearts were an enigma under Tommy McLean. On one hand, we were struggling, plus he was such a grumpy looking little man. The club was skint and we were bringing in bargain players like Colin Miller and Willie Jamieson. But often, the football was really good and there was something temporarily refreshing about Tynecastle and its new stand. Stevie Frail, the talented right back was in scintillating form, and I remember him scoring a stunning goal versus Aberdeen. Yet history will show Hearts as a floundering side, teetering towards relegation, and not many Jambos revere old 'Hamster Chops'. It was as if we knew we were crap and in transition, but nonetheless, ready and waiting for something better to happen.

I was waiting for something to happen; anything really. Like Forrest Gump, I would sit around waiting for 'my Jenny' to appear: even though there was no actual 'Jenny' or anyone else for that matter. I ghosted around the house, avoiding my mum and her partner. I walked to work in the dark. I mopped the floor, and listened to the same crap songs on Virgin (I swear they had Sheryl Crowe's 'All I Wanna do' on some sort of loop). I served the customers and waited for the shift to end. Then came my favourite time, around 5am. It was close enough to feel the coming of the end of the long, ten hour shift: but quiet enough to get the kettle on and read the morning papers, looking for Hearts stories. I'd put the flower stand and the fire extinguishers outside, ready for the rush hour and the walk home, to Saughton Mains Bank.

Snowy December came and went, bitter January arrived, and still I waited for something exciting to happen. And in arctic February, something did happen; something good. Sean, Allan and I were in the Wheatsheaf, when I pointed out a girl I fancied. She was young and cute, had curly hair, a beautiful big smile and round blue eyes. She looked strangely familiar, as if our paths had crossed, but I didn't know her. Whenever I was in the pub, she would smile at me and I would sheepishly approach the bar, tuck back my curtains and bashfully ask for a "lager and lime, please". I didn't think she fancied me, but I fancied her. It was *coup de foudre*. I would look out for her, always timing it so that she would be the one to pour my pint and dash it with lime (hey, I'm from Saughton Mains. My brother wore a shell-suit. Deal with the fucking lime!). I would go back to Allan or Sean and nudge their arm,

"nice, eh?"

Allan gave me the low-down. Her name was Lesley, same age as us and most importantly, single. A real point of interest though; she was a massive Hearts fan, and even worked at Tynecastle on match days. As Allan was next in line for his 21st, he suggested I asked 'Les the Barmaid' out. Ask her out? It was time for a history lesson. G1 and G5 just kind of happened; the other three Gs asked me out. I had never asked a girl out; or at least had one reply with the words, "oh why yes, sir". Allan turned up the heat.

"Fucking ask her, ya poof." This was not a time for political correctness.

"If you don't ask her, I'll do it for you", he warned me. And from his threat, he made it a promise. My heart sank. Allan was walking over to ask Lesley out, on my behalf! It was like being back at Stenhouse Primary School.

"Will you go out with my mate?" he asked. Lesley looked severely unimpressed from where I was perched.

"Does he not have a voice of his own", was her far-from-impressed reply. Allan came reporting back to the round table. Sean looked on unconvinced by the whole incident. I was genuinely scared, but I gulped down a mouthful of lager and lime, tucked back the curtains and slowly walked round to the end of the bar. Like Hugh Grant's 'David Cassidy' key speech in Four Weddings, I stuttered and bumbled my way through asking the lassie out.

"I don't suppose you're free next Friday?" I asked.

"I'm not, sorry no."

"Right, right (confused pause); well are you free on Saturday?"

"Sorry, no."

Fuck me, I was running out of days of the week here and dying the death of a sweating bastard. A 'mild' feeling of panic came over.

"What abut Sunday?" I blurted.

"Ok", Lesley replied.

Bloody hell, I pulled the barmaid! After twice confirming my third-choice proposal, I thanked her and sauntered back to my table. The lads knew I had scored, word spread and a full house awaited us the following Sunday. On February 19th 1995, I tried to act normally by going to the pub to watch the footy (Man Utd 3: Leeds 1 if I recollect). Inside though, I was nervous and everyone kept reminding me of my impending date. When Lesley finally finished her shift, I waited for her behind the pillars near the door, but the lads knew my game and as we swiftly left, a full round of applause broke out, as did a cheerful rendition of the TV advert "There may be trouble ahead..."

For some reason, I decided to take Les to The Golden Rule bar, in Polwarth. The strange choice had something to do with me wanting to go for a quiet drink in unfamiliar surroundings, but the regulars were as interested in Les as they were in slagging off my hair. We then headed to Dan Mackay's bar at the West End. We hit it off, and the dubious state of Heart of Midlothian featured heavily in our conversation; as it did too, when I took her for our first ever meal – to Marvid's Cafe on Gorgie Road! Lesley was a cute-looking twenty-one-year-old from a middle class family in the south-west of Edinburgh. She attended Boroughmuir High before moving to Glasgow to study. At weekends, she came home to work. Lesley's parents were retired, and she had a big sister, Fiona, who was also a student, and a fifteen-year-old younger brother, Andy, who was then attending George Watson's College (such an awkward age for a young man!). One of the old biddy barmaids felt compelled to ask Lesley,

"Why the hell are you going out with a laddie from Saughton Mains?"

Lesley though, was no snob. In fact, she was as down to earth as I could have hoped for. She was funny and charming, but best of all, she was actually willing to go out with me! The more I found out about Lesley, the more I realised that she was just like me, though with some obvious differences! She talked to me on a level I hadn't experienced before. She had charisma and conversation. Les was cool, and I was most impressed that she'd once met Darth Vader (yes, the real one) in John Menzies circa 1983. She had walked the same pavements, lived the same era and hoped for the same things as me. But she got to perform on the castle esplanade in the 1986 Commonwealth Games Opening Ceremony; and was even in a TV trailer for it. She wore the Nike trainers and did the dance routine numbers at Meadowbank Stadium. She ran down the Royal Mile as I slagged her off from my living room. She had even gone to Dens Park, and stood just feet from Albert Kidd as he stuck a knife into both our twelve-year-old hearts. She got up for school one morning, like me, to hear that John Lennon had been murdered. She went on to get seven 'Highers' when I had seven schemies at the night shift serving hatch. She was the girl on the back of The Sun's "Wayne's Whirl" cover when I had all of Grant Marshall's sixteen stone lying on top of me. She and I had probably walked by each other a hundred times at Tynecastle Park in the past. But most amazingly of all, she was the girl in the turnstile booth when I got myself arrested at Tynecastle. How romantic, and we know this because after one of our long conversations, it suddenly dawned on her that she had written about such an incident, and indeed I was "the cute guy" she described in her diary entry, August 17th 1991 (her words, not mine).

Chapter 35
The end of the road

'Love' was once more kicking my head in. Lesley and I were smitten (or at least I was). With my hair cut short to mark my new mood, we'd bound along Gorgie Road as white vans tooted their horns. We were a Wheatsheaf love story. But the real reason why Les agreed to go out with me soon became apparent. Hearts were playing Rangers in the fourth round of the Scottish Cup and Sky TV was broadcasting the game. It was the day after Les and I went on our first date, and thus the reason for her still being in town. She had only gone out with me because she had a spare night to kill in Edinburgh, before working her shift at Tynecastle. Just as well I was free too then, eh? (Yeah right.)

The game will go down as one of the great Tynecastle nights; a sensational and at times, chaotic roller coaster of a match. Hearts looked well up for it from the start, and the home fans were behind their team like I'd never seen for years. We raced to a 2-0 half-time lead, only for Rangers to peg us back to 2-2. But then John Robertson scored on the hour to make it 3-2 and it left Allan and me jumping for joy (although I think I accidentally kneed some poor kid in the back whilst celebrating). The game was heading for full-time and Rangers were piling on the pressure. But with about a minute left on the clock, Dave McPherson, our giant, gangling defender produced one of the most brilliant flashes of inspiration that I've ever seen from a footballer. As a deafening noise bellowed from the old and new stands, Big 'Peas and Gravy' collected the ball from deep inside his own half. The lanky one then proceeded to depart on an astonishing 'mazy' run up the field, beating several Rangers players on the way. As he played a one-two with Kevin Thomas on the right wing, the entire Hearts support were on their feet roaring him on towards goal. But just as he looked up to shoot, he stopped to think (never a good idea for a 'Davy Mazy'), and squared the ball back to Thomas, who slotted home to make it 4-2! The Shed was gone, but bodies still flew in the air. It was beautiful bedlam. What a goal: what a victory. A fantastic first date coupled with a Jambos win over Rangers in the cup? Not a bad twenty-four hour's work, that.

If my love-life was looking as good as a Colin Miller thirty-five yard free kick, then back home at Saughton Mains Bank, things were going from bad to worse. I managed to sneak Les back a few times, but my mum barred her from staying over. My mum was going through a difficult time and her partner had become tired of me being there. I felt like the person the other two blamed for the ills of the world and their growing resentment of me made my life extremely uncomfortable at home. I even offered to live in the caravan by the side of the house like some sort of trailer park hill-billy! But that offer was declined quicker than you could say 'Tonya Harding'. By the spring of 1995, not a day went by where I wasn't getting blamed for something, even when I wasn't there. And I started to get the hint that I wasn't wanted when the shed skin of my mum's partner's tarantula spider ended up on my bed!

My relationship with Lesley was great. I worked through the week on night-shifts, as Les went to Uni in Glasgow. I'd go through there, and I loved staying at the massive student flat in the Hyndland area of Glasgow that she shared, but the memory is tarnished. When I think back to that time, what really stands out was the crushing disappointment of losing to Airdrie again in the Scottish Cup Semi-Final. It was truly awful, and I remember sitting shell-shocked on the 'Clockwork Orange', and heading back along Byres Road. Although Albert Kidd and Dens Park 1986 would forever be the worst experience, as an adult, that semi defeat was as bad as I'd ever felt supporting Hearts. It's difficult to even begin describing how bad Hearts were that day. So I won't. But I was devastated, because that cup run, which included a splendid win over Dundee Utd, represented the hope that I had in my life at that time. It made no sense to lose.

On the occasions I'd sneak Les back to my house at Saughton Mains Bank, I would code-name it 'Operation Nightcap'; this involved me giving Les a tip-toed piggy-back up the stairs to my room whilst trying to balance a donner kebab and two bottles of Hooch on a tray! In May 1995, just as Hearts were fighting for their survival in the Premier League, I was struggling to maintain my own existence at Saughton Mains Bank. On a spring morning, my mum went out for the day with her partner. I arose some time later, hungover and spent the day chilling with Max (our beloved Alsatian dog). Much later, mum returned home. Within seconds of her arrival, she went berserk at me because the water-heater had been left on all day. Not that it was me who had left it switched on. It was her. But I got the blame, simply because I hadn't noticed it in the brightly lit kitchen. I stood up to her, but it was no use, she was raging and unable to see reason. My hurt turned to frustration, my aggravation to anger. It was a bad moment; worse than the time Henry Smith took a penalty in the Coca Cola Cup tie at Dens Park and sent the ball so high over the bar that it probably ended up inside Tannadice. She wouldn't let it go, and I clenched my fist and threw it forward, smashing it into the wall, just as Bobby had done several years earlier with the Argos punch-bag. Only I meant to miss.

As my boss, Lewis, had split up with his wife around that time, he moved out of his Shandon flat and I moved in with his ex-missus! Besides, Mrs V, as I knew her, gave me no say in the matter. It was decided: I was moving into her spare room at the cost of £180 per-month. As Blur took on Oasis in the battle of the crap song contest, I had my own battle to fight on the home front. But in the end, I had to retreat, as I was ousted from my home by war of will. Domestically dispossessed, I was never to return to live there again. And after twenty-one years of Saughton Mains Bank, my time was up. The 'Three Point Plan' was two-thirds complete.

Chapter 36
Learning to fly

Before the 1995/96 season, Jim Jefferies had Hearts fans in knots over his vacillation as to take (or not to take) the reigns from the desolate Tommy McLean. We all wanted JJ, as he was 'the right choice' for the club, having dutifully captained the team during the dire 1970s and carving out a bright career for himself in management. But as Jefferies went to hand in his resignation, he dramatically declared he wasn't coming, after what appeared to be a crafty emotional ambush by the Falkirk chairman, George Fulston. But then Jefferies spectacularly changed his mind again, and realised that his dream job was the path pointing towards Tynecastle. It had all the suspense of the OJ Simpson murder trial, but after three years of struggle and apathy, the feel good factor was about to return to Gorgie. But for Allan and me, the summer of 1995 signified another change in direction of our friendship.

Like his father and my brother, Allan was a joiner by trade. I worked in a petrol station. Allan was a man's man. He lived for the job and accepted the social upshot that came with it. A lot of my friends were now established tradesmen or suchlike and it was often difficult for me to exist in that environment, as an underqualified outsider. The social scene at the petrol station was quite different though. Despite the bleakness of the job, my colleagues were great and quite middle class; like McNaught, Lewis and Gary. Gordon was more working class, but he lived in a big house. Another great friend was Yolanda; she too made the Commonwealth Games Opening Ceremony, and was caught on TV shoving some poor little kid right out of her way. I was essentially leading a double social life. As in Cooley's 'looking-glass self', I fitted in to whatever setting I became situated, becoming all things to all men. I was a lad with the lads, but I was never in a tradesmen's club. Allan and I now had differing social patterns. After four years of intense alliance, a degree of autonomy began to grow between us once more.

I was free from the manacles of Saughton Mains Bank, but renting a room from Mrs V was not going to be the answer. As she couldn't afford to return my deposit, I spent the last month living rent free. The atmosphere caused by that agreement provided me with the inspiration to get the fuck out of there, and fast. So, in the autumn of 1995, I went to the bank to get a mortgage. My petrol station wages amounted to just enough to purchase a cardboard box; and that's a pretty accurate description of what I ended up buying. To be able to buy my first flat in the booming capital, I needed help; and the answer lay not in Edinburgh, but in Livingston. I asked my father to become my guarantor, allowing me to borrow a little bit more from the bank. He, along with an inquisitive 'Stepmom', nervously agreed to my request and with the money in place, I bought a shoebox-sized property in Dundee Street, Edinburgh. Out of all my friends, I was the first person to buy my own property; not bad for a twenty-two-year-old 'petrol pump attendant'. Staying with Mrs V should have been fun, but I had almost jumped from the frying pan into the fire. I only ever saw her once after that. I wish her well with whatever she is doing now, but I'd rather set fire to my balls before beating them with a rolling-pin than become some pre-menstrual woman's lodger again.

On January 12th 1996, I moved into my Dundee Street flat. It was cold, small and had a strong aroma of stale takeaway food. My building was full of nutters; single men who lived out their lives on the fringes of society. The guy opposite was a hopeless alcoholic who at no point ever came to recognise me when I said hello. The myriad of squatters next door reminded me of some sort of G8 protesters' campsite. At the end of the landing were two flats, both containing men who seemed to be jostling for first place in the 'Crackbrained Psychopath of the Year Award, 1996'. One was a tattooed and pierced Sid Vicious type, who guzzled Special Brew for breakfast with his pet rottweiler, 'Gunga'. And he was the decent one! The other was as mad as a bag of ferrets. In all seriousness, he was a danger to himself, but it was his interest in me that was most alarming. My flat was mine though, and it was officially warmed with one almighty party. The morning after, I found my sofa outside before pouring so much dead booze away, that I experienced the hideous phenomenon of tenement sink burp-back. I didn't know whether to laugh or cry. In the end, I think I just crawled back to bed.

Yet curiously, although I had moved to within a mile of Tynecastle Stadium, I actually found it difficult to let go of Saughton Mains Bank, and it was then that I started having recurring dreams about the place. At least one night every week, I would walk down Calder Road, by Sighthill and then Parkhead. Then I would cut through the alley behind Saughton Mains Loan, past the little field by Saughton Mains Grove, and left onto Saughton Mains Drive. Finally, I'd turn towards the overgrown lane that leads to Saughton Mains Bank. I was now a man, with my own kingdom, starting to make a better life for myself. But in my dreams, I was stuck at home.

Chapter 37
Us nearly men

Football means so much to me, yet the game itself comes in many different guises. Watching Hearts lose in the rain at Pittodrie on a cold day in January can hardly be the same sport that those lucky, long-haired, kipper-tied connoisseurs witnessed at Mexico 1970. Likewise, standing in a pub in Gorgie, drinking lager and having a laugh with my friends is a million miles from those World Cup 'love me I'm an idiot' fans who wear national-dress costumes that the BBC cameras love to zoom in on. No cameraman has ever found reason to zoom in on me. Likewise, I don't envy the Old Firm. As I mentioned earlier, they see loads of trophy wins, but do they ever know what it's like to really savour one, as if their life is defined by it? But one thing I'm not is one of those glorious losers. I hate losing. It's just that they win so often, what exactly does it mean to them? Is it just to get one over the other lot? And would they put up with not winning? It's all a bit repetitive and confined. Football to me isn't about pretty passing, or glorious failure; or even dressing up like a prat. Football to me is about winning, or at least trying to win: and daring to believe. It's about winning and celebrating, having a laugh and drinking lager, singing and friends taking the piss out of each other. But that dream of winning has to count for something. It has to really matter. It's about being there and living it. I wouldn't have it any other way.

When Pele feigned touching the ball before proceeding to run right round the back of the Uruguayan goalkeeper, only for him to then just miss out on scoring, the watching world held its head in its hands. But they did so not in agony: but in awe. How could this cheeky, wiry Brazilian have had the audacity to attempt such a feat on the biggest stage of all? I guess it's because he believed it could be done. Yet, had he scored, the magnitude of such brilliance would have set him apart from all his peers; the perfect goal, but confined to just that. But because he missed, his outrageous attempt made him fallible, and it allowed an adoring public to imagine, to dare to believe that maybe such greatness could be achieved. It was the fact that he nearly scored, and that Pele was after all, mortal, which makes the clip so utterly gorgeous. There is almost a touch of samba effrontery about it too, as was Pele's decision to lash another keeper's kick-out straight back towards the goal it came from. The 'dummy' footage looks simply sublime on its sharp cinematic frame, but the hazy early colour of 1970s TV is equally splendid; as the British commentator blurts out "oh what genius!" But although Pele's dummy belongs to all fans of football, it's really part of someone else's memories on the other side of the world, and a generation before me. I only knew Hearts, the long ball and miserable weather; the Old Firm hoovering up all the silverware, leaving Hearts with just a silver jersey. And if winning (and in Pele's case, scoring) isn't everything, well then maybe that's fair enough: because by 1996, I didn't know any different anyway.

The first 'big win' of the Jim Jefferies era came in the form of a sensational 3-0 victory at Ibrox in January 1996, just a week or so after I moved into my flat. There was an exciting feel to this Hearts team. Our smattering of foreign players such as Pasquale Bruno and Gilles Rousset, added a new, glamorous and continental touch to contrast stalwarts like Mackay, Colquhoun and McPherson. We also had a batch of kids in McManus, Ritchie, Locke and the hat-trick hero of Ibrox, Allan Johnston, who was quite outstanding that day. I was working until three o'clock, but I remember how Les and I leapt about the flat as the second and third goals went in. It was a stunning win, and even 'Sid Vicious', the perma-drunk anarchist from the end of the landing, would have been nervous if he'd witnessed my hysteria. The Hearts were back.

On the back of the flat guarantor gesture, and the fact it was my little brother Ian's birthday, Lesley and I went through to Livingston. My father and 'Stepmom' didn't appear to be very happy. We went to see Ian play football for his primary school, but my dad sat in the car for the entire game reading his newspaper. Ian ran his heart out for me, but the game ended 0-0, as twenty little outfield dudes chased a full-size ball on a full-size mud bath pitch. Twelve years after I stood ankle deep in various quagmires and still we hadn't learned. No wonder this country is lagging behind. On the side-lines, the parents who could be bothered to watch shouted their frustrations at the kids, the ref and at each other. A couple of weeks later, 'Stepmom' left my father for a man who spent years pretending to be my dad's best friend. It threw my father into a downward spiral from which he never really recovered. It was a West Lothian love tragedy.

It was also an exciting time, with good things happening. I 'found' my cousin, Stuart (he of the karate pyjamas), and we started a great friendship watching Hearts together and socialising. I was also painted a giant 'impression' of the 'Abbey Road' album cover for my flat. My brother, Bobby put it up on the wall for me, and proceeded to point out all the little errors he could find from the CD cover. I roped in Les, John, Andy and Gordon to help paint the flat (although I kind of turned into a cross between

119

Genghis Khan and Jack Sparrow – tyrant bastard in a bandana). Les and I went to Killie for the fourth round tie in the Scottish Cup, and it was refreshing to hear modern Britpop being played in a football stadium, as we only ever heard 'The Final Countdown' by Europe at Tynecastle. The good times rolled as Hearts won a battling contest 2-1, and the pies weren't too bad either. The semi-final meant another trip back to dreaded Hampden Park, the haggard stadium where we hadn't won for ten years. But on an emotional and nerve-racking day, outnumbering the Aberdeen support by about three to one, a last minute goal from Allan Johnston won us a place in the final; our first since the days of those silver jerseys. Hampden was due a new roof, and we almost took the old one off. It was carnage: beautiful carnage.

Ten minutes previous, Aberdeen had scored a late equaliser, but now we had an extraordinary feeling when pouring out of Hampden victorious, and being swept along Mount Florida with twenty thousand other frenzied Hearts fans. We may have been celebrating, but collectively, we seemed to do so with a pugnacious snarl. Heart of Midlothian had shown Aberdeen who was boss outside the Old Firm. Strathclyde Police though, showed Hearts fans who was boss at the old stadium: one hundred and thirty-three arrests would prove that. Back at the Wheatsheaf, the party went on long into the night and eventually, Les and I stayed over at her family home. With an abominable hangover, I awoke in the stifling living-room early the next morning, and with a mouth like a camel's hoof. Dear old Donald didn't do Irn Bru or Red Kola, so as naked as the day I was born, I stood in the family vestibule and proceeded to guzzle down my potential father-in-law's Schweppes' Bitter Lemon. With no other route back to the living-room, it was with some dismay that I became aware of Donald's presence as he came down the stairs to take the dog out! With only an empty bottle of fizzy gin mixer to shield my embarrassment, I stood silently in the dark shadows of the lobby as he wearily grappled with the dog's leash. Even though the dog knew I was loitering there (and it probably wanted to sink its teeth into my white ass), the old mutt was too frail to make much of a scene, and in the end, I got away with a late scare in a big semi. Just like the Hearts.

...and so to the final:

We had high hopes. Rab Ewan from the Wheatsheaf, a lovely guy, was adept as always at putting on the bus, and we left thinking this could be the day to end thirty-four years without a trophy. As we made our way inside Hampden, the noise generated by the Hearts fans was mind-blowing; the best I've ever experienced. It was raw and emotional. The singing from our fans produced a magnificent reverberation around the embarrassing

'National Stadium'. Rangers fans for their part were slow on the uptake, just another cup final for their nine-in-a-row generation. For us, it was wonderful to be there, a decade on from those tears. We felt we had a chance to win it too, having merrily disposed of Rangers in our last two league meetings. With the inspiration of having twenty-year-old Gary Locke as our Jambos-mad captain, we took to the field to 'Cum on feel the noize'. Feel the noise? We were the fucking noise.

With a great roar the final kicked off and we were ready for a scrap: but with just minutes on the clock, Locke's enthusiasm took him into an early challenge, and his knee gave way to leave him sprawled out on the Hampden turf. Such a savage and early blow was compounded with the realisation that the Hearts bench was being warmed by two pocket-sized forwards and a spare goalkeeper. Our shape had gone, with Allan Johnston pulled back deep into midfield, and there were still eighty-three minutes left to play. Sadly, it was eighty-three minutes too long. Rangers were already leading 1-0 at half-time, when early in the second half, Gilles Rousset let a horror goal right through his legs. The heads of our outfield players went down and Rangers won 5-1, with Durie, Gascoigne and Laudrup running riot. Locke's injury was catastrophic to our cause. He was a young lad living the dream, perhaps slightly punching above his weight. But his passion and drive made the team tick: Mr Bonnyrigg Hearts. He did come back, but he was never quite the same player again.

We left somewhat routed, but all-in-all, it was a good season. Cup final defeats I can handle. Those are the days to remember with fondness, because we see the potential of the support and the fervour they generate. Losing is crushing of course, but not as crushing as seeing a team lose hope. I just missed out on the 'relegation years' of 1977, 1979 and 1981, but I saw some really bad times too. There were moments when it seemed that Hearts had no hope; no apparent way out of the mire. Those were the worst days. The most crushing day of all was the last league game of the 1985/86 season, but even that was for different and more personal reasons altogether. Which is why this cup final defeat then, almost pales into insignificance. And as disappointing a game it was, the pre-match atmosphere made me realise once more how lucky and how proud I was to support Heart of Midlothian. Like I said, I hate losing: but I'd rather be one of us, than one of them.

Hearts finished 4th at the end of 1995/96. And although we strengthened with quality players like Colin Cameron (my all time favourite Hearts player), David Weir, Neil McCann and er, Jeremy Goss, we weren't quite as consistent the next season. There is a strange phenomenon in that Hearts, since re-establishing their Premier League status, seem to only do quite well every other season. And if the season ends on an odd numbered year, Hearts are usually average to crap. We did however, get to the Coca Cola Cup Final in 1996/97; again we travelled to Glasgow in massive numbers, and yet again, we faced Rangers. I got pretty drunk before the game, but I remember that it snowed all the way to Glasgow, with a slushy pitch inspection required before kick-off. Rangers were favourites, again, and they raced into a two-goal lead, again. Things, it seemed, were looking as bleak and predictable as the December weather. But there was one notable difference between here, and the previous cup final back in May. This time, we got angry! And as we picked ourselves up from the ground, we wiped off the mud…and got stuck right into the bastards!

Hearts, wearing a dashing, deep maroon strip were starting to get at their opponents with a newfound daring determination. With the game teetering towards half-time, the ball skidded towards Stevie Fulton. The midfielder controlled it, spun round and scored a terrific goal to make it 2-1! It was by my estimation, the first meaningful goal that Hearts had scored in a decisive match in my lifetime and it was game on at Celtic Park! The start of the second half saw Hearts, and in particular, Neil McCann set a breathtaking pace. We were really going for it and McCann was playing like the devil down the wing, leaving a trail of defenders in his wake. Again and again, he caused havoc, and on one fabulous dart, he beat Petric, Bjorklund and Moore to cross in, and there was Robbo to slide the ball home for 2-2! It was bedlam: sheer bedlam. The celebrations were immense. Oh my God: this was it! At 2-0, we looked buried. But now we were so close to victory. The feeling of elation was incredible; and for four magical minutes, we could reach out over the steep terraced stands and put one hand on the cup.

But then came Gazza; the infamous Geordie remembered for his tears at the 1990 World Cup. He entered stage left, found one extra gear and two sharp elbows and won the trophy for Rangers. It was a wonderful game, and Hearts played so well. But fundamentally, it was yet another near miss, as Hearts rolled on towards thirty-five years without that trophy. As we returned to the Wheatsheaf, I drowned my sorrows. With Les one side of me and Scott on the other, I cried like a baby, as Gazza had done six years before me. I was crying over yet another lost opportunity. Now there was a broken record. My journey supporting Hearts was my life. So nearly good, but never once being able to touch upon greatness. But then maybe I was missing the point. Perhaps the greatness that I sought was there already, but I just didn't recognise it? Maybe this was as good as it gets supporting Hearts? Maybe life didn't get any better. But all I knew on that Sunday night was that my team had failed again, and it was getting tougher to take. There I was, still dreaming, yet still working at the petrol station. My dad's life was in chaos and he would deliriously phone me about a dozen times a day in despair. Ten years after Albert Kidd, we were the class of 1996 – The Nearly Men. Pele nearly scored after his dummy on the keeper. But my life wasn't a metaphor for Pele: I was probably the keeper.

Chapter 38
'Flight of Fancy'

1997 was the year of New Labour, Cool Britannia, 'OK Computer' and the rather dubious death of Diana, Princess of Wales. For me, it was the year we beat Hibs four times. 'OK Computer' was important too: more so than Cherie Blair and less so than Hearts. It came to represent the colossal album I was waiting for; better even than 'The Bends'? Well, maybe. But music and football (along with booze and socialising) were mere smokescreens for my calamitous flat and mediocre job. A Nightmare on Dundee Street began a few weeks after I moved in:

1. We had a mouse, or at least we thought it was just the one. We never spoke of them in the plural sense in those early days (ah, ignorant bliss). I had to get Allan to help me seal round all the skirtings with a mixture of plaster and broken glass. Bobby alternatively suggested catching one mouse and pouring Tabasco sauce down its throat. This apparently sends out a signal to all the other mice that it's being held captive by the fifth craziest person on the landing. Bobby knew all about hot sauces. He carries a bottle to work and once made me taste a spoonful of something that bore the slogan, "Who Dares, Wins"! The only remedy for that was to drink a litre of milk. Lesley's mum suggested a 'humane' trap. But what's humane about a slow, claustrophobic death of no light, no space, no food and no water. One day, the mice disappeared, and hastily so. But the very reason for their sudden departure would be the basis for my yearning their return...

2. The windows in the flat didn't pull up more than a few inches from where they rested at the bottom. That was fine until I nearly poisoned Les and me one Sunday morning, and bang in the middle of the big chill outside. The January temperatures in Edinburgh in 1996 plummeted to around -15C, yet we had to squeeze our heads out of the window and then leave them there, as I had accidentally melted two plastic (and highly poisonous) trays onto the top of the grill, whilst attempting to make breakfast. Yet the entire time we were stranded there, a woman in the flat across from us just stared at us. At no point did she actually bother her arse to ask us if anything was the matter, so I just used the time to stare the bitch

out!

3. The flat had a strong aroma of food, not that surprising really when one finds oneself living above a takeaway. However, Les and I stopped noticing it after a while; until that is we went on holiday. When I opened our suitcase, I was hit by the realisation that all our clothes were permanently hooching!

4. The industrial extractor fans used by the takeaway may have been conveniently attached to their ceiling: but this subsequently meant it was bolted to my floor. Whenever they turned them on (which was every daytime and all evening), my entire flat would shake like a scene from Dante's Peak. I had to resort to resting a 30KG canister of butane gas on the middle of my bedroom carpet to stop the bloody floor rattling. The Environmental Health people reckoned the vibrations to be something like ten times over the acceptable noise limit!

5. The nutty neighbour at the end of the hallway kept trying to befriend me (not the drunk I call 'Sid Vicious': the other one). He asked me repeatedly to have a drink with him, so one night I reluctantly agreed, making it clear to him that my girlfriend knew my exact whereabouts. I swear, I thought I would never leave his flat alive. He poured me a glass of cooking sherry from a chipped whisky glass. He had lino in his living-room which surrounded an open tank, home to some sort of reptile! It was my first and last drink with him. But after I continually gave him the cold shoulder, he resorted to emptying the contents of his cat's litter tray on my doorstep! I banged on his door asking why the fuck he did that, but he actually had the brass-neck to deny having a cat! To clean up, I had to pour bleach on my doorstep, but things then took a turn for the worse when he banged on my door shouting,
"You killed my cat!"
I yelled back through the letterbox to him, "But you don't have a cat, remember?" I can laugh about it now, but deary me, the guy was howling mad and after he managed to set fire to his flat, I never saw the raving loony again!

6. When Allan laid down a new wooden floor for me in return for putting him up for a couple of months, we threw the old planks out of the window. To my eternal shame, I left them lying there for over a year! When I had friends round for dinner, I would show off the new floor to them, before offering them a gallery view of the old one! The backyard was little more

than a dumping ground for Sid's pissy mattress and the squatters' broken sofa anyway, and no one seemed to give a damn until our stairwell was stormed by the fire brigade. I moved the planks the next day, but as I made my first ever trip into my own backyard, I was horrified by what I saw.

7. ...and so, worst of all, and about three tumultuous years after moving in: a little food shop round the corner shut down. This pretty much meant that the mice moved out and the cockroaches moved in! Les and I didn't know what had hit us; and at its peak, we had to sleep on our living room floor... inside a tent!

One of the grimmest days in the advancement of my professional career came in the guise of a tantalising office job in town. The girl who interviewed me was pretty and young and asked me questions regarding attributes like 'enthusiasm' and 'positive attitude'. As I had no issue with either of these things I qualified for the 'second interview stage' and was told to report for duty at 7am the next day. I adorned my atrocious shiny grey suit and horrible pattern tie and headed into town. But it was during the bus ride that my nerves made way to suspicion. The problem was I had no idea what the job actually involved. 'Sales & Marketing' was the banner in the paper but there was no mention of what sales I'd actually be marketing. I guessed it probably involved me having my own office and shouting loudly to my assistant: "Get me London on the phone!" By 7.15am, it became apparent that there was no London: but there was a Fife. I was introduced to my 'partner' and we hopped on a bus to Inverkeithing. He was carrying a giant holdall.

As we approached our destination, he opened the bag to unveil a huge booty of cheap radios and crap ladies handbags. Basically, we were to spend the whole day flogging them and by any means possible. He got the money, and I got to watch. It was a freezing day and the weather was all over the place: certainly not shiny grey suit weather. As we traipsed around grim industrial units, people were literally telling us to "go and fuck off". Like I said, we were in Fife. Others just stared at us in embarrassed disbelief. Yet my 'partner' was unrelenting in his 'enthusiasm' and 'positive attitude'. And so was I, in my pursuit of the 11.10 train back to Edinburgh. I remember stopping off at Somerfield on the way home, stocking up on comfort food and beers; desperate to get home and shut the world out. I jumped straight into my trackie bottoms, cracked open a Corona and played 'Sensible Soccer' on the Megadrive. By the time Les got in from work, I relayed the entire humiliating episode back to her, realising that the other guy was probably still out there, flogging his bag of shit to bemused Fifers. Les was always great in a crisis and an amusing footnote to this sorry incident is that my dear friend Allan went for the same initial interview a couple of weeks later. I think he was fed up with being a joiner for a spell, but I couldn't wait to warn him of what he could expect at the next 'interview stage'. Yet Allan being Allan, his pride flatly refused him to believe it was the same job and I think he probably felt embarrassed. Maybe like me, he thought he'd be in his office shouting: "Get me London"!

If my job search was exasperating, then the footy was a real source of dissatisfaction too, and I lost it big time at Tannadice. Hearts hadn't won a trophy since 1962 and I was getting beyond desperate. I cried sorry tears when Albert Kidd's goals ruined my childhood; I sat in stunned silence when we lost not once, but twice to bloody Airdrie. Now I was watching Hearts make a ham-fisted attempt at a Scottish Cup Fourth Round replay. Poor Donald still never lets me forget my behaviour as all of my frustrations boiled over in the front row of the main stand. We spent eighty-seven minutes aimlessly chasing the game and when the whistle blew, United's manager, Tommy McLean turned round from his dug-out, and gestured right into my eyes to 'get it right up me'. I was ready to leap over the fence and build 'Hamster Chops' a new hutch, but instead I chose to sit back down, without realising my chair had tipped back to its upright position. As I fell flat on my arse, I questioned whether I'd ever see Hearts win a bloody trophy. It was one of those moments when a fan's love for his team is sternly examined. Within those last ten years, Hearts fans had to endure watching St Mirren, Raith, Kilmarnock and even Hibs pick up silverware. Were we to be forever cursed?

If the football and the job search proved fruitless, then I could at least galvanize myself with a tilt at indie-rock-stardom. It all happened on the back of 'OK Computer', 'Coming Up' and 'Urban Hymns'. Pete was the brother of my workmate, McNaught. After hearing me sing on Gordon's karaoke machine, he suggested we start a band, as not only was he a talented guitar player, but he knew plenty of other musicians. I wasn't exactly Richard Ashcroft, and this wasn't Spinal Tap, but my hair had grown longer again over my ears and I was well up for this. Pete asked me to write the band a song, before going to see him. So with pen and paper, I wrote the beautiful anthem, 'A Flight of Fancy'; an angst-ridden sonnet about getting dumped by a heartless bitch because I wore white jeans. I travelled up to Bonaly and nervously blurted the words out to Pete. He was so impressed, that he never called me again. And my last, desperate act to stay in the band was to leave Pete a four-minute long phone message, with me singing 'Blinded by the Sun', by The Seahorses. I'm surprised he never got an injunction taken out. By the age of twenty-three, I was a washed-up singer/songwriter.

The new 1997/98 season had arrived. The team looked fresh and talented. Colin Cameron, Neil McCann, David Weir, Paul Ritchie, Stevie Fulton, Stefano Salvatori, Stephane Adam, Thomas Flogel and latterly, Gary Naysmith were all at the top of their game. Interestingly, I went through a spell of inadvertently stalking our Italian midfielder. In the space of a few weeks, I had seen and spoken to him in three different restaurants. On the fourth occasion I saw him, in Castle Street, I think he did a double-take when he spotted me coming, which then compelled him to cross the road and pretend to look into a shop window! It wasn't my fault Stefano: I live here! Hearts were playing brilliantly and had the form of potential champions, like twelve years previous. Still we watched, and still we waited in hope. Hearts were once again teasing and torturing us; tempting us to believe in them. By the turn of 1998, we were still challenging with Celtic for the title, as 'nine-in-a-row' Rangers trailed behind.

When Celtic visited Tynecastle in February, their narrow lead over us in the league didn't allow any terminal slip-ups from us. Hearts/Celtic games have always been spiteful affairs and Tynecastle, the bear pit of Scottish stadia, provided a perfect setting for such aggression. Celtic took a deserved lead, and seemed to be coasting to victory, as Hearts' title hopes faded with the light. But as the game drew to a close, both teams began to throw caution to the wind. Hearts went for broke, leaving huge gaps in their defence. But Celtic surprisingly kept pushing forward too, looking for the killer second goal. All cards were on the table: except Hearts had a cheeky little joker up their sleeve in the form of chirpy Angolan winger, Jose Quitongo. As the game reached its ninety-third frantic minute, Jim Hamilton launched the ball into the box, sparking one almighty scramble. But the ball broke to Jose and he swung out with his shin. The ball took a twist, and then a deflection, before nestling into the net for an unbelievably late Hearts equaliser. The poor Celtic fans, who were all there to the end, couldn't get to the exits quick enough. What they were then forced to endure, was the sight of thousands of Hearts fans celebrating riotously as pandemonium broke out all over the stands and spilled onto the pitch. There was a real esprit de corps. And my own position in Section G allowed me to reach out to the travelling supporters to offer them my sympathy, whilst wishing them a pleasant journey back to Drumchapel. Celtic fans may be a spoiled bunch when it comes to winning trophies, but man did we give it to them tight that day: and bhoy did they not like it up 'em?!

Yet the entertaining football didn't veil my personal struggles. The petrol station situation was becoming unbearable. All throughout the 90s, it was the guys who I worked with that kept me happy; our laughter and chemistry binding us to one another. Yet it was that bond that became the problem. They weren't just keeping me sane: they were holding me back. We had all been there for so long, it was as if we were an aging, washed-up rock band, and I needed to get the fuck out. My 'Three Point Plan' was still incomplete, and to achieve that, I had to be the one who 'broke up the band'. That was my 'Flight of Fancy'.

Chapter 39
It's getting better, man

Like Jimmy in Quadrophenia, I didn't know whether to walk back from the cliff or drive right off it. I was twenty-four, and had reached the nadir of my job, with little sign of a way out. Yet my maddening situation at work was alleviated with a really good Hearts team, and such wild oscillation can often lead to outrageous thinking. On February 14th 1998, Hearts defeated Albion Rovers in the Scottish Cup. That night, the club held a St Valentines Ball in the newly opened Gorgie Suite at Tynecastle. There were plenty of people I knew going, so Lesley and I got tickets. It was an enjoyable night, and a great roar went up when it was announced that Hearts had drawn Ayr United at home for the quarter-final. There was though, a little devil playing fiddle in my head. In front of a packed house, the DJ gave me the microphone and got the attention of the room. I summoned Lesley over, and just as she approached, I dropped down onto one knee, and asked her to marry me. With tears in her eyes, she said yes. Our friends and family came rushing over to congratulate us, and the rest of the night was a drunken haze. But poor Les, when she saw me grab the microphone, she thought I was getting up to sing!

I awoke with another one of those hangovers which no doubt meant that certain death would try and visit me in the early hours of Monday morning. My enjoyment of the engagement stunt was only slightly tempered by the fact that Les cried for three days and hardly spoke to me for another five! That though, was just a blink of an eye compared with the twelve months it actually took me to buy the bloody ring. The Ayr United game was negotiated with much less fuss, and the 4-1 win set us up for the semi-final against Falkirk, who were traditionally thorny opponents. The game was played at Ibrox and all seemed well as we took a fifth minute lead. Falkirk though, started to dominate and their diminutive, veteran winger, Kevin McAllister was turning Gary Naysmith inside-out.

We spent most of the match hanging on by the skin of our shins but essentially, with our lead still intact. However, with just minutes to go, McAllister looked up and chipped a sublime goal into Rousset's top-hand corner: and I just lost it.

"Bottlers!"

"Fucking Bottlers!"

I was not a happy little Easter Bunny. As I bawled, I stood up and kicked the seat in front of me and the searing pain in my shin drew some blood. Like Tannadice the previous season, I was enraged, with much abuse spouting from my mouth. I was sucked back into semi-final defeats from St Mirren and Airdrie. I saw the travesty of Dens Park. And once more, I was living out the same recurring Groundhog Day of watching Hearts snatching defeat from the jaws of victory. I sank to my seat, my team negligent, my worst fears realised, my mind numb and my leg in agony. It seemed so sad that one thing in life would forever be certain: this would always be the scenario. We were perpetually doomed. With time up on the scoreboard, Hearts broke forward and suddenly, Neil McCann was racing through on goal. Now just hang on a minute, Sir. He looked up and dinked the ball to the back post, where waiting was a gleeful Stephane Adam...who made no mistake in making the score 2-1 to Hearts!

"AAAAAAAAAAHHHHRRRRRRRRR."

My cousin Stuart and I grabbed each other and we went wholly mental, and his momentum threw me over the very seat that I'd kicked in anger just a few minutes before. Throughout the celebrations, I was almost in an upside down position, and just as I got back to my feet, McCann was clear through on goal again: only this time by himself. He calmly looked up, picked his spot and swept the ball home to send Hearts into the final with a bit of style. As the whistle went for full-time, I actually felt a tinge of embarrassment about my behaviour, and my cousin has never been slow in performing his "Bottlers" impersonation back to me. My team had won a Scottish Cup semi-final; almost it seemed, just to spite me. And to forever remind me of that lesson, in a certain light, I can see the faint scar on my leg to this day.

But sadly, our league challenge died a death after the semi-final. Stuart, Lesley, Donald and I sat in the most exposed corner of Easter Road. I remember looking down to see two small mountains of hail stones balanced on each of my legs as Hearts lost to Hibs. But it was to be a defiant moment of cheer for our Edinburgh rivals because Hibs were relegated a couple of weeks later. Despite the result, Hearts fans still managed to sing with a degree of foresight the lament; "We'll meet again, don't know where, don't know when". Our league challenge was over. But Hearts were in the final of the Scottish Cup, where they would meet Rangers, again!

My mate Franco declared that "Gorgie was buzzing", clearly in a confident mood; and when I hit Gorgie Road, I could see why. There were so many Hearts fans, bounding. Struggling shops had 'good luck' messages in their windows. Flags flew from the windows of the tenements. It was a gorgeous day, but I wanted a perfect one. And the clock hadn't hit 09:00hrs when I marched up to Callum in the Luckies Bar and requested my first pint of lager-n-lime. Perfect day? It was going to be a long one. The bus was packed and for the first and only time in my life, I headed to a Hearts game...topless! No wonder there were children crying along Calder Road, as sightings of a were-wolf spread across the Edinburgh West. We booked into our bar in East Kilbride and the welcome was superb and the atmosphere electric; one of my all-time favourite pre-match singing/drinking sessions (along with Liege 92 & Hampden 95). By the time kick-off arrived at Celtic Park, I was feeling slightly tipsy. It wasn't the drinking that did it: it was walking out into the sun! It was hot: damn hot.

The twelve years since Albert Kidd and Dens Park had given Hearts fans many moments to celebrate. But those 'moments' were goals and games. They were never cups or championships. It was never silverware. Fortunately, I now had Lesley. She made my life good. She encouraged me and gave me hope. Hearts and Lesley were two of the things that I loved most. Lesley had never let me down, and I was going to need her here because Hearts always let me down when it truly mattered. With a deep breath I stood high above the Celtic Park pitch, and I wanted to see much more than just a football match. For once, just once, I wanted to see my beloved/be-hated Hearts win a trophy. Just once, I wanted them to be winners. Because if Hearts could be winners: then I could feel part of that. I could taste it. On May 16th 1998, Heart of Midlothian played Rangers in The Scottish Cup Final at Celtic Park, Glasgow; and I no longer hoped or prayed for success. I fucking demanded it.

Chapter 40
Voice of an angel

Trembling with adrenaline once more, I stood as part of a vast army of Hearts fans, of which there were twenty-two thousand of us. We were a glorious sight, stretched high along the massive two-tiered stand that ran the length of the pitch. I was soaring, my position was at the building-site end of the unfinished stadium, and I looked over towards my people; people that I knew, and people with whom I shared so much, without knowing them at all. We puffed out our chests and sang our hearts out as the team emerged in dashing white with maroon. The cup final was upon us. Hearts kicked off, what seemed a little early, and immediately went on the attack; the ball broke to Stevie Fulton, our captain for the day. Bloody hell, 'Baggio' didn't mess about either, heading straight for goal and he wasn't stopping to ask for directions. We had only just started, but there was Stevie...and he went down in a heap...tripped on the edge of the box. Well blow me: the ref gave us a penalty! 'A penalty kick to Hearts!' We couldn't believe it and there were only thirty seconds on the clock. The intensity was incredible. There was Les and me, her brother Andy and her dad, Donald. My cousins Stuart and Linda were there also; my friends, and Bobby smattered around both tiers. For the last thirty-six years, Hearts had never been ahead in a cup final. Yet here we were, playing Rangers on the day their celebrated 'nine-in-a-row' team was breaking up. I took another deep breath, and held onto the people either side of me. Every Hearts fan watching held onto something!

Colin 'Mickey' Cameron had been my favourite player for two years leading up to the penalty. He was such a fabulous little attacking midfielder and his beaming, goal-scoring smile was always a sight to treasure. I liked him, and he was regarded as one of the most popular and respected players in the Scottish game. But none of that mattered now. Like Bobby hissing towards me at the Broomhouse v Saughton take-on, "you'd better not fucking miss!" Mickey was now in charge of the most important kick of a ball in my lifetime. He steadied himself and ran forward; I gripped Lesley's arm with all my strength. He leaned back and stroked the ball high in to the net.

"YYYYYYYYYYYEEEEEEEEEEEEEEEEEAAAAAAAASSSSSSSS!!!!!!!"

One minute gone, and 1-0 to Hearts! We went absolutely berserk; the roof of the Celtic Park Stand was shaking, and it was hot: damn hot. It was a sensational start, and I don't think a Rangers player had even touched the ball and Donald didn't even think the hour mark of 3pm had struck yet! Get in there! 1-0! Rangers of course, came roaring right back at us. Laudrup, McCoist, Gough, McCall, Goram and manager Walter Smith were all playing their final games for the club. But Jim Jefferies had spent a week in Stratford creating a robust system set to frustrate Rangers, and so far it was working. Rousset, McPherson, Ritchie, Weir, Naysmith, Salvatori, Fulton, Cameron, McCann, Flogel and Adam all had superb seasons. Jim Hamilton was on the bench, as was legendary striker John Robertson, who was also saying his own goodbyes that day. But nostalgia had to wait as the game raged on, and Rangers were making chances, hitting the post at one point. Hearts though, held firm, and went in 1-0 up at half-time. It was time for a cigarette, or maybe four.

The second half began, and Hearts were attacking the goal towards us. But it was Rangers that were now looking the business. We'd stung them early in the first half, but now they were ready to pick us off, as they had done in the previous two cup finals between us; and done so with an inevitability, like the unrelenting dead eyes of a shark. Their fans were now getting behind them and it was a worrying time as I had bitten all my finger nails off. But Gilles Rousset looked to take some pressure off Hearts with a free kick seven minutes into the second half and launched the ball forward. As the ball bounced to Lorenzo Amoruso, we could catch a breath as the danger was cleared for another few seconds. But someone hadn't read the script. Amoruso dallied on the ball for a second too long. Stephane Adam sneaked in from his blind side and pick-pocketed the ungainly Italian to set up a chance for a second Hearts goal. We leaned forward as he fired his shot; he struck it true and low, but Goram got a hand to it and the ball bounced up. For a split second, I thought that we'd won a most welcomed corner. But the ball didn't run for a corner. The ball ended up in the net. "AAAAAAAAAARRRRRRHHHH!!!!!!" It was 2-0 to Hearts!!! Pandemonium on a scale not yet known to Hearts fans!

The noise was mind-blowing. I was jumping up and down with four or five people attached to me. We were bouncing and laughing and screaming; a very aggressive joy. Heart of Midlothian were beating Rangers 2-0 in the Scottish Cup Final. I could barely believe it: but it was true. And so the game raged on. Flogel should have buried a header to make it three and easy, but then he turned it on later with an outrageous overhead flick. But Rangers came at us again, and with eight minutes left, Rino Gattuso set up Ally McCoist and he struck to get a goal back. It was horrible, nauseating; repulsive. Their fans sent a wall of noise towards us, and rallied their team again, throwing everything at us. With just three minutes to go, McCoist was through on goal once more. I was shaking, my heart in my mouth, my stomach tied in knots. He bore down on Rousset...but was tripped on the edge of the box, just like Fulton had been at the start. The referee immediately pointed towards the spot and the Rangers fans went wild – a penalty kick. We'd blown it. I froze in the baking heat. Just minutes before, we were 2-0 up and edging towards victory. But now, we had let them back in and victory was now certain to be theirs. Even with a four goal cushion, I wouldn't have been confident of not losing 5-4 to Rangers. But this was sickening, truly sickening. Our two goal lead was always precarious. Not because two goals is a pitiful advantage: but because it's Hearts. Those seconds after the referee's decision left me shattered: again!

As the roar from the Rangers fans engulfed us, Hearts fans around me groaned, barely able to comprehend another savage blow. Time stood still in the history of Heart of Midlothian. But "out of chaos, comes order", according to Friedrich Nietzsche; and although his cogitations weren't wrong, no existentialist could ever encapsulate what it takes and what it means to follow Heart of Midlothian. Yet it was then, that salvation appeared. Something happened. Something miraculous happened: something that changed the course of my life. From a few rows behind, I heard a voice; the voice of an angel. It might have come from another Hearts fan. Maybe it was in my head. But it was a soothing voice. It was a voice of clarity: a voice of truth. In my darkest hell, it spoke to me words of pure deliverance. Without panic, without fear and in no certain doubt; it said, "It's not a penalty". And it wasn't.

From where we sat, almost everyone thought the ref had given a penalty to Rangers. But Willie Young had actually ran in, pointing to the edge of the box. It was almost too much to bear and I wouldn't have lasted if I'd been one of those Hearts fans in the sun. I could hardly breathe in the shade. McCoist had gone down, but the replay showed his remarkably collapsible legs had folded half a foot too soon. He was actually twice fouled: once outside the box, and once in it. It was a foul, yes. But a penalty it wasn't. Laudrup took the free kick, and it hit the wall before going out for a corner. We had survived another momentous scare, and Rangers weren't done yet. However, one crucial fact remained: Hearts were still winning. The dream was still alive, and now it was within touching distance, closer than ever before: closer even than 1986. But as the game teetered towards full-time, the bastards kept on coming. Chance after chance, McCoist again; Porrini stopped with a last ditch tackle from Weir; Jim Hamilton, winning everything in the air for us in a heroic cameo;

Robbo, itching to get on to fight for us; Gordon Durie, slamming a shot just inches over the bar. There was a shrieking of whistles, a calamity of hoarse voices and a million prayers skywards. Hearts fans: we were begging for the end: begging.

I clasped my hands. I was juddering uncontrollably and sweating like Meatloaf. I pleaded over and over again for the ref to finish it, and to end my agonising wait. All my life flashed before me, all my let-downs, all my pain; still waiting there, in the pits of my mind, ready and willing to pounce. I hated it. 'Please ref, blow the fucking whistle'. Don't do it to me again. But this was to be a red letter day, and as Gilles Rousset sent his 94th minute goal-kick high up into the gods, there was to be no heartache, and the referee finally blew for full-time. 'We've done it'. Heart of Midlothian had won the cup. For the first time in my life, we were winners; and as we grabbed each other with raw emotion etched across our faces, tears stung our eyes. Stuart was inconsolable; weeping uncontrollably. Lesley cried too, and held her dad, who had waited a long, long time for Hearts. And then there was me. Having sunk to my knees, my arms were stretched upwards and my head looked skywards. I had a thousand emotions; but I cried just one tear from each eye. For the first time, these were tears of joy – one for joy, and maybe one for relief! Over and over again, I kept saying to myself a looped message:

Hearts have won the cup
Hearts have won the cup
Hearts have won the cup
Hearts have won the cup

Still we hugged one another. And when I looked around me to try find out where that angelic voice had come from, the voice that had won me the cup, all I could see were thousands of other Hearts fans, stretched right along the stand; each with their own tears of happiness, and all at their own very personal journey's end.

Chapter 41
By the time I got to Gorgie

I gazed over to the thousands that bedecked the stands in maroon and white and saw a blizzard of twirling scarves. I now had the best view in the stadium and what a sight it was. What potential this club has. The trophy was held aloft by Stevie Fulton and Gary Locke like two kids fighting over a selection box. The players did a long lap of honour to celebrate with us, and scarves and hats were thrown down on the pitch. We danced to the tune of 'Carnival de Paris' and sang many more songs before slowly heading for the exits. Forty miles to the east, the greatest party of my life was getting underway.

As soon as we left the stadium, the sun hit us and suddenly I felt drained. In the confusion we lost Donald and Andy. We also had to find our coach. But before all that, I needed to quench my thirst, so I bought seven cans of juice; such was my confidence in finding our transport. We walked for miles, but it was no use. The bus was nowhere to be seen. So we decided to cut our losses and get a taxi to Queen Street Station and return home triumphantly by rail, but I nearly got arrested as I jostled with Rab C Nesbitt's twin brother for a taxi. The atmosphere in Glasgow's main train terminal was incredible when we did eventually get there. Our depleted group of four managed to get a seat, and as the doors closed and the train pulled away, we gave each other a look of accomplishment. We were finally on our way home. What was waiting to greet us was the stuff of dreams: the party we spent a lifetime fantasising about. Choo choo!

About forty-five minutes later, the trained pulled into Haymarket and as we piled off, my once dry mouth now drooled with anticipation. I climbed the steps and kept my head down, trying to build the suspense. This was it. This was it: the moment. I reached the top of the stairs, and there it was: the sight I had longed to see; the entire Haymarket area awash with Hearts fans; a mass of noise and songs reverberating in the warm evening air. Now it was time to really celebrate. We bought beers and champagne and stood there for a while, immersing ourselves in the chaos. But then Les got a call on her mobile regarding the team coach. We swiftly made our way to Gorgie Road, and there we saw the main body of the crowd, celebrating and giving the victorious team a hero's welcome. We got there just in time, and I yelled my gratitude, as Robbo, Ritchie, Adam and the others stood on the roof of their bus, like the triumphant parade of ancient Panathenaic athletes aboard their chariots; as old ladies hung out of grey tenements, how we cheered.

The bus squeezed its way round past the Tynecastle Arms and slowly etched down McLeod Street, where the acclaim continued. I was just a face in the crowd, but I'll forever be glad just to have been part of the gathering who hailed the great men of 1998. It was thrilling, and afterwards I bought a Pink News, which carried the headline, "Hearts in Paradise". Hearts were in Paradise, and for two hours, Paradise was Celtic Park. But this Paradise wasn't exclusive to just one specific place, and certainly not a half-finished football stadium in the east end of Glasgow. Paradise was a state of mind. And right there and then, Paradise was Gorgie Road. There was nowhere else I'd rather have been. There was no one else I'd rather be. And it was then time to walk along it, to the Wheatsheaf (where we found Donald and Andy) and a night of celebration, drinking bubbly and singing ourselves hoarse. The festivity however, didn't end there. With a kebab in one hand and half a bottle of flat champagne in the other, I clambered over a fence, made my way up some steep steps, and enjoyed the splendid tranquillity of Tynecastle Stadium from the comfort of the commentary box gantry. That was Paradise; such a perfect day.

Such was the ferocity of my hangover, it actually took me a few seconds to remember what had happened the previous day. But despite the thumping headache, I just laughed aloud at the realisation; Heart of Midlothian FC had won the Scottish Cup: and I kept saying it. Within minutes, I had bought nearly every newspaper I could get my hands on, and watched the whole game over again. Les would one day fall out with me over those newspapers. She asked me the hypothetical question: "Should the house ever catch fire, what one thing would I save?" To which I answered without hesitation, "My Scottish Cup winning newspapers". Oops, the correct answer was in fact 'her'. By lunchtime, my flat was pre-parade HQ as family and friends touched base before we headed down to Gorgie. It was yet another gloriously hot day and perhaps the only time I've ever gone to see Hearts whilst wearing sun protection! The open top bus snaked its way along a three mile route from the Royal Mile, Princes Street, the West End and into Dalry. By the time it got to Gorgie, it was suggested that the crowd could've reached the two-hundred thousand mark. That's where I was waiting.

There's a photo, like Morgan's Instamatic snapshots in time. I am standing in Gorgie Road with a 'man-bag' (very cutting-edge for 1998). The bag is holding three bottles of bubbly. In one hand is a cheap cane Hearts flag: in the other, a can of the cup sponsor's lager. My arms are aloft. It was the happiest time of my twenty-four year life. When the bus came past, I bounced up and down with Stuart, singing, "There's only one Stephane Adam". The man himself looked down to us and gave us a grateful thumbs-up. It was fleeting, but I will never forget the thrill of seeing an open top bus pass through Gorgie, with the Hearts players aboard, proudly holding aloft the Scottish Football Association Challenge Cup, the oldest trophy in world football and last spotted down Leith in 1902!

The Wheatsheaf beer garden was our next port of call. Les had stopped working there a couple of years previous, but such was the scale of the revelry, she offered to help out behind the bar for an hour, which meant free beers for me all afternoon. Lots of friends were there, soaking up the sun. We were singing and laughing and enjoying the banter. As the Salvation Army Band marched past, one punter decided to add some tail-end percussion with the help of a beer tray, inviting us all to join him! But he was too late. We didn't need salvation anymore. We had that yesterday. Now we just needed more lager and there was plenty of that coming. We were toasting the Heart of Midlothian football club and each other. Eighteen months previously, I had cried in the snow after the League Cup final. Six months before that, I endured Hearts taking a cup final five goal hammering. A year before that, I sat stunned as Hearts lost dismally to Airdrie in the semis. Three years before that, we had watched Hearts lose to Airdrie again. I recalled horrific late Hampden defeats in 1987 and 88. And then there was the greatest let-down of all; Albert Kidd, the silver strip and Dens Park 1986. I wasn't over Albert Kidd, but he had no place here today. He wasn't invited. This time, Hearts were the winners, and as the party went inside for a long and special night, I realised the love that I had for my team, was perhaps symbolic for maybe just a morsel of self-respect that I began to allow for my own existence. My higher sense of them that wonderful weekend was epitomized by a growing sense of myself. It was much more than just a cup.

Chapter 42
The third point

I always thought that if Hearts won the cup, I'd party for a whole week. That was the plan. But after four days of drinking, my body was shot to shit and it told me "no more!" The summer was spent watching the Coupe du Monde, ushering for Bobby at his wedding, trying to forget that his Best Man gave poppers to a donkey in Blackpool, and listening to Pele talk about erection problems, whilst waiting on my annual hay fever prescription. I was happily engaged. Hearts had finally put me out of my misery and I had my own flat. All I needed now was to get the hell out of the petrol station. At twenty-four years old, I was no longer the long haired skinny rake I used to be. My hair began to thin as my body became thicker. Yet I still dutifully worked the night-shift in the petrol station; I still mopped the floor and put the fire extinguishers and the flower stand outside in the morning. Though I could blame other factors, I began to realise that the world was never going to come to me. The world didn't owe me a thing.

Allan told me about a well known 'parcel delivery company' (let's call them PDC) who were looking for drivers. The job may have been blue collar and low pay, but at least it would get me away from the bloody petrol station. I got into my suit and went for the interview where I was offered a position right away. I remember a feeling of both shock and mild jubilation as I went home. I was so pleased with myself. Not for the glory of joining PDC, but for finally breaking free from the petrol station. Lewis, Gary, Allan and Gordon were some of my best friends. But I had to leave them. I had to break up the band. On the early morning of Friday 23rd October 1998, I mopped the floor, put out the fire extinguishers and the flower stand; serving the early rush hour customers for the last time. Nearly ten years had past since the scraggy, undereducated boy scooped horrifying gunk from the jet wash drain. The last point of my 1994 'Three Point Plan' had taken me four years to realise. I just hoped my new job would bring me some happiness.

Most of my PDC colleagues were good guys. Jim, Brad, Andy, Graeme, Stevie and David were all nice lads, as were my gaffers John and Rab. There were a few tossers as well, but that's life. It was though, the quality of the vehicles that was most prominent. They were appalling! The guy in charge of them was one of the most miserable sods I've ever worked with in my life and he had a face that could bloody freeze petrol! A colleague of mine was driving along the A1 near Haddington, when his side door fell clean off. But such were the stringency of his deadlines; he simply turned to evaluate the gaping chasm that had appeared in his van, shrugged his shoulders and thought 'fuck it'; and kept on driving! My own diary of disaster was nearly as impressive. I was never really cut out for PDC. It was all 'them and us' and petty resentments. I had one mishap after another. But then, I was the guy who smashed the gruesome jar of beetroot, had the biggest spillage since Exxon's Alaskan tanker and electrocuted the boss whilst mopping the floor. My list of bumps and scrapes was quite long.

1. I took out a chunk of roof when performing a U-turn in Bathgate. I was convinced that the van would get under the maximum height crossbar. I can still hear the sickening crunch of fibre glass to this day. And earlier that afternoon, the van broke down...on the Newbridge Roundabout. I called it 'Black Wednesday'.

2. I got stuck in a field just outside Bathgate. I had got lost and driven over a service bridge on the Edinburgh Road. Again, I did a U-turn, but this time I ended up sinking the van into a boggy marsh. I spent about an hour trying to free it in fading light by wedging cardboard underneath the wheels. I failed, so I ended up crossing the squelchy field to plead to a JCB driver working in the concrete dome plant. Half an hour later, he got me out. But I don't know what shocked him more: the sight of a PDC van in the middle of a field or the sight of me; head to toe in mud!

3. I somehow managed to crash into a van on the long, straight, dipping expanse of East Fettes Avenue. His front light was a little loose, but the only real damage the impact caused to his vehicle was the shattering of years worth of rust. The chap wasn't bothered, but later that day, up the hill at affluent Ann Street, I took my seven-and-a-half tonne truck into a street where I had no right to be. The police said I hit four cars. I called it 'Black Friday'.

4. Upon pulling away, I slightly uprooted a bus shelter in Whitburn. There might have been someone standing in it at the time.

5. A drunk in Stockbridge staggered in front of my van, and began attacking it whilst accusing me of stealing his bike! What a bullet: but in an unbelievable twist of fate, I actually had the 'pleasure' of delivering his

new one. It was the only time I asked a customer to sign for a parcel after threatening to kick their ass. He sure sobered up.

6. Having crammed the final few parcels into my side door, I drove my one thousand cubic feet truck all the way to Livingston; while leaving the back door open. I remember receiving a phone call as I approached the Lizzie Bryce roundabout. Although I discovered several parcels scattered along the side of the A71, most of the damage had been done on the first bend back in Edinburgh and the driver of a rival firm kindly delivered them back. Doh!

7. I was involved in a wild-cat strike. It happened because one of the drivers got punted for failing to engage the handbrake of his vehicle whilst delivering a parcel. It wouldn't normally have been a problem, but for the fact that the van was positioned on a hill. It was the sort of thing that I would've done, and his oversight must have surprised the shopkeeper who received a surprise delivery – right through the glass frontage of his establishment. The driver was actually under severe volume pressure and as the union got involved, all we needed was Red Robbo and Arthur Scargill to turn up and we could've strung it out for days. But in the end, the whole thing died out after lunch and we all got back to work. Ok, so he left the handbrake off. But at least his back door was shut. I doubt anyone would've called a strike in my honour.

When I look back on the major events in my life, I try to comprehend a sort of logic, that it was all 'meant' in the name of 'career progression' or 'character building', or both. I became as miserable at PDC as I did in the petrol station. I know this because I'd dream of PDC on a Sunday night as often as anything else. The dream always involves a horrible workload in impossible circumstances. During one Sunday Night Dread, and during a PDC dream, my shower curtain pole actually collapsed in the bathroom at about 3am. I thought it was the end of the world. I couldn't blame my 'Three Point Plan' though. That only stipulated that I find another job. I got into some horrific situations working at PDC, and it was a strange job; one in which I was undeniably not 'meant' for. And that's why me being me, I stuck it out for three and a half wretched years.

Hearts capitulated the following season after winning the Scottish Cup. It was to be the start of another downfall of the club and the beginning of the end for owner Chris Robinson as debts rose to unimaginable levels. The very existence of Heart of Midlothian would come under threat. The heroic team of 1998 was broken up and sold on as Hearts went from cup winners to relegation candidates. And the happy, tight-knit gang of 97/98 seemed all too ready to jump ship. The season started with a fine win over Rangers, and the pub afterwards had talk of another title challenge. But by the following March, we had gone four months without so much as a win to our name! And after an abysmal defeat at Dundee, Hearts were three points adrift at the bottom of the SPL. That particular day is ruefully known to some as 'The Mohammed Berthe Game'; who played his one and only match for Hearts doing an impression of a man running through maple syrup. Yet we rallied in the final six weeks. My man Colin Cameron came back from his long-term hip injury (bizarrely cured through wearing a gum-shield), and the fresh signing of Darren Jackson galvanised the team. Gary McSwegan finally found his scoring boots and Hearts stormed up the table, finishing sixth. But although we had recovered in time to stay in the SPL, something was rotten inside Tynecastle. The pies, it seemed, were off.

By the time the 98/99 season was ending, Les and I had the appalling cockroach situation to deal with in the flat. We had defeated the mice, nullified the vibrating floor and silenced the bam at the end of the corridor. But when our flat became home to a thousand cockroaches, we came up against a force so powerful, that even Indiana Jones would've snuffed out his torch and said "fuck this". A phone call was made to the Environmental Health and we spent about a month sleeping in our tent on the living-room floor, before buying a mosquito net. But when something landed on my head on my twenty-sixth birthday, I knew it was time to sell up. Thankfully, the next fumigation worked, but the whole experience gave me nightmares for a year afterwards. Even dreams of Saughton Mains Bank were put to the back of my consciousness. By August 1999, at the time when people were looking to the sky for a total eclipse, I was looking to the floor, trying to avoid stepping on things that could make a grown man scream.

Hearts found a bit more consistency in 99/00. We were never in any sort of blistering form, but we were good enough to challenge for a place in Europe again. It was however, events off the pitch that had Hearts fans scratching their heads. It seemed the club had struck gold with an £8M investment from The Scottish Media Group (SMG). Chris Robinson hailed the deal and instructed Jim Jefferies to immediately spend some serious dosh in the transfer market. But by then, Jefferies' relationship with Robinson had taken a nosedive. It was revealed that Robinson had mooted the idea of sacking Jefferies the previous season. It appeared that the marriage between CEO and Team Manager had ruptured beyond repair. Jefferies, it seemed, felt he'd been stabbed in the back by Robinson. But he got his own back. We signed Gordan Petric.

Les and I finally got the hell out of Dundee Street in October 1999. Carrick Knowe Avenue was a street I knew well from childhood excursions. It represented scorching summers and happy memories. Whenever I walked across the shaky metal bridge that separated Carrick Knowe from Saughton Mains, I knew I was heading for something better. It was the straight, tree-lined route to another world: The Zoo! Bobby was now my brother and my neighbour. And even though he could be a right bastard, Bobby was thrilled that we'd moved so close. With everything we'd been through together, I think he was glad that I was getting on with my life. He even put some laminate flooring down in the living-room for me, but that resulted in him missing out on the Carrick Knowe barber shop before he went to the pub. So in return, I cut his hair with my clippers, and without him knowing, I threw in a couple of complimentary MC Hammer tramlines. That was for ruining my Argos punch bag. You can't touch this.

The 1990s was a time when I went from disillusioned youth to manual worker with calamitous Frank Spenceresque tendencies. I was dispossessed at Saughton Mains and infested in Dundee Street. But I had also met Lesley. We were so young: just twenty-one years old. And from the moment I found her: she saved me. She made me want to be better than Frank Spencer in chinos. And in my heart, I knew that the job I ended up with at PDC wasn't for me. Much of the past still hung over me, reverberating throughout my twenties, and I had never experienced an elongated time of happiness. Yes, there were moments of joy, like Hearts winning the cup, but that was only a glimpse; a taster. I still had ghosts to exorcise, and I still had to walk a long road, in my search for something better. And for now, that long, straight road was Carrick Knowe Avenue. I just had to decide if it was pointing towards Saughton Mains Bank, or pointing away from it.

Chapter 43
Bohemian like you

"God is a concept, by which we measure our pain." – John Lennon

The Millennium was crap. In previous years, all the Wheatsheaf gang met at the, er, Wheatsheaf. But for some reason, people were doing their own thing that year and the pub began to go a bit downhill. It was all a bit of a damp squib, but then there's always next time. At least I took to the new century better than Bobby and his Millennium flu bug. My image of him pacing the bitter pavements of Carrick Knowe wearing a big leather jacket invoked the strains of Bruce Springsteen's 'Street of Philadelphia'. But ill health was ubiquitous. Hearts were reported to be haemorrhaging something like £250,000 per month, and the SMG pot of gold wasn't all it seemed. Of the £8M, only £3.5M was actual investment. The remaining £4.5M was little more than increased borrowing, and money that eventually had to be paid back.

The final game of the 99/00 season was against Hibs, who had enjoyed a decent return to the SPL. Hearts had to win to secure a place in Europe and there was a great feel to the day. The sun was shining and new retro team strips were debuting. With the game flowing along nicely, our talented, if inconsistent Spanish winger, Juanjo, collected the ball and dribbled his way from one side of the pitch to the other. He then cut back across the field again before stopping outside the edge of the box. The fans didn't know what to make of it, and I'm guessing at this point he must have got bored, because he stopped pissing about and duly stuck the ball into the net. For a team of so-called cloggers, it was a fabulous goal and Tynecastle erupted. Hibs equalised in the second half but Hearts held strong and won with a glancing header from Gary McSwegan. A place in Europe was clinched, a derby match won and we finished the season on a sunkissed high.

That day had it all, including a fine post-match session. It was almost reminiscent of the whimsical weekend in 1998, though there was neither a street party nor open top bus. We gave The Diggers a body swerve in order to soak up the sun outside the Ardmillan Hotel. We had our current heroes to thank, Antti Niemi and 'Mickey' Cameron. Lager was consumed with great verve, songs were sung out to the street and that great love of Heart of Midlothian became apparent again. Even with moderate success, supporting this fabled football club was worth it. It was days like these that I'd feel grateful for every February away trip to Motherwell in sub-zero temperatures. But maybe the reason I enjoyed the day so much can be credited to a more subconscious level: because in the coming two years, there would be little to cheer about.

My father married for the third time in the summer of 2000; the latest venue being the Church of Jesus Christ's Latter Day Saints. Not many people can say they've been to two of their father's weddings: I'm guessing he likes the icing! It was a strange affair. The wedding took place on a dark rainy day at the Mormon Church in Deans, Livingston. My father is a religious man. Yet strangely, unlike my brothers, I wasn't christened (officially), so I feel nothing in that sense. My father didn't believe in 'living in sin', but Les and I were in no rush to get married and not least for that stupid reason. There were dark clouds too over Tynecastle. The 2000/01 season was stuttering along unremarkably. We drew a lot of games and the football was uninspiring. Something was badly wrong with Hearts. The fans didn't like Chris Robinson as quite frankly, CPR's PR was FR. Traditionalists were horrified at his rebranding of the club. The debt was getting bigger and Robinson stated that Tynecastle might not be suitable in the future. Jim Jefferies demeanour was that of a man who'd been slapped across the chin with a slippery pike and our beloved captain, Colin Cameron, was another one tripping over his own petted lip. But perhaps most disconcerting of all, was Hibs playing their 'flair' football, and stealing a match from us in the league. By the time we played them in October, it was win or bust for Hearts in their attempt to peg back their greatest rivals. We chose bust.

Some of the nicest and funniest guys I know are staunch Hibbys. I have cousins who are Hibbys. I don't see them much but they're top blokes. As are other mates such as John, Scotty, Dale, Murray, Joe, Paddy, Neil and Peter. Kerrin too is a Hibby, and I met him when he started to date Lesley's sister, Fiona. He's a brilliant guy and really witty, but his team were flying when I got to know him and that impending game at Easter Road was way more daunting that the prospect of a Hibby brother-in-law. And so it came to pass that October 20th 2000 was one of the most painful days in the history of Hearts. Our pedestrian team actually got in front early on through Andy Kirk and we were heading for half-time a goal up. But just before the break, we completely and comprehensively submitted, and it only got worse after that. Goal after goal was scored, and by the time Cameron pulled one back, Hibs had stuck six past us in what was an embarrassing rout. The only fortunate thing for me was that I didn't go to

Easter Road that night. Les and I decided to watch the game in The Westfield Bar. There was a mixed crowd in, and to be fair, I was leaping around in front of the Hibbys when Hearts scored after three minutes. But I could only handle five of their own celebrations before leaving. By the time we got back to the car, the commentator declared that Hibs were gunning for a seventh goal! Seven: like a broken record, it's the number Hearts fans will forever hear from gloating Hibbys. The Hibby at work with a face like a Halloween Cake; the ghoulish rattlings of my Hibby mates; and the guise of a future Hibby brother-in-law were all to be avoided for some time, as Hearts were buried alive.

Les and I decided to leave Carrick Knowe. Anyway, my work there was done having painted my mate Scott's shed maroon in the middle of the night after a party. I just felt it needed cheering up a little, but alarmingly his wife guessed it was me straight away the next morning. Les and I spotted a little house in the Corstorphine area and we just had to have it. From Saughton Mains to Shandon, from Dundee Street to Carrick Knowe and then to my present house: yet I would still only ever dream about living at Saughton Mains Bank. My 'work' recurring dreams are rainy days at PDC with a hellish schedule, or long, sleep-deprived night-shifts at the petrol station. The other dream I'd have regularly was the Saughton Park struggle, trying to run across the field to reach the Astroturf pitch, but never quite being able to make it. And then there are the really weird dreams, like nursing Adam Ant or the Pet Shop Boys football club, accessed by the Balgreen tunnel. Recently, I had a great dream about doing backing vocals for a Michael Jackson concert (and we reached some lovely harmonies on 'Leave me alone'). But there's always room for more recurring dreams. On a gorgeous September day, I got a call from Les. She told me there had been a plane crash in New York, and that I should get to a TV screen. When I got back to the PDC depot, it was deserted. Everyone, as I discovered, was huddled around the TV. I could hardly take in what was happening, and by the time I managed to digest some of the fragmented information given to me, I watched the second tower collapse. The next three days were spent overloading on 9/11. I should have eased off, because I've been dreaming about that ever since. That is, when I can get to sleep.

A far lesser tragedy, but cutting none the less, was that my last ever footballing hero, Colin Cameron decided that he didn't want to play for Hearts anymore. He'd been unhappy for a while. So in September 2001, he was transferred to Wolves for £1.75M, and his smile returned. When I was a kid, I always imagined that Hearts players would walk around in some bubble of awe: stunned at their good fortune upon wearing the famous maroon jersey. But the only awe they have is for themselves. I was lucky in a way. Henry, Levein, McPherson, JC, Robbo, Mackay etc were kicking around for bloody donkey's years! Children these days can hero worship players for what, a season or two? And as for adults, anyone who still frets over the commitment of individual players is simply wasting their time. What's the point in bothering about some overpaid, underperforming prima donna? I'm sure Jonny Premiership doesn't give a flying fuck for me. I loved Colin Cameron, and he was neither underperforming nor overpaid. But he didn't idolise me, and in his last year at Hearts he had a face like fizz. The new world order was a harsh place indeed.

The season was long and tough, and as Hearts were struggling through the winter, I was slogging away in my new house, and working my backside off at PDC. It was dirty work. When January arrived, the New Year should've been a time of renewed vigour, but that didn't seem to apply to Hearts. First Division side, Inverness Caledonian Thistle came a calling in the Scottish Cup and it was one of the most wretched days I've ever had supporting Hearts. And by 2002, I'd had more than a few of those. In fact the Caley game completes my top five worst ever Hearts moments (two semi-finals v Airdrie, Hibs 6-2, and of course, Albert Kidd, the silver jersey and 1986). The 1-3 defeat made me want to do something: anything really. I knew I had to make a change in my life, because this defeat was just too damn depressing to be put down to 'one of those things'. It was nothing against Inverness. They deserved to win. But Heart of Midlothian shouldn't be losing at home to a team which were formed just eight years previous. And in the twenty years I had supported Hearts, it was the first time we'd lost at home in the cup.

I left Tynecastle early that day, and battled my way through the cold sleet that flew in horizontally, drenching my hair, soaking my skin and numbing my glum, blue face. There were already a few locals in The Diggers, and they didn't need the TV to figure out how the game was panning out down the road. One look at my sorry puss said it all. A while later, Les and Donald sat quietly chatting: but I could barely find a word to utter as teardrops of condensation ran down the steamed windows. The bohemian element of The Diggers were murmuring quietly into their beer; each with a sad story to tell. Long coats and scarves lay draped over seats and a drift of smoke hung in the air. The TV beamed a picture from the Santiago Bernabéu. How I wished I was there, rather than this dark place. But eventually, the first sound of laughter broke, and as cold ears thawed slightly, the beer flowed and normality crept back into the bar. Businessmen chattered with Lord Provosts, fans ruefully bantered and poets sat daydreaming in corners. Only so much can put a dampener on the soul. Human nature survives. To be completely broken by a football result means that it's time to leave the bar. The crushing defeat didn't break me. Instead, it made me take action. Hearts really disappointed me that day, and I remembered John Lennon's words "I don't believe in Beatles". Who knows, he might've written them having just had a day like mine. I didn't know what to believe in anymore. I just believed in me.

Chapter 44
Escape to 'Victory'

The morning after the Caley game, I awoke early and watched the classic 1981 film Escape to Victory. Ok, so John Wark was never going to win an Oscar, but I liked it. It was comfort viewing, and it cheered me up a little; not least when beer-bellied Michael Caine reckoned World War II merely 'interrupted' his glittering West Ham and England career. There was hope for Stevie Fulton yet. After the allied POWs had beaten off the Germans, I drove Lesley to Dirleton Castle in East Lothian. The castle looked absolutely stunning, in its eight-hundred-year-old ruined state. The drawbridge, leading into the arched gateway, the barrel shaped vaults and the magnificent grounds made it an easy choice. One hour and thirty miles after leaving the house, Lesley finally discovered why she was standing in a dark, cold medieval castle in January. And thanks to Inverness Caledonian Thistle FC, the wedding would become a reality, now that the venue had been chosen.

Back in the days of Saughton Mains Bank, I had made my 'Three Point Plan' to leave the petrol station, dump my girlfriend and move away from home. Things had now progressed somewhat. My wedding date was set and my new house was coming along nicely. But as I turned my attentions to leaving PDC, I realised that once more, the job part was the defining and most laborious part of this updated 'Three Point Plan'. The 'Three Point Plan': it had become my very own Lord of the Rings trilogy; which was all the rage in 2002. Edinburgh was Middle Earth: Saughton Mains, The Shire; Bobby, the 'Ork' big brother. The rings for my wedding though, were not forged on 'Mount Doom', but at Robert Anthony, in Rose Street: the same place where I got my ear ceremonially pierced all those years ago and to the strains of 'Karma Chameleon'. So would that make Boy George the Lord of the Rings? Well I guess it would.

As for leaving PDC, my moment of clarity came in the form of a massive whack to the head outside a shop in Main Street, Kirkliston. I had jumped out of my van and thrown down a couple of heavy boxes on to my spindly, metal barrow. Unfortunately, the barrow was just in the process of falling back as I hurled the boxes downwards. It resulted in an act of physics similar to standing on a garden rake (and yes, I've been there too). Such was the pain endured, I recalled a quote from Kurt Cobain when he once said "I hate myself and want to die". And as I lay parallel to the pavement, matters were then made somewhat worse when an old lady passing by informed me that "that was a stupid thing to do". I looked at the appointments in the Evening News that day and one caught my eye, a job working for a large corporate company. I had never worked in an office before, and could barely use a computer. But with a stutter and a smile, I passed the interview and my notice was gleefully handed into PDC. It was a major change for me. From the mucky, miserable, manual grime of PDC, I was moving to the steady, sanitised safety of office work. And I even got to call 'London'.

The following season, we played Hibs in our first home game, and Hearts fans didn't really know what to expect. Maybe we'd lose. Maybe we'd win. Maybe Mark de Vries and Jean-Louis Valois would turn out to be half decent. In the two previous seasons, we had beaten Hibs only once (and that was one more victory than any game we played against the Old Firm). What we did get that afternoon was an unexpected yet thoroughly exhilarating performance, on a day when the goals rained in as the rain poured down.

At that time, my seat overlooked the enclosure of Tynecastle's 'notorious' Section N, and that's where I found Bobby waving up to me from. It was a day that he and I would never forget. Hearts went two goals up through Andy Kirk and new boy de Vries. It was a brilliant first half, but Hibs pulled a goal back early in the second. Mark de Vries though, made it 3-1 shortly after and Hearts looked comfortable seeing the game out. But as the derby entered its final throes, it was announced that the Man of the Match was Jean-Louis Valois. The Frenchman had a fantastic game and looked sublime and skilful. But a few minutes later, his award seemed a travesty, as Hearts launched another attack. Mark de Vries rounded off his hat-trick with a superb goal in injury time. From below, Bobby was jumping about and snarling up to me, as was I, in the row up above him. Hibs had fallen to pieces, but it wasn't over yet. With the game about to end, Hearts had one more charge left in them, and when Gary Wales chipped a delightful cross to the back post, there was Mark de Vries again, leaping almost in slow motion, to nod the ball back across the wrong-footed goalkeeper.

Bobby and I were bawling to each other; our faces contorted with disbelieving joy. We were swaying about, bouncing around and attached to random people: but the connection was there, and it was real, until he finally got swept away down the tunnel at the final whistle. Despite years of arguments and fights, it was our love for Hearts that bonded us together: love for a football team that could drive a sane man barking. People I know that don't 'get' football (or me, for that matter) are well within their rights to think I'm some sort of 'sad-case' football fan. And they're right: I am a sad-case and an anorak too. But when was the last time they ran about, celebrating like a lunatic in Ikea, and screeching with joy when something was actually in stock? Football might be a pain in the ass for much of the time, but every so often, a game comes along which makes all the crap worthwhile. The final score was Hearts 5 Hibs 1; avenging somewhat, the 6-2 drubbing we suffered in 2000. As I headed to the pub, some remaining Hibs fans defiantly sang 'Sunshine of Leith' to us. I very much doubt there was anything other than dark clouds in Leith that day, and I find that song something of a dirge anyway. I'll never forget a young lad, about twenty-one and just ahead of us, when he shouted back "The Proclaimers are what happens when you sleep with your sister". My tears, were crying.

The next time we played Hibs was at Easter Road in November 2002. Stuart was in Edinburgh for the weekend and he wanted to spend some time with me, having a beer and watching the game. We chose the Wheatsheaf as a nostalgic venue, and the pub was brimming with Hearts fans. There were a couple of folk wearing Hibs scarves, one of whom was in a wheelchair. In Edinburgh, Hearts and Hibs fans can generally socialise and mix together in most pubs, and isn't that the way football should be? The Hibbys had every reason to cheer, as their team headed for a comfortable 1-0 victory. Hearts simply hadn't turned up and the game was coming to a close when the two Hibs supporters made for the door. I was in one of my angry and frustrated moods; shouting at the telly, and cursing my team, calling McKenna "fucking useless". Well, did he not just go and score with two minutes left! The pub went fucking mental, and as I leapt off my seat, I accidentally landed on a glass which shattered into fragments, and showered the poor Hibs supporting woman in the wheelchair!

Les got hold of me and pointed out what I had done and instructed me to apologise. I felt genuinely bad about it, and I eventually turned to the Hibs fans to say sorry: but the look on their faces said it all. They fucking hated me, but as I tried to apologise, the game went into stoppage time and something caught my eye on TV. Hearts were through on goal again and now we had a chance to win it! The ball broke to chunky midfielder, Phil Stamp. The Englishman looked up and thumped the ball past the goalkeeper to win The Edinburgh derby for Hearts! At that moment, I could've jumped through a glass window like Adam Ant in the video for 'Stand and Deliver' for all I cared, as I deserted my Hibs-supporting antagonists to embark upon a crazed, bouncing lap of honour of the pub; shouting at the very top of my voice. Not my finest hour, and there was certainly no honour in my lap. But I have to say I enjoyed that moment;

one of my finest non-attendance celebrations. And it was the first and only time I've ever apologised to a Hibs fan as a result of a Hearts goal, but it wasn't the last time that season that all the surprises were saved until the end.

The third and final part of the epic derby trilogy, 2002/03 took place on January 2nd. If the previous two games versus Hibs were steeped in drama, then it was nothing compared to events that were to unfold at Tynecastle on that cold day. Yet I have mixed feelings when looking back at the game now. I had been away for three days at Loch Rannoch on the piss and I was feeling rougher than a hedgehog's chin. I was also feeling very jangly about returning to work, early the next day. And my paranoia increased somewhat rapidly as Hibs stormed into a 2-0 lead; their fans giving us pelters. But Hearts fought their way back into the game, with Steven Pressley and that man, de Vries getting us level. We should have gone on to win, but as the game seemed destined for a 2-2 draw; it was a result not too displeasing under the initial circumstances. But in the last minute of the match, Hibs went ahead once more. It was a crushing blow, and matters were compounded in injury time, when Hibs scored from a penalty rebound to wrap up the match. My close proximity to the celebrating Hibbys was more than enough to convince me to escape. I announced to Les and Donald that I was leaving, and they had little choice but to follow me out.

As we reached the bottom of the stairwell, we heard a faint cheer and someone confirmed that substitute, Graeme Weir had scored a consolation goal for Hearts. Les looked at me for a long second, but I kept walking. As we got past the nursery and onto McLeod Street we heard another roar: the final whistle, no doubt. Hibs had avenged our previous victory, just like we avenged their '6-2' with our '5-1'. But as I trudged away, something didn't seem right. I turned to look up to the top of the old Main Stand, and there through the old frosted windows, was the sight of silhouettes. Those silhouettes were of people, and those people seemed to be moving, and jumping up and down, punching the air. I shouted to Les and Donald.

"Look. Up there!"

I ran back and grabbed someone coming out.

"What the fuck is going on?" I demanded.

"Weir scored again! Last kick of the ball!" shouted the man.

I couldn't believe it. I ran up dark, chilly McLeod Street like some sort of latter-day Marco Tardelli; celebrating as if it were me who had scored. But not only did I not score, I hadn't even stayed on to witness someone else's good work. I had turned my back on Hearts at a time when all was not lost. Looking back now, I had no right to celebrate, hence my mixed feelings. And I'm gutted that I missed all the commotion. There were dozens of Hearts fans hugging each other on McLeod Street. But Les and Donald weren't happy with me at all. By storming out on ninety-one minutes, I had denied them, and myself the chance to witness (and celebrate) the greatest comeback in the history of the Edinburgh derby. Weir's goals, according to Londonhearts.com came astonishingly in the ninety-fourth and ninety-fifth minutes of the game. I had to apologise and grovel to Les and Donald in The Diggers afterwards, and promised never again to leave a match early. I never did, and Graeme Weir, to my knowledge, never scored another goal for Hearts, but I will always blame him for having Les and Donald growl at me for weeks after that game. And Hearts fans will forever be grateful to him, for pulling off a remarkable and unlikely comeback; something akin to a Hollywood script. But as in Escape to Victory, the famous match that felt like a triumph, was in fact a 4-4 draw.

Chapter 45
Touching greatness

To anyone that loves the beautiful game, the terracing that lies aging away at Cathkin Park is perhaps as haunting an image as there's ever likely to be in football. It is nestled within a suburban park near Hampden in Glasgow; and for ninety-five years it was home to Third Lanark FC. The club was indiscriminately run into the ground in 1967, yet the old stadium was left standing, becoming a silent symbol to football's yesteryears. Trees and bushes now lean up against the crush barriers, where men in flat caps once stood. And when the breeze blows through them, faint whispers of the past can almost be heard, like the shrill pitch of a cheering crowd. Football anoraks like me don't remember the past in calendar years: we remember it in seasons. And with each ephemeral season ticket, the past slips further away; and its players recede one by one until teams are completely recycled. Memories of last season become the season before. A couple of seasons ago become five, then ten years ago. Of the team of 1986, only one made it to the bench in 1998. The rest are part of a memory that is now a generation ago. The things we did, and the way we looked, become benchmarks of that time, and still forever slipping further away.

Every memory of past seasons reminds me of where I was at the time. It's sad really: sad as in we'll never be as young as we were then, or even now. And it's only when I properly contemplate my past that I realise the only value that it holds is an inherent one. It is nostalgic to evoke memories of the past; like flicking through newspapers from the 1998 Scottish Cup win. But the past serves no real functional purpose; apart from maybe a few harsh lessons learned here, and recalling a twang of heartache there. Like the bulldozers that ripped apart my beloved Tynecastle Shed, only the future counted for anything. What became of the terracing and crush barriers at Tynecastle, or the giant 'Tynecastle Park' sign on Gorgie Road, I'll never know. Maybe the new Tynecastle still has bits of the old resting underneath. I didn't know it at the time, but Hearts would soon be faced with the very real scenario of having a team, but with no stadium: or a stadium, but with no team.

Time slips further away. Hearts beat Celtic at the end of the 2002/03 season with a spectacular last-gasp goal from Austin McCann. That game seems so long ago now, and the team is unrecognisable from what it is today, just a few seasons later. I was several years younger, and probably two stone lighter with maybe twenty-five per cent more hair coverage. In football, it is games, goals, players, fashions and hairstyles that give identity to our memories. It was such an incredible finale to a game; with guys like Severin and Stamp in the team. The victory over the UEFA Cup finalists effectively sealed Hearts return to European football, whilst dealing a fatal blow to Celtic's league hopes (so a tremendous day all round then). But looking at that team line-up, it leaves me with nothing to link the past to the present. Pressley and Webster left under a cloud and have now tarnished their reputations with the fans. The powerful Scott Severin joined Aberdeen because we couldn't afford his wage demands and they could. Maybury and de Vries jumped ship at the first opportunity and the rest became surplus to requirements. But the game itself is still treasured, if the players themselves aren't. As with any form of nostalgia, we pick out the good bits and wipe off the bad.

The day before the wedding was akin to the sort of military operation that the A-Team would've been proud to have been hired for (although sadly, I had no requirement to build a tractor-like machine that fired out cabbages at communists). It was also the day in which my younger brother, Ian, came to the fore. Ian was eighteen, a real gentleman and something of a lay-deez man. I needed someone to help me, and because I was his older brother, I could order his skinny ass around. I drove to Livingston to pick him up. Naturally, he was hungover, but nonetheless the next eight hours were spent:

- Driving to Edinburgh
- Driving through MacDonalds!
- Picking up the flowers
- Picking up the kilts
- Driving to North Berwick
- Picking up the wedding licence
- Driving to Dirleton Castle
- Setting up the candles (all 100 of them)
- Setting up the flowers
- Setting up the chairs
- Driving back to Edinburgh
- Getting a hair cut
- Picking up the luggage/the cake/other stuff
- Driving to the hotel to deposit the luggage/the cake, etc
- Driving to the BBQ King chippy
- Getting changed
- Going out for a Wedding War Council/lagers

Saturday, June 21st 2003 was a drizzly day, initially. Ian and I had set the alarm early and got dressed into our bluey/lilac kilts. A while later, I was in The Horseshoe Bar for an early morning lager-n-lime, just as I had done in 1998 for the cup final. As we waited for the coach, guests arrived fairly rapidly. Scott turned up and it became apparent that collectively, we bore a striking resemblance to camp TV designers, Colin and Justin! I'd never known a feeling like it. I was so nervous but it was fantastic (I'm back writing about the wedding here: not Scott and me). At high noon, we all piled on the coach and headed for Dirleton.

By 1.30pm, the guests were seated inside and waiting for the bride to appear. And when Lesley arrived, the piper led her and her dad, followed by her sister, through the grounds and along the winding path to the castle drawbridge. It was a spectacular setting, and yet somehow eerie at the same time. The barrel-shaped vaulted chamber where I stood looked magnificent, if maybe a little bit like a Meatloaf video! As the pipes faded away, the heart-felt strains of 'Con Te Partiro' brought Les down the aisle towards me. It was such an emotional moment. We had planned it for a year and a half, and I thought it would never arrive. But it did arrive, and it was superb. Getting married, and in such a setting, was a real achievement for both of us. Of course, it was the bride's day, and she looked so beautiful. For me, I became Andrew-Henry Bowie: married man. I had come a long way from the cleaner who scooped the gunk out of the jet wash drain and the miserable Hearts fan who had left the Inverness game early.

It was a really nice ceremony, with lots of laughter, but isn't that always the case when the minister looks like Don King? There were touching moments too, and the women cried as did some of the men. We signed the register to the haunting melody of 'Vide Cor Meum', which I loved from the film Hannibal, as Dr Lecter attends the opera in Florence. The dark music may have complemented the old ruin castle, the flickering candles and the overcast skies, but this was a happy occasion, and the drizzle stopped as Les and I made our way back down the drawbridge as husband and wife. We had our photos taken, and then we joined everybody else in the pub across the road. It was one of the most enthralling hours of my life. A great cheer went up when Les and I walked in and I got a free pint! I felt elated and I socialised and circulated without my feet touching the ground. Bobby, Kerrin, Ian and Andy all did a great job in ushering, and Les had a great time too; she even liked my Convict 99 hairstyle!

But there was a problem. Allan was having a bit of a nightmare. He was going through a bad time in his personal life. In fact, he was battling against alcoholism. He was my Best Man, as I was his a couple of years previous. Whilst at Dirleton, he admitted to me that he hadn't prepared a wedding speech. I wasn't angry. I was just disappointed for him. For all we'd gone through, it was sad to see him looking so pained, but I had to get on with my day. There was more revelry when we got back to the hotel in Edinburgh and then it was time for the meal, and the speeches. Donald gave a moving and funny speech to Les, which included a charming story of her giving Rangers fans the V-Sign at Ibrox aged twelve. My speech to Lesley was kept short and sweet. I thanked people and got down to the business of declaring my love for my woman! My speech ended with a romantic rhetoric:

To recognise greatness, you have to touch upon it first.
And in order to reach greatness, you have to hold it.
When I saw Lesley walking down the aisle: that's when I recognised greatness.
When she got a bit closer, I got a sniff of her perfume (!)...
...and that's when I smelt greatness!
When she said "I do": that's when I heard greatness.
And when I kissed her: that's when I tasted greatness!
...and as I stand here holding her hand: I touch upon greatness.
Ladies and Gentlemen – I LOVE MY WIFE!

ALL RIGHT! So I'm a big sap, but come on, it was a groom's speech: not The Comedians with Bernard Manning! Bobby, the big brother from hell and fellow baldy, then stepped in, slapped my newly shaved head, and told the audience that his wee brother "spoke a lot of shite". He then went on to talk about the bunk-bed that hovered above me for several years, the one that "shook a bit from time to time". He was a fine stand-in if ever there was one and even old Bernard would've been proud. Andy was brilliant too, and enlightened people that I used to impress him by "eating half a dozen raw eggs and cold chicken soup out of a tin" in my "cockroach invested flat"! Well I thought it was a good initiation ceremony for the young lad? The time then came for the first dance; and Les chose 'Kiss Me' by Sixpence None the Richer (as if the day wasn't soppy enough!) The night got into full swing as evening guests arrived, wrestling for dance-floor supremacy against inebriated day guests. And is there a finer sight than drunk Scottish uncles at a wedding dancing to The Beastie Boys 'Intergalactic'? It was a great party, and only my mate Colin made use of the buffet when he awoke on the Sunday to find his rucksack stuffed with pakoras.

The next morning, Les and I got up and ready to go on our honeymoon.

I was concerned that Allan hadn't called me about the lift to the airport. I called him but there was no answer. We were due to leave by about midday, but still I heard nothing. Eventually though, I got through. Allan wasn't driving me to the airport anymore, despite him insisting on doing it beforehand. This time, I was angry. But I just said "no problem", and that was the end of the conversation. Another plea to Andy was made, the second in twenty-four hours, and he kindly drove us to Glasgow. When I look back on my wedding day, I remember it for being as much about my struggle with Allan as it was about my marriage to Lesley. It was a fantastic setting for a wedding: but in the end, I suspect the timing was wrong. Some things about it were good and some not so. I didn't want to hurt Allan because he was my best friend, but he had an absolute shocker that day. But now, as time fades into the distance, I've realised that I shouldn't have allowed things to go on as they did. Not because I didn't want him to be my Best Man, because I did. But he was in no condition to carry out the role. His pride was at stake, but he was let down by me for not being strong enough. I put a lot of effort into that wedding, and it all seemed so important at the time. Les and I only just made our honeymoon flight but my friendship with Allan was left behind, in tatters. My wedding day though, gives me fond memories, for all it's worth. And with any form of nostalgia, we pick out the good bits and wipe off the bad. It is in the past and remains there now, slipping further away. Like those overgrown trees that cram the terraces of Cathkin Park, there's nothing anyone can do about it now.

Chapter 46
The light of day

As the light of day broke through the curtains, my mobile phone awoke me, and once more I found myself in 'The Old Town', Albufeira; hungover. I had already spoken to Bobby on the phone when we landed the previous evening, and he told me what a great time he'd had. I was grateful to him and was glad he was proud of me. He was texting me again, enthusing over something that had happened at the wedding. Over the next fortnight, Les and I had a brilliant time and I didn't want to return home. It had a quaint beach and nice places to eat. At night we sat in or outside Sir Harry's Bar where a guy played songs on his guitar. And while Les spent about an hour getting ready to go out, I'd chill out on the balcony with a few beers, watching the world go by. It was an excellent honeymoon, despite losing Barry White halfway through.

I knew Allan would be looking to contact me, but I wasn't ready to speak to him yet, and besides, I'd only been back for a few days when my Aunty Veronica died. It was a manic week, and Les and I were off again on our travels: this time to Sandwich in Kent, where we did our yearly stint working at The Open Golf Championship. By the time we returned from that, it was almost a month since I had last seen Allan, the *persona non grata*. I spoke to him once on the phone, but the conversation was brief, and eventually, the calls stopped. But then one day in August 2003, he came to my door. Les chatted to him for a bit in the hallway before showing him in and leaving us to it. I was surprised to see him. It was friendly enough, but he looked bad, and although I felt for him, I didn't say it. He could barely keep eye contact with me and I think he might have been in trouble. His phone kept ringing but I had no idea what the nature of the business was. He was only in my house for around twenty minutes in all, but I did manage to speak my feelings to him near the end. I told him that if we were to continue to be friends, then he would have to change and get serious help. I told him to call me, but only after he was ready to sort himself out. He agreed to this but he then told me he had to leave. Even as kids, we would always shake hands when we said goodbye, but this time there was no hand shake. There was no embrace. There was no banter and there was no smile. Although he was agreeable to what I had said, he probably knew in his troubled heart that I had demanded too much from him, just like his role of Best Man. I stood by the door and watched him shuffle away as if he was carrying the weight of the world upon his shoulders. I didn't know it at that moment, but it would be the last time we'd ever speak.

I turned thirty years old on August 26th 2003. Les threw me a BBQ at the house and we had a few folk round to see Gary's premier of the wedding video. He did the full works: trailers, title credits, music and lots of good fades; helped greatly by having two cameras rolling. It was a splendid evening, though later on, Les had to go round asking folk as to my whereabouts (I was found lying in the garden at 3am). At work, my transfer to another office was a disastrous move. I had only been there a few weeks but I was deeply unhappy. I also hadn't heard from Allan since our chat. Maybe I had asked too much of him in our conversation. Yet I decided to stick to my guns and await his phone call. I had to be tough on him this time. On September 22nd 2003, just three months and one day after my wedding, I did get a phone call at work. It wasn't Allan on the phone, but it was regarding him. The voice on the other end of the line told me the news: Allan had died.

I slouched down, numb with shock and utterly speechless. I tried to let the news sink in, but I just couldn't comprehend it. I was shaking. Instead, I got up and told the boss I was leaving. I made phone calls to my mum and to Bobby. I went to Les and she left work also. It was a blur. Allan had died in a car crash very early that morning, just outside Perth. It was too surreal. Just moments earlier I was going through the motions of a dire Monday at work. But now there was only one place to go, and ten minutes later, I was back at Saughton Mains Bank. My mum was in, and Bobby arrived shortly after. There was no hugging or solace, just a lot of unanswered questions. I phoned around and got Scott. We then headed to Allan's mum's house. It was so grim. Les and I then went to see Allan's sister, and we had an honest chat about it all. The day was spent in The Horseshoe Bar and even the Wheatsheaf. By the evening, I ended up plastered, crying my eyes out in The Oak Inn. My tears were of sadness and of guilt. I ended that terrible day watching his wedding video, with a six-pack of beer and a kebab. I guessed that was how he'd have wanted it.

I spent the next three days off work. As I was miserable there, I didn't really care about going back anyway. I spent time with Scott and DD, and we talked through the ins and outs of everything. All along, I felt that overwhelming sense of guilt: guilty, because I had fallen out with him at the last hurdle: guilty because I ignored his texts when I was working in Kent. Guilty, because I knew in his last hours, he might have thought of me being pissed off with him. On the Sunday, Bobby, DD, Scott and I went to the site of the crash. We laid down some stuff, Hearts scarves, etc. I wedged in a photo of us from a night out. It was so sad. We had grown up together and gone through some tough times. Friends were together again, but in the worst of circumstances.

A week and a half passed until the funeral and I found the pressure almost unbearable. But there was one thing that tied him and me, plus our friends and family together. Midweek, Hearts played Zeljeznicar in the UEFA Cup, and it was a good time for the 'Hearts family' to get together and have a few beers either side of the game. For the first time in years, a few of us went to the game together, in an effort to stay close, and in memory of Allan. Although we won the game 2-0, things were still very sombre in the Wheatsheaf, and I was still meeting up with some of Allan's good friends, many of whom I hadn't spoken to since his death. Then Franco came out with a funny story about Allan and the atmosphere changed. Scott then told us of the time he and Allan did a midnight run in Tynecastle, which resulting in them being nabbed by the police for taking rolls of turf, which were being dug up due to the pitch being altered. The policewoman wanted to arrest them, but her male colleague was a Jambo and he knew the intrinsic value of a good 'midnight run', so he just let them off. Astonishingly, Allan then had the audacity to ask if they could still have the turf! The poor bloody policeman, shook his head and said "You can have one roll each"! But Allan was never one for half measures. I remembered back to Spain, when he was so drunk he went back out at night wearing just his boxer shorts and a baseball bat: and in Greece, when he went walkabout and ended up sleeping in a different town. We argued and fell out all the time. But the good times were funny.

On the Thursday, Bobby, Scott, DD and I went to say goodbye to Allan. I was extremely anxious at the thought of it. Bobby and I nervously smoked a cigarette as we waited for the other two to arrive. Scott and I took a deep breath and we shuffled inside. Allan was there. Scott and I took a seat but we kept our eyes down.

"We have to do this", he said to me. He was right and we both stood up and looked at Allan. I was trembling, and in my head, I managed a few words of apology. I was sorry. So sorry.

The funeral was on the Friday. It was a crisp day and Les and I were together. She had been a great support to me during that time, and had booked us a break to get away from it all after. There were maybe as many as six-hundred mourners at the service, including Hearts legend Gary Mackay. I have a photo of Bobby, Allan and me from 1984. Allan and I are standing at the front, whilst Bobby is getting playfully strangled by two young Hearts players, John Robertson and Gary Mackay. The next time I spoke to Mackay was when he played football with us at the Corn Exchange. I saved a shot from him in the warm up, but I staved my thumb so bad, that it hurt for six months. Allan found that amusing, and he'd try to bend it back. Now Gary was here again, to pay his respects to a young guy from Stenhouse who idolised him. He was there, I guess, representing the Hearts community at the funeral. Allan would have loved that because there was no bigger fan of Heart of Midlothian than Allan.

The service was conducted by a minister who happened to be Allan's uncle; the same man who had conducted the marriage service for Allan just two and a half years previous. He spoke honestly about Allan. He gave special mention to Bobby, DD, Scott and me. But strangely, he said "there are no old friends here today: just pals." I was taken aback by that because he was wrong. Allan had lots of friends; many he knew for years and I was an old friend: the oldest friend of all and more than just a random pal. For twenty-five years I was his friend. Friends, who grew up, played football, tasted beer, met girls, got knocked back, scored (occasionally) and loved Hearts – together. A quarter of a century of friendship, laughter, tears, domestic problems and fall-outs. And although it had ended with a fall-out, I was still an old friend for fuck's sake. Later that evening, The Wheatsheaf was heaving with people, giving Allan the rock-n-roll send off he deserved. I spoke to many people that night. Those closest to Allan were distraught. There were dozens of Hearts Boys there. I did my best that night to pay my respects and act accordingly. But eleven days had passed, and I wanted it to be over.

I went to the Hearts versus Dundee game at Tynecastle the next day. The atmosphere was flat. Les and I took the car as we were due to drive to Killin after the match. But I could barely find the will to watch the game. About half an hour into the 2-2 draw, we were heading back to the car and we got the hell out of Edinburgh for a week. By the time the game ended, I was back at the place where the awful events of the previous twelve days had begun. I wanted to let Les pay her respects, as she was his friend too. There were no words spoken, because no words made sense from the death of a twenty-nine-year-old Hearts fan. Half an hour later, as the sun began to set and the fresh autumn air brought a chill to the outdoors, we reached our pub in Killin with its roaring log fire. I switched off my mobile phone, and for the rest of the week, it never saw the light of day.

Chapter 47
The lost weekend

Trouble was brewing at Hearts. Debts were spiralling out of control and CEO Chris Robinson proposed the sale of Tynecastle. He claimed that the stadium was no longer "fit for purpose", but the reality was that debts were insurmountable and drastic action was his final solution. The consequences for Bobby and me weren't quite on a par to Cain and Abel but we disputed the future of Heart of Midlothian. As Murrayfield became the prospective home of Hearts; my stance was thus: If Hearts were to move there, I would still support my team, both unconditionally and wholeheartedly. Bobby said he'd never set foot inside Murrayfield and branded me a "Pieman loving Bastard!" I was of course, nothing of the sort, but my team still needed me, and that was imperative. Bobby fought a hard battle along with many other prominent dissidents of the Murrayfield proposal. I emphasised that the team would still need supporting, and that Heart of Midlothian is older than Tynecastle. I felt that my opinion was valid and representative of the reason why we all had such high-running passions in the first place. Both of us cared about Hearts. I wasn't in favour of selling Tynecastle: in fact I was against it, but I was all for supporting the team if we did. I was looking for pragmatism and functionalism beyond the scope of popular opinion and the point of no return. But Bobby was part of a revolution that was ultimately successful. The 'Save our Hearts' movement won the day and I didn't need to take up my lonely residence at Murrayfield. I backed the 'Save our Hearts' cause and I paid my £10 to became a member. But Bobby had reached a grandiose stage whereby he'd already made up his mind on me. Any active involvement that I might have participated in would have (in his eyes) made me his disciple; and I doubt he would ever let me forget that. For the record, Brother, I am delighted we stayed at Tynecastle.

The 2003/04 season didn't have nearly as many thrilling moments as the previous term, and most of the drama happened off the pitch. But Craig Levein's Hearts were a tough nut to crack and ground out a lot of victories, whist also being extremely difficult to beat. One such match was easily the highlight of the season. Due to my honeymoon and golf open commitments, I didn't have any holidays left to take for Bordeaux, but I was told that even in early November, it was still a balmy evening, as three-thousand plus Hearts fans marched towards the stadium. How I wished I was there. As I worked until the early evening, I just came home and watched the game in my house with a few beers, and with little expectation.

Hearts were under tons of pressure for most of the game, but we soaked it up and our young goalkeeper, Craig Gordon produced a dazzling performance. With the first leg heading for a highly credible 0-0 draw, Hearts got a free kick deep in foreign territory (that being anywhere over the halfway line!). I was shouting at the telly, "Come on the Hearts!" Hartley delivered the free kick, and from it, Kevin McKenna won the header. Bloody hell, that's going right for the top corner! I lurched forward off the sofa, but the keeper tipped the ball onto the post.

"Oh fucking hell", I shouted in expectation; and then Mark de Vries came piling in, and battered the ball into the back of the net. "YEEEEEAAAAAAASSSSSSS!!!!!!!!!!" I went absolutely fucking berserk, screaming at the top of my voice as I jumped around the living room. "GET FUCKIIIIING IN THEEEERRRREEEE!!!!!!!" What a rush! Bordeaux of course, came back at us. But after what seemed like an age, the referee blew for full time. Hearts had beaten Bordeaux, in Bordeaux, a tremendous result. But the best bit about the TV replay was not the game or even the goal itself but the wonderful, chaotic sight of all the Hearts fans celebrating like lunatics. Eventually, after a bottle of red, I knocked on my neighbour's door to apologise for all the noise I'd made, but they just laughed and as Hearts fans, they too were delighted. We discussed the goal, and although they had the sound way up on the TV, the only thing that they heard – was me!

Now if the Bordeaux away leg was the one trip that I wished I hadn't missed, then the home leg left me wishing I was in Bordeaux, preferably getting sloshed on some local plonk. But then I'd have happily been anywhere but Tynecastle on that cold November evening. It was such a disappointing night. I remember reading beforehand that no Scottish team had ever been knocked out of Europe having won the away leg first. Well that's just great! One nil up against one of the better sides of the tournament left us just ninety minutes away from post-Christmas European football (something Hearts have only ever experienced once). I was at the game with Les, Donald and my usually non-football-attending friend, Colin. Below us in the enclosure were around a hundred and fifty Bordeaux fans. Some of them looked like they weren't all that bothered to be fair. But one brave, bare-chested chap consecrated his entire evening by turning his back to the game in a desperate attempt to rouse his fellow Frenchmen and woman.

It was a scrappy start, and Hearts looked really nervous. One Frenchman we wanted to be on form was Jean Louis Valois, but he gave away possession in midfield after eight minutes. The loose ball was picked up by Bordeaux's Riera, who took one touch before viciously lashing a speculative, yet dipping shot towards goal from all of thirty-five yards. Young Gordon frantically dived to his right, but only succeeded in wrapping himself around his goal-post, as the ball bounced back out into play. But...did they...off the stanchion? I simply couldn't comprehend what had just happened and the entire stadium was in stunned silence. But most strange of all, was the reaction of the Bordeaux fans below me: in that there wasn't one! The Bare-chested One had whipped his followers into such a frenzy that the rest hadn't taken any notice of what had just happened. It was a most surreal moment, and despite it being one of his first ever attendances at any football match anywhere, I was forced to lean over to Colin and anxiously enquire:

"Did they just fucking score?"

To which the answer was, "I think they fucking did".

There was little doubt as to their second (and killer) goal scored on sixty-six minutes. It was such a frustrating experience, and I'll always remember the confusion their first goal caused that night. Even after twenty-one years of supporting Hearts, there were still some things I just didn't get.

Although I was unhappy at the office, one good thing about working for a corporate company was the football scene; and in early 2004, I had a couple of cracking trips away. The expedition to Aberdeen was the first round of the cup. The plan was to have to have a few beers in the Granite City, before playing the game on the Sunday morning. But by the time we reached our hotel, there became apparent one major problem. There were only seven of us. In fact it was six, if we included a Senior Business Analyst who couldn't kick his own backside and had planned to buy his footwear on the day of the game. None of that bothered me too much though as I conceived a tactical plan for a 'Christmas Tree' 3-2-1 formation (and the "1" had better track back). Such planning meant I was elevated to team captain there and then in a pub near Union Street. We eventually ended up in a nightclub and our copious squad began to split. I ended up with my two best friends from work, Scotty and Eadie. They got talking to three girls and it was quite apparent as to which two of the three they were most interested in. As they went off to dance, I was stuck standing with the one that was about four foot tall and had a face like a robber's dog! Kick-off was in eight hours.

I slipped away to the bar but when I returned, the poor wee lassie was still there. It soon became clear to me that she wasn't going anywhere soon, and worse still, she barely uttered a word to ease the awkwardness of my position. So in the best traditions of chivalry, I asked her on to the floor. There I was, dancing to The Boogie Pimps' 'Somebody to Love' wondering how the hell I'd got myself into such a situation. It was cringe-factor 10 stuff, so I thought it best to at least try and speak to her, by bending down to ask a couple of generic questions.

"Alright?" I asked (nice easy start, nothing controversial).

- "Aye, fit like." (Eh?)

"What's you name?" (Ok, so Parkinson, it wasn't)

- "Blah."

"Where do you work?" (What? Am I conducting a survey here?)

- "Blah Blah."

Barely a response was articulated and a few moments passed. I tried to think of something else to ask. Though I had no interest in this sullen Jimmy Krankie, I was reminded of my single days, when talking to women was so difficult, such a grim task. Then I thought of something. Yes, I'll ask her where she lives; just a generic, conventional query to break the monotony before I got the hell out of there. I bent down again:

"Where do you live?" I asked.

But she wasn't there! She had gone, and gone some time ago, leaving me stranded, humiliated and dancing there on my own like Kevin Bacon in Footloose. Scotty and Eadie were poorless when I told them what had happened. The next morning, with just an hour or so to kick-off, we were sitting in MacDonald's eating junk food, still more or less in a drunken state. I contemplated the game. Could we keep our defeat down to single-figures? Or could an Aberdonian team finally avenge that world-record 36-0 defeat? I then got a phone call from Paul, the manager. He had some good news and some bad news. The good news was that the game was cancelled, due to frost: but the bad news was that as an alternative, we would play them in a five-a-side challenge, and the result of which would stand. Suddenly we went from seven drunken no-hopers, to five-a-side footballers with subs to spare! We turned up just in time for kick-off, hungover to hell, with burgers and milkshakes churning through our stomachs. One of our guys couldn't score in a brothel and another two almost did just that eight hours previous. Forty minutes later we were back in the changing rooms, feeling physically sick and shot to shit after a chaotic experience. By the time I got home, I could barely believe I had yet another, more intense, indoor tournament to attend the following week. And nor could I believe we had beaten the Aberdeen lot by eight goals to five. Rock-n-roll football: it's the only way to play the game.

The prestigious Amsterdam Euro Five-a-Side Tournament took place the week after Aberdeen. The night before the competition, we gained an advantage over a rival team when one of our guys proceeded to knock ten bells out of one of theirs before chasing him down the corridor in his pants. His crime? Staggering into my mate's room and trying to pee on his bed! It set the tone graciously. We spent the next morning, and the actual day of the tournament having a party in my room. We were changed and ready to play with hours to spare, but with plenty of booze at our disposal, what else were half a dozen lads supposed to do in an Amsterdam hotel? Have a bed-in with Yoko Ono? By the time the tournament began, and unlike Aberdeen, we weren't at the hungover stage. We were pished! It was a most unprofessional way to prepare for a football match.

When we eventually got there, the heat inside the hall was horrendous, and the Dutch referees didn't appreciate our physical style one bit. In the first few seconds, and as captain, I ran towards a guy with every intention of sticking him, and maybe the ball, into next week, but I lost my footing completely and he ran unchallenged towards goal and scored. That got all our backs up, and we were bickering with each other as the booze poured from our foreheads, stinging our eyes. The guy that got punched the night before then took another sore one when he got hit in the kisser with the ball…when carrying a tray of water; the poor sod. But I also remember feeling embarrassed, when I missed an astonishing open goal from just one yard! Yet somehow, we managed to win our games, and with it, the trophy. The cup was presented to me and that felt good: and not at all bad for a man who was quite drunk at the start of the tournament and near death by its end. It felt fantastic being there, and I lived not for that day or the next: but for the next lager, my next ciggie and the next laugh with the guys. The football was a bonus, an excuse even: but it was the bond between the lads that gave me a great feeling; Jamie, Joe, Scotty, Reilly, David and me. Every hour was precious and unpredictable; dangerous and brilliant. Whose round was it next? Where are we going next week?

The Aberdeen victory was the first step towards reaching the cup final at East End Park, Dunfermline. When we got to the lounge we found our opposition sipping water, wearing suits off the pitch and all black on it (a bit like those well drilled Nazis in Escape to Victory). We were a motley crew, watching in dismay as the other went through their star-jumps and synchronised warm-up. I was captain in a cup final at an SPL stadium in front of a crowd pushing three figures! Although my Hutchison Vale sorrow could never be amended, I at least had the chance to taste some glory on the football field; albeit at amateur level. This game meant a lot to me. I said a few words of encouragement to the guys before kick-off, as did Paul, our player-manager. We were under the cosh for most of the match, but I enjoyed the 'siege-like' nature of the game, making some great tackles, despite losing three years worth of skin off my knees. It was quite an exciting contest, but when it was all over we were tied at 1-1, and penalty kicks ensued.

I decided then, to lead by example and take the first penalty. It was a long walk, and I had quite a few friends and family watching. I thought of my penalty miss in the Broomhouse v Saughton mass take-on, all of eighteen years previous. I looked over to the enclosure. Les was there and she smiled over to me. I kept walking; my head was down, trying to concentrate. But I looked again, and I saw standing on the red seats of East End Park, the baying mob at St Joseph's Primary School; the kid on the bike, the dog; the drunk with the Special Brew, the breakdance mat school crowd, the Commonwealth Games ghetto-blaster, my dad and Albert Kidd. And it was then that I made my run forward...

Les and I went on holiday in April 2004, but I caught a really horrible cold on the first day and I was ill for the whole week. I also missed the birth of my niece, Rebecca; but I doubt Bobby and Denise would've wanted me around anyway, spreading my germs. It was a pity, and the rest of the summer seemed so self-centred. I went six months without even bothering to speak to either of my parents. I hadn't seen my dad in two years. My socialising had gone into overdrive. A 'lost weekend' occurred when Lesley went off to Prague and Eadie moved in and pretty much stayed there for four days. We drank solidly. We went out more than a few times, including the 'Save our Hearts' night at The Corn Exchange and some crap clubs in George Street. And when we weren't out, we were in, drinking lager. It was a brilliant laugh, but deary me, I was out of control. By the Sunday morning, we were tucking into a slab of Tennents lager, playing topless table-tennis in my living-room! It took me back a decade or more with Allan; where we'd live from beer to beer, night to morning, weekend to holiday. Eadie, though younger than me, began to fill the void in my life left behind by Allan. He called me his "work wife". I had a work's night out the next Friday, which got me home at four in the morning. Three hours later, Les woke me up. My taxi for the airport was waiting. As I was still wearing the same clothes I had on from the night before (including my jacket), I only needed to grab a pair of boxer shorts and my toothbrush before making the early morning flight to Nottingham. And as I boarded Easy Jet, they could've flown the plane using the fumes from my breath as I headed out for a stag night!

Nottingham was a good night out, but I was on an even better stag weekend a few weeks later; this time in London for Kerrin, my Hibby supporting brother-in-law-to-be. It was an amazing trip, but what stag-do wouldn't be when the groom is made to join in the Gay Pride march wearing nothing but a Bernie Clifton ostrich outfit? In fact, half of the marchers seemed to be staying in our rundown Piccadilly hotel where the rooms didn't even have toilets. I remember being forced to take a pee at five in the morning standing next to a trucker called Dave who had the butt-cheeks cut out of his leather pants. I'd never seen that in The Busy Bee before! There were lots of laughs and high jinx, scrapes and near-disasters. There were also pubs, clubs, curries, strippers, dodgems and a nightclub brawl. And bizarrely, it all ended at Waterstone's Bookshop! Then there were the weddings that followed the stag nights, and various other nights out and football trips. Bloody hell, I was in the last throes of youth; living the life of a twenty-year-old, but aged thirty.

Post wedding, post Allan, post Saughton Mains Bank. I drank the whole summer away, and by the fall of 2004, my liver felt like The Stone of Destiny. I stopped caring about career progression as the office job that I'd always craved felt shallow. My 'lost weekend' wasn't just about hanging out with the lads and drinking beer for breakfast. It was my denial. I was miserable, and the only thing I cared about was the next booze session with the guys. I had a wonderful wife but I was out all the time. I was out of control, yet I felt as though I had to get busy living, even when it hurt. And had it not been for a locked door, my penalty kick would still have been bouncing down the Halbeath Road as I write this now. But I didn't just miss the penalty: I completely ballooned it, high and wide; effectively costing my team's chance of winning the cup. The penalty miss left me with the sort of frustration that can only be eradicated by beating oneself with a birch branch underneath the canal overflow at the Slateford viaduct. But instead, I just got pissed. The 'lost weekend' was merely a temporary vacation, because the past would inevitably be found lurking again, soon enough.

Chapter 48
The loneliest kebab
in the world

At the start of the 2004/05 season, it was reported that Hearts had sold Tynecastle Stadium for the sum of £22 million. I was on my way to a wedding in sunny Paris, but the Evening News headline at the airport left me cold. The club was lurching into crisis. I wanted Hearts to stay at Tynecastle, but what was the point in having a stadium if there was no team to play in it? Amidst the passionate demonstrations of some, and the succumbed indolence of others, every Hearts fan had to decide if the club was more than the ground it played in. Was 'Tynecastle', 'Hearts'? Could Hearts survive without Tynecastle's frenzied atmosphere? What Hearts needed more than anything, was a knight in shining armour. Chris Robinson had been in charge for a decade, but instead of turning the club's worrying debt situation around, he presided over it spiralling out of control. The most daunting question of all was now becoming reality. 'Just how bad would Murrayfield be anyway?' As participants in that season's UEFA Cup, we were about to find out.

For the second year running, Hearts had finished the season in third place, amassing a club record sixty-eight points and making a mockery of their incredible knack of never having two decent seasons in a row. For the new 2004/05 campaign, Craig Levein's sturdy team drew Portugal's Sporting Braga in the UEFA Cup and the club announced that the game would have to be played at Murrayfield. It was such a strange notion: going to a Hearts home tie in the west of Edinburgh, but not at Tynecastle. All of the pubs around the vast rugby stadium were rammed and the rain was pouring down. I managed to get a beer in the Westfield, before heading to the game. Up until that point, I had never actually set foot inside the Murrayfield, and instead of turning right into nostalgic 'Puddle Lane', I went left under the railway bridge. But untried as it was, the sight of all the Hearts fans milling around, climbing the steps into Murrayfield made for an impressive sight.

As for the match, Hearts played really well, and the atmosphere was electric. A tense 2-1 lead was a good enough result for me, but in the last minute, Patrick Kisnorbo smashed home a third goal to raise the roof of the

East Stand and complete a superb victory over tricky opponents. The fans poured from the stadium, singing loudly and we joined the human traffic-jam back under the railway bridge. Murrayfield felt ok. The stadium was way too big for us, but with the right performance, the atmosphere generated was excellent. But in the end, it was a case of 'first time lucky', with perhaps a touch of novelty thrown in. Hearts played competitive football at Murrayfield another five times in the next couple of years. Some of the attendance figures we pulled would better the likes of Newcastle United and Juventus plus a host of other 'big teams'. But ultimately, playing there was never as good as it was on that wet September night in 2004. Our one good/one bad season pattern re-emerged, forever a curse to our European campaigns, and the team was never able to get its game together on the expansive pitch. It was as if the players forever longed for the intimate surrounds of Tynecastle. The fans certainly did, and a couple of years after that Braga game, I realised that my declaration of unflinching support for the team should we have moved to Murrayfield would have been pointless. Blind loyalty can only go so far: Hearts belonged at Tynecastle, and Bobby was right all along.

In addition to the welcome result and the historical sense of occasion, there was one other positive aspect to the Braga tie, in that the winner would qualify for the first ever group stage of the UEFA Cup, guaranteeing lucrative European football up until Christmas. Despite the pastel shades of their away kit, Hearts looked mean and focused in Portugal as they posed for an iconic team photo before the game: but they got off to a horrific start, conceding an early goal; the result of early Braga pressure. Les, Eadie, Andy, Donald and I were watching the game in The Caley Sample Rooms. The pub was packed, with everyone screaming at the TV, contesting every decision and roaring the team on as our nerves shredded. Outside, a couple of hapless tourists (possibly North American) had walked by and stood there, looking in through the window in awe at our demented, angry ritual. Well a few minutes later, they must have got a right eyeful as the pub went absolutely fucking berserk, as Mark de Vries scored the equaliser.

Eadie was in tears, crying with laughter, but not at the goal. He was laughing at me and my frenzied reaction. I often imagined what those tourists made of it all. They were certainly fascinated by the whole spectacle. I wonder what it was about watching a pub full of Hearts fans, that made it a more appealing (and perhaps slightly less intimidating) experience than actually coming into the pub and watching the game. They were still there, watching with astonishment, as Hearts scored again; and once more, we went crazy, with cask beers and lagers being thrown into the air. It was excruciatingly tense, but Hearts finally made it though to the group stages, the first British team ever to do so. What a night it was, one of the best ever and very much part of the 'lost weekend' summer season. I had never watched such an important Hearts game from the comfort of the pub. But although it was a fantastic experience, I so wished I'd gone to Braga. The Hearts fans over there had a great time, and as the game ended, the tourists standing outside slipped away. Soon, I would be in their shoes. It's strange, but often, it is Hibs and their fans that are solely painted as the Edinburgh 'romantics' and 'warrior poets' by the media and their celebrity/fan writers. Yet, whenever I recall these games from the past, it is always with a sense of romance, and a feeling of dare; we dared to dream that our team could be something more. What's dour and Protestant about that? What's 'establishment' about the way I leap around?

The next morning, The Scotsman proclaimed the arrival of Vladimir Romanov, the Russian-born Lithuanian banker who had previously been courting all Scottish clubs that began with the letters 'Dun'. Romanov had been in Scotland for an international match the previous autumn and was impressed by the passion and heritage of Scottish football. It was suggested that he wanted to use a Premier League side to market his Lithuanian players. However, when the bigger fish of Hearts came up for grabs, he began to reassess his ambitions which included a declaration of making the Jambos European Champions within a matter of years! It all sounded a bit too good to be true; and perhaps the real extent of his ambitions lay somewhere in between. But what we needed was someone who wasn't Chris Robinson. And a more realistic challenge for Romanov was to reverse the sale of Tynecastle, which he did without fuss. It was an act that instantly made him a hero to Hearts fans. Vladimir had arrived, and with him were his bright-young-thing lieutenants. It was the start of a new revolution, and yet another tumultuous chapter in the history of Heart of Midlothian. If Hearts fans thought they'd been put through the mill in the previous year: then they hadn't seen anything yet.

The 'lost weekend' continued in the form of a coach trip to Rotterdam to see Hearts play Feyenoord in the UEFA Cup. I remember leaving McLeod Street. But by the time I woke up in Dover, it seemed I had upset half the bus with my drunken behaviour, which included a springboard dive off the coach, head first; peeing in front of the entire service station; asking the driver for a "square-go"; and demanding to know who had drunk my port. I had drunk it, along with several cans of Stella. Our hotel was like something out of The Crystal Maze, with a series of bamboozling corridors and dead ends. I fully expected Richard O'Brien to jump out on me with a sardonic put-down. Half an hour later, after giving up, I put my bag (and my beer) down on the counter and demanded to be carried to my room!

Like in Liege twelve years previous, I got that feeling again. There is nothing quite like being abroad, supporting the team that means so much. The songs were being belted out and the beers were sunk with ease, as Eadie, Stuart, Les, Andy, Donald and me stood by the pavement at the front of the Big Ben pub. It was all going well, when suddenly we were treated to the sight of at least a hundred and fifty Feyenoord casuals, marching past. And it soon became apparent that they weren't there to exchange phone numbers. The Hearts fans started chanting "Who are you!" The Feyenoord boys retorted with a charge and a volley of bottles, several of which were thrown in our direction. The police were already in place, and waded into the Dutch hooligans with batons, boots and fists! In over twenty years of following Hearts, I had never been as close to the action as I was at that moment. The police then hastily shut the pub, and buses were laid on for us, ad hoc. Once we got to De Kuip, it was chaotic, and they wouldn't let me in as I had lost my ticket after passing though the first turnstile (yes that's right, I was pissed again). It took Andy to scrunch his ticket up, and throw it back to me as I distracted the steward to get me through the gate! Andy was always a good man to have around in a crisis. When I eventually got in, everyone had fallen out with me again and as there were no seats left, I stood the entire game and watched Hearts lose 3-0.

The 'weekend' wasn't over yet. On Hogmanay 2004, I headed up to Loch Rannoch for a two-night New Year party. I had been there in 2000 and again in 2002. This time, I organised it all myself for my friends and it was a bit like the video for Wham's 'Last Christmas' but with drunken hooligans. It was a brilliant party, and on the stroke of midnight Stuart asked me to be his Best Man. For two days, we got stuck into the booze, and Kerrin's London stag-do mates were there also. 2004 had ended, but 2005 would have plenty of dramas of its own. It was a time when the world was still mourning the devastation of the Asian Tsunami; which occurred just eight months before the New Orleans flood. 2005 was the year Al-Qaeda bombed innocent commuters on the London Underground; and Bob Geldof held more Live Aid concerts, as a bunch of unwashed, lentil-eating anarchists ripped up memorial park benches in Princes Street Gardens.

Hearts were to make the news too in 2005, despite our inconsistent season. Craig Levein had left suddenly to go to Leicester and his replacement (yet another Hearts legend), John Robertson, was having a torrid time. His behaviour seemed a little erratic and he managed to get himself into one or two scrapes along the way. Our next two games at Murrayfield drew large crowds, but they became non-events as Hearts lost both matches, silencing the fans. There was controversy in March as Lithuanian winger, Saulius Mikoliūnas barged into linesman Andy Davis. The Govan based assistant referee flagged for an inexplicable last gasp penalty for Rangers at Tynecastle. I was only a few yards away from the entire episode and I can confirm the linesman was indeed a complete trumpet. Miko lost the plot, and went for Davis. But although I was raging at the linesman, I knew my protest was as futile as Miko's. There was nothing any of us could do about it. We all knew what had just happened and frankly, it's been going on for years. Rangers won the game, and ultimately, the championship. Hearts were furious with the verdict, and launched an appeal against Davis, questioning the "integrity of the decision": a stance which then turned the media against the club. Miko, who had been one of our best players, was banned for five games and was never to rediscover his scintillating early form for Hearts.

A month or so later, Hearts were in hot water once more when a section of the crowd booed during the one minute silence held in honour of Pope John Paul II. The very structure of the fixture was against us from the start: an early afternoon kick-off on a Sunday and in the opposition's backyard. It was always going to be a powder-keg situation; especially as the opposition was Celtic, and in a Scottish Cup Semi-Final. Les, Donald, Andy and I stood silent; but many Hearts didn't. It was ensnarement on a grand scale. So why have a minute's silence that was always going to make the Hearts support look bad? Well the answer to that one of course, is in the question. The Celtic fans were morally outraged, and roared their team on to a 'just' victory, accompanied with their usual barrage of traditional 'folk songs'. In all probability, it would've only taken a handful of the twelve thousand or so Hearts fans to have spoiled the silence. But many more than that did. The SFA should've foreseen what was going to happen: but they left us out to hang; our very own Bay of Pigs. God bless the love triangle that is the SFA and the Old Firm of Rangers and Celtic.

It was a sorry end to our season, as the self-styled flair team of Hibernian and the media dah-lings of Aberdeen stole a match from us in the league. I was glad 2004/05 was over. Vladimir Romanov, to his credit, had stepped in, and he had done more than just buy the club. He'd saved it. And as he saved Hearts from becoming the next Third Lanark, he also saved Tynecastle Stadium from becoming another Cathkin Park. There would be no trees sprouting out on the Gorgie Stand; no bushes in the Wheatfield; and the threat of luxury flats was replaced with talk of rebuilding modern Tynecastle for the second time. From the start, Romanov was outspoken, and maybe even eccentric. But then he wasn't the only one: for it was around that time that Delia Smith made her excruciating half time "where are you?" rant. One sherry pie too many, me thinks.

But despite the end of a long season and the encouraging noises from the Romanov camp, I needed to get away from it all and far, far away from the place I was at. It wasn't the football that was bothering me though: it was the person I saw staring at back from the mirror every morning. Aged thirty-one, I had never fully removed myself from the life I was leading. I had never switched off, or switched on for that matter. I had never really done anything exciting. In the spring of 2005, I was still trundling along, working in a job I cared little for. I was still living for that Friday night in town, and that Saturday at Tynecastle and The Diggers. In order to assess my everyday life and evaluate the person living it, I had to remove myself from it. I needed away from dull Saturday footballers like Dennis Wyness and Neil MacFarlane. I needed away from the Sunday Night Dread dreams of Saughton Mains Bank and the petrol station night-shift. I needed away from Monday morning hangovers and Tuesday morning meetings where I'd fight sleep and often lose. I needed away from crap rainy Wednesday and penultimate-push Thursday. I needed away from rubbish Friday nights; watching drunken workmates snog, fall-out, cry-over, make-up and then throw-up with and over each other; before I headed home £60 poorer and one kebab richer. And that was if I got a taxi. Sometimes I'd be the one waiting in a doorway, escaping the rain with a foam carton in one hand and a plastic fork in the other: waiting for the orange cab light that would never appear. Living the life of a twenty-one-year-old some ten years too late left me feeling empty inside, despite the best efforts of the kebab. I needed fewer days like Stephen Simmons and more like Colin Cameron. I needed a vacation, to get away from the 'Humdrum Town' of my mind. And that's exactly what I did.

Chapter 49
America was, America

It had been coming for months, but I was dreading it. The plan to travel around America was both psychologically daunting and strategically challenging; but that's not what kept me lying awake at night. As the archetypal insomniac, lack of sleep wasn't anything new to me anyway. What really had me disconcerted was the thought of being strapped into a steel test tube that was built by the lowest bidder, forty-thousand feet in the air, travelling at six-hundred miles per hour and praying that neither terrorists nor mechanical failure would all but end my chances of making my Hearts debut by my thirty-second birthday. Poor Les, she had to put up with my sleepless nights, panic-attacks and involuntary hand movements anytime we boarded a plane. But a transatlantic flight was a whole new game of 'tie me down'. She reassured me: yes, the plane had passed all its safety checks; yes, the pilot was indeed fully qualified; and no, he was not in the least bit suicidal. The take-off is always the worst bit for me: the drinks cart is the best; and two or three cups of van rouge sorted me out. The flight was to be seven hours long, and I'd saved Mike Smith's book, Follow the Hearts for the Glasgow runway. But nothing bad happened, and eventually I made it. I was in New York City.

I had never been outside Europe. The closest thing I'd ever had to adventure was going to The Gyle for some shopping one morning with Lesley and ending up on a flight to Spain just hours later. The United States of America had everything I was looking for in terms of excitement and escapism. I didn't bother to bring my mobile phone charger, and when Bobby texted me to say that John Robertson had been sacked, I wasn't especially interested. Only New York had my attention now. Les and I don't dress like tourists, but it's difficult not to act like one when taking in the sheer vertical scale of the place. I had never seen a skyscraper before. I had stood on the roof of Tour Montparnasse in Paris, but this was incredible. We had such a great time there; walking in Central Park, standing on top of the Empire State Building, looking back at Manhattan from the Statue of Liberty, wandering around the shops of The Village; Les spending all our money in Macy's and Bloomingdale's. I even bought her a Tiffany necklace: and she bought me a kebab at the Lexington Sunday market. My wife always knew the way to my heart, but there were a couple of things I had to do above all else.

I stood by the sidewalk and gazed into the tunnelled archway of The Dakota Building, the very location where Mark David Chapman murdered my hero, John Lennon. It was a place that always seemed very far away from my bedroom in Saughton Mains Bank back in 1990. But I had made it to West 72nd St and it felt like something of a pilgrimage. I didn't say much, or stay too long. The doorman was looking at me funny and as Yoko Ono still lives in the building, I didn't want to appear as though I was hanging around, like a bloody Mark Chapman! Standing in the spot of an infamous crime scene is eerie, but in some small way I felt privileged to be there. Despite Lennon spending childhood holidays in the Murrayfield area of Edinburgh and often visiting the cinema in Gorgie; as well as having first cousins living in Balerno, all just a couple of miles from Saughton Mains Bank, I never felt close to John Lennon. I only shared this world for seven years with him, but never on the same island. Yet here, outside the Dakota, and twenty-five years after his murder, I felt close. A whole quarter of a century had passed and yet it still seemed such a pointless waste. And his killer, as I deduced, was rotting away in his cell just a little bit up state from where I stood. Les and I walked over the road to Strawberry Field, and breathed the sweet free air that Chapman will hopefully never inhale again. Whatever bullshit reason he had for killing John Lennon, I just hoped for his benefit, it was worth it.

A couple of hours later and a few miles downtown, Les and I stood back and away from tourists posing for pictures; some jostling for the best shots of the former World Trade Centre. I was technically a tourist too, but I didn't use a camera, or walk around like a tit wearing ridiculous shorts with white socks and sandals. I went there to see it, but did so with at least a bit of respect.

The WTC site had become a swarming, ghoulish tourist destination, even though it was no longer there. It was now just a hole in the earth and I could only imagine the scale of the towers, standing twice the height of the skyscrapers that surrounded it. And like the vast empty void of Ground Zero, the real essence of my trip wasn't something I could see: but something I couldn't. The thing I needed from my journey wasn't something I could've once paid $10 to ride to the top of. It was something on the inside I had to discover and it was in the USA that I could make a clean break from the rest of my life and find it. The more I took in New York, the more I grew to love it. Amidst the chaos, it was a place that made sense to me.

As the hotel limo drove us to the airport, I heard 'Leaving New York' by R.E.M. It was such a sad feeling, not only to be leaving, but the thought of another long flight; this time to San Francisco.

My first hour there was a shambles. Les and I fell out at the airport. I then fell out with the taxi driver because he was a tosser. At the hotel, the service was useless and I fell out with them! I was in a shocker of a mood, so we threw down our cases and immediately walked to Pier 39. But as it was quite chilly, I went into another mood and had to turn back to get a coat. I told Les I'd catch her up. Now it should've been time to calm down and de-stress, but on my way back, a 'street-person' lurched out at me from behind a makeshift bush! This, to my discovery, was supposed to be a harmless bit of kerbside entertainment; much to my horror, a crowd of tourists laughed and took pictures of me from across the road. The 'street-person' then waved to them before having the audacity to shake a tin can in my direction, inviting me to pay for the privilege of having the shit scared out of me. I took a quarter out of my pocket and placed it in the can; grimacing through embarrassment. The man shouted up to me in a loud Californian accent,

"Hey man, aren't you having fun in our city?"

To which my Saughton Mains reply was "Go fuck yourself ya tramp". But just as things couldn't get any worse, I stumbled into a gift shop on the famous pier. Les knew I was at boiling point, and left me at the door while she wandered around. Two spotty bastards behind the counter then called me over and asked me to "pick a card". I wasn't in the mood for games, but as I reluctantly put my hand to the pack, the guy holding the deck gave me an electric shock. Seconds later, as I had him by the throat, I wasn't sure whether to throw him off the pier towards the sea lions; kick his ass there and then; or buy the cards as a present for Bobby.

Fortunately, my ability to fall out with every person I met in the first hour was the nadir of my time in California. Les and I loved San Francisco; there's a fabulous 'feel' to the place. I don't quite know how to describe it: it's just so cool. We did all the 'sight' stuff, like Alcatraz and Lombard Street, and I now know why people stand on the trams: because the vibrations go right up your backside! Best of all though, was cycling over the beautiful Golden Gate Bridge and continuing right round Marine County in an epic journey. At nights we ate out in China Town, and it was in San Francisco that I discovered the joy of cold Guinness on a warm evening. Ah, San Francisco: what a groovy place and I was sorry to be leaving. When we did, we made our way to Oakland to pick up our RV. This was the daunting part. I had never driven an RV, nor an automatic. And I had never driven on the right side. Yet, I had two and a half thousand miles and six states to get through; at first I made a calamity of wrong turns, ending up at one point down the dodgiest of dead-end side streets.

Eventually though, we found our way to the open road and high into the Californian wine valley. It was frantic at times, but after six hours of driving and one incredibly precarious mountain ridge, it felt very good to get to our first stop near Yosemite National Park. The adventure was well under way, and not least because this was big ass bear country.

The next day was perhaps one of the most momentous in my life. We were up at 5.30am to drive through Yosemite and then on to Death Valley. After hurtling along the first two miles on the wrong side of the road, we headed into the beautiful national park before climbing the steepest of ridges. As the road reached a summit of around ten thousand feet, we found ourselves driving above the snow line and this caused us a serious snag. The snow was old and coloured a highly disturbing black as it sat stacked up and compounded by the road. And when we finally reached our junction, we were forced to turn back as the melting ice closed our route. We then had to find another way off the mountain towards the deadly desert of Death Valley. As I had the entire journey mapped out before we left, we simply had to make each leg of the trip to have a chance of making the next one. On that day, I knew I was up against it, so I drove and I drove and I drove.

By around 2pm, we were in the desert. The change in scenery was bewildering and all around us was the starkest of landscapes; with only mile-long trains, snaking their way along the basin floor to give away any sense of scale. I needed a break, so we pulled up just outside the middle of nowhere. I remember stepping from the RV. The last time I'd left my cabin was above the plague coloured snow line in crisp Yosemite. This time, I popped out and lit a cigarette in blazing heat. With my one and only draw, I somehow breathed in all of hell's fury! We still had hundreds of miles to drive. Through California, and into Arizona, hours of empty, straight road and beautiful desolation lay in front of us: and Les fell asleep! It was scary, but a good scary. It was adventure, and it was change. But best of all, it was time. Time that is, to think. By around 8pm, we made it to our camp in Arizona and I finally pitched up the vehicle. I can't remember what I ate that night, but I remember cracking open a cold bottle of lager. After fifteen hours and seven-hundred-odd miles, Les and I sat on top of a picnic bench and sipped our drinks. Sunset was upon us, and the stars appeared as the sky turned lilac, and then maroon. The temperature was just perfect and for as long as I live, I will never forget that moment.

Driving the open roads through the South-West cast such a spell on me, it was as if the Navajo had intended it to be that way. The rest of the week was never as colossal as that second day, but the scenery was like some sort of geologist's wet-dream! We drove to the Grand Canyon the next day and it was a glorious sight. It was windy, and all the 'copter rides were grounded. It was supposed to be the highlight of the drive, but we saw a couple of places that we considered to be even better. Later that day, we got caught in what can only be described as a sandstorm, as we headed through Monument Valley, a place straight out of those old Cowboy and Indian movies. I bought Bobby some hot sauce, called 'Fire in the hole' (I'll bet), and we visited ancient sites like Mesa Verde in Colorado and Aztec, New Mexico. We even stood on the one spot in the USA that had us in four different states at the same time. Of the four, Utah was the best.

Canyonlands National Park was so empty; it felt like we were the only people on the planet (though what planet, I'm not sure). We drove the road over 'Island in the Sky', a long, thin and rising plateau of some six-thousand feet. When we finally got to 'Grand View Point', I realised I had stumbled upon the most awe-inspiring sight I'd ever witnessed. For as far as I could see, a stunning image of crumbling, decaying pre-historic Earth. And unlike the Grand Canyon, with its whipping winds and jostling tourists, this was peace on Earth; a glowing red nirvana. The serenity and reverence kept us transfixed for hours. There was hardly another soul there and the very road we'd driven on wasn't long built. Les and I sat alone, on the edge of the cliff. Sometimes we talked. Sometimes we just stared out. Who knows: she might have even thought about pushing me off! I had a few thoughts of my own. In the tranquillity of Canyonlands, I made another life decision. My surroundings demanded it.

I recalled the words I read on an in-flight magazine by Colleen C Barrett, boss of an airline similar to the one I was strapped into. "Work is either fun or drudgery". Fun or drudgery. When I was shovelling sludge out of the jet wash drain, or when I got stuck in the boggy marsh at PDC, I always thought that office work was the pinnacle of vocations. Any old office job would have done for someone like me. But when I finally got one, I became conscious that it wasn't all it was cracked up to be. For me, working in such an Orwellian environment was 'drudgery' and I knew I wasn't having much fun. Its career ladder was no longer something I wanted to climb or walk under. I had to change, again. So I declared to Les that my job was now in a period of probation. I sat quietly for some time more, mulling over my verdict, and then eventually, we headed back to camp. The next day, as we drove through the Utah desert, we almost ended up crashing the RV into the deepest of ditches, many miles from anywhere. As I drove, Les wanted to take a photo of my wing mirror, which showed clear blue sky against the backdrop of red rock desert. But in order to achieve the perfect angle, Les asked me to take the photo while she held the steering wheel and watched the road. Let's just say I held my side of the bargain and as the RV swerved all over Highway 24, I reckoned that if the twenty foot ditch hadn't gotten us, then the desert would've in our very own version of The Flight of the Phoenix.

Bryce Canyon must be one of the weirdest places on Earth. As the sun began to set, we watched in amazement as a giant amphitheatre of spiked shaped rocks glowed white, pink and orange. The 'hoodoos' stood side by side, like a melting sandcastle army regiment or perhaps even a group of football casuals. They were magnificent, yet odd; much like the red-neck waiter who served me the next morning, when he eyeballed me the question, "What kin ah git you boa?!" Driving the RV was great. With stunning scenery, straight roads, automatic gears, cruise control and a bench-seat to cuddle up to the wife, the most difficult part of the journey was remembering that I was actually driving! And every five miles or so, there'd be a slight bend in the road before the next straight expanse (a bit like Comley Bank Avenue). And I had time, lots of it. I had time to think, time to plan and time to reflect. Our final destination was Zion National Park, with its monster cliffs and waterfalls. After a week of rock formations, canyons, cliffs, rivers, scrapes and heatwaves; and not least sleeping in an RV: Les and I headed for the relative luxury of Las Vegas. We handed back the keys; fortunately for us, they didn't notice the missing glass microwave plate that I had smashed when driving over a bump. But unfortunately for me, it only took the bastards two minutes to swipe my Indian fudge that I'd saved up yet left behind in the fridge. Like the journey itself, I guess what goes around, comes around.

Las Vegas was the kitsch, final leg of the trip. Les had booked us into a massive hotel that was shaped like a giant, naff glass pyramid. It was so hot when we got there and I was so exhausted from the road-trip that I keeled over! The rest of the first day was spent in bed and I could barely move. When I did wake up, Les ordered me to slow the fuck down! I needed to chill out now, and we did that in Vegas, by the pool. There was an incredible moment of coincidence when I bumped into old mates Scott and Nicky in the hotel. They were on a stag week and we all sat and watched Liverpool's famous Champions League victory over AC Milan. We went to the Elvis museum (where I managed to lean over and touch The King's car), and a Titanic Exhibition (where I managed to lean over and touch 'The Big Piece'). We went to Caesar's Palace and watched showbiz types arrive to see The Contender, but I didn't touch anyone there. Siegfried & Roy were back in town, despite Roy's recent mauling from a tiger. And I too mauled all-you-can-eat-sushi, before we cringed at an ultra-PC 'rap-off' between rival ships at Treasure Island (what the hell's wrong with a good old-fashioned sword fight I ask?). And when the light show ended above our heads at Freemont Street, I knew the trip was over.

Just before I went home, I took a final walk round the hotel to get some shots of what is the world's biggest and most spectacular atrium. As I strolled across the floor at the mezzanine level, I noticed a man and woman walking towards me. The man was none other than Colin Cameron, my favourite Hearts player who had broken my heart when he no longer wanted to play for my club. I was shocked to see him, although not because he was there: but because I was. For all I knew, this could've been his annual beano and that he spends his summers hanging out with P Diddy at the Mandalay Bay Four Seasons. This wasn't Colin Cameron in my world: this was me in his, and at that precise moment, I was right in his path. Now the natural thing for any football fan to do (especially when they're five thousand miles from home) is to interrupt the footballer, ask probing questions and maybe even pose for a photograph. But he had left me to join Wolverhampton Wanderers, not the other way round. And as wee 'Mickey' and I approached each other; something suddenly occurred to me and I stepped aside to let him pass by, without me saying a word or even looking back at him. My realisation was that Colin Cameron didn't owe me a thing: not his time nor his explanations. He was forever a Hearts' Hero, and I was just a fan. That was all that mattered and that's the way it's meant to be. Footballers are footballers. What the hell can I do about it? By not bothering or disturbing him, I made my peace with him. The way I saw it was: he was he, and I was me.

The sight of Colin Cameron reminded me of Hearts, and indeed home; and it was time to get packed up anyway. But for me, America was stepping out from the norm (apart from bumping into mates and footballers) and getting far away from the only things I had ever known. America was as much a journey of the mind as it was a road-trip along Route 66. Because whenever I drove the mother road, or walked along the edges of canyons, I had nothing but time to reflect and deduce; contemplating what had gone before and calculating what had to come next. Of course America may well have a dodgy foreign policy, a bumbling president and national psyche that involves talking loudly and eating rather a lot: but it's also a country of overwhelming natural awe and iconic man-made splendour. But the most important discovery I made driving across the desert states, was that the end of my voyage had ultimately led me to one almighty crossroads. That was the best thing about America.

Chapter 50
Hearts this, hearts that

The week after I returned from America was a bad one. I hardly slept due to my old problem with insomnia and my new issue of jet-lag. I also found a lump on my body, which was going to need to be removed. I had a night out on the Saturday, which was fine, but I wasn't looking forward to work on the Monday and that meant only one thing: Sunday Night Dread. As I lay in bed, I felt ill. I hadn't slept a wink, and I became aware that something was happening with my heart. It felt wrong, very wrong…as if it was coming to a stop! As 1am became 2am, the palpitations got worse. At 3.15am, I jumped out of bed and declared to Les that I was going to call an ambulance! Les called a number for me, and the lady on the phone told me to get my ass into the A&E pronto. By around 4am, I was being driven round the Edinburgh bypass. Bypass: now there was a word on my mind. What if there was something drastically wrong? What if I needed major heart surgery? What if I was going to buy the farm? I was seen to right away and they hooked me up to an electrocardiograph machine. The doctor hesitated for a moment, but then said I was ok. I was allowed to leave and incredibly, I went straight to work despite having had no sleep and one major health panic. For the next couple of days, my heartbeat fluctuated wildly and I was scared.

Another cause for beating hearts was the acceleration of the newly dubbed 'Romanov Revolution'. A new 'big name' boss was hired and George Burley got down to the task of signing a number of players for the new season; as did Romanov himself. Les, Donald and I went to Kilmarnock for the opening game of the campaign and it was exciting seeing a new look team play difficult opposition off the park. Hearts won 4-2 and Rudi Skacel, Roman Bednar and Edgaras Jankauskas all played exceptionally well on their debuts, as did Julien Brellier in the following game as Hearts routed Hibs 4-0 at Tynecastle. It was the time of the 'Easy, Easy' chant and after the game, I found it easy to celebrate with my friends. The sun was shining down on Gorgie once more.

The next morning I awoke at 6am and rushed to the computer to read the derby match reports online; like a kid getting up early for Christmas. I was hungover, but three cups of coffee sorted that. Big fucking mistake! I recognised the feeling. My heart jolted and then jolted again. 'Oh fuck', I thought. This was bad. My heart started to palpitate wildly, and my entire body began to seize up into a paralysed, clammy shell. I burst into the bedroom and declared to Les that I was having a heart attack, and that I was going to fucking die! I didn't die. Nor did I have a heart attack. But when I envisaged life-changing events on the cusp of 'Grand View Point' in Utah, developing heart problems wasn't one of them. This second attack was worse than the first one and a day or so later, I received a phone call from the doctor who treated me the first time. After consulting her colleague, she decided she wasn't happy with my test results, telling me she thought there was maybe a chance that my heart had become enlarged. No wonder: Look at the bloody football team I support. And so I had to go back in for another scan.

Hearts were running riot in the league as my heart was causing commotion in my chest. The irony wasn't lost on me, nor was any match at the start of that season. Winning 3-0 at Tannadice was brilliant: though Utd did give us a tough old game. Livingston was a stroll, and we dug out the three points at Inverness. At home, Hearts saw off Aberdeen and Motherwell (thanks to Craig Gordon's 'Save of the Century') before taking on Rangers, in what would be the first real acid test of the season. After our fifth straight win in the league (against Motherwell), I was standing having a laugh with Kevin, 'Gigalo-Aunt' and Mozzer. Gary Mackay then walked in.

"How good is it to a Hearts fan right now?" he demanded to know.

"Very", was my reply. It was all happening. Rebus star, Ken Stott was there, as was our cheerful chairman, Lord Foulkes. But then George Burley and his assistant, Simon Hunt walked in, and to a great cheer. They elected to come over and stand with us for a short time and I asked the Hearts boss why he never made it onto the cast of Escape to Victory with his Ipswich Town team-mates?

"Because my wife wouldn't let me!" It was all going very well until some big fat sweaty guy with B.O. came bounding over (the kind of fat bastard, as said in The Sopranos, that when he goes camping: the bears hide their food). Fatty pushed in among us, spilling my Guinness all over my trainers and demanded to know if Burley was "just another yes-man like Levein". Burley looked far from impressed (as were we), and the Hearts manager left after downing his pint. It was still a great night though.

Cold Guinness, warm weather, great banter and a winning Hearts team: it was all too good. And when Roman Bednar rose to head home the only goal of the game versus Rangers, the roar from the crowd was deafening; as was the pub and the after-match party that went on long into the night. It was so tempting. Could Hearts win the league in my lifetime? Such a question was forever rhetorical; but to many, it was one needing answering. The 'Mount Rushmore' of Hearts: Vladimir Romanov, Phil Anderton, George Foulkes and George Burley, were looking unbeatable. Even Simon Hunt looked the business in The Diggers, with his big black book of contacts under his arm. Heart of Midlothian had the look of potential champions. It was enough to make any man's heart palpitate.

One day, I got the lump removed from my back and sent off for testing. An hour later, I had more heart tests. The doc hooked me up to the ECG again and examined the results there and then. Although one of the lines read a little high, he told me I was fine; and that I just needed to chill out a bit, slow down and take it easy. But later that same day, I was told at work that I was being shipped out to work for another department that needed help. My new role was 'peripatetic'; meaning that I had to work away from home, in some sort of 'systems testing'. Slow down maybe: but after a day like that, I needed a beer. But at least Hearts were going well at the top of the league and that's what made that whole time something of a paradox. At almost any other period, my personal events were *un temps de terrible*. But it wasn't a bad time. It was a fucking great time. Not because I enjoyed having heart problems and lumps removed. I was scared beyond belief. But it really was the best of times because Hearts were not only top of the league, but they looked like they could go on and actually win it. Ask any Hearts fan under the age of fifty, and they'll probably say that some of the best times in their lives were during the 1985/86 season, May 1998 and the beginning of the 2005/06 campaign. If Hearts are doing well (and I mean really well), then we as fans can put up with a whole load of other shit.

But then as the glorious late-summer turned to autumn, it all went a bit 'Pete Tong'. Hearts may have been sitting top of the league, but there were growing rumours of major problems behind the scenes. It appeared that Romanov didn't take too kindly to Burley's methods (or was it his celebrity?), and that the two men's working relationship had apparently disintegrated. The media began speculating as to whether or not Vlad was trying to interfere with team selection and questions had already been raised over the 'moral' validity of his 'loaning' system which supplied Hearts with players via his Lithuanian nursery club, FBK Kaunas. I had another eventful day when Hearts played Falkirk. The night before, I was out with Eadie in City nightclub. I left very drunk and ended up getting a taxi home. I wasn't able to hear the taxi driver, but I did hear the walkie talkies, as the 'Old Bill' gladly completed the final leg home from Corstorphine Police Station. The next four hours were spent snoring, before having to play a game of football in goal while still quite drunk (a most underrated experience for any goalkeeper). I then made it just in the nick of time to catch the Rainbow Hearts bus to Falkirk…and still drunk! Hearts winning streak came to an end, but we did manage to stick it up taunting Falkirk fans by scoring two very late goals which salvaged a draw, which was a better return than I got in my own game earlier. On the way home, I learned that I'd become an uncle again. When Fi and Kerrin told me little Joe was born, I raised a toast for him in The Corstorphine Inn; but only after I'd paid for my taxi at the Police Station.

The next day was good, as I found out that the lump in my back was benign and Les and I flew off to Paris for a short break to try and give us a bit of time to relax and get away from it all. I don't know about the relaxation part, as we walked for miles round San Suplice, Musée du Louvre, Musée d'Orsay, Musée Picasso and the Centre Georges Pompidou, but it was a nice trip and Paris is the best city in Europe by a mile in my humble opinion. The next weekend, Hearts drew with Celtic in the slightly less cultured surroundings of Glasgow's East End, but the three point lead at the top of the league was still intact and every Hearts fan enjoyed singing "We are unbeatable" upon being kept in at the end. It was a very good result, but the rumours about Burley and Romanov intensified. The next weekend, Hearts were playing Dunfermline and I was on my way to The Diggers when my brother Ian sent me a text message. It read:

UR NOT GOING 2 BELIEVE THIS BUT GEORGE BURLEY
HAS BEEN SACKED

It was sickening: the thought of my brother resorting to 'text speak'. And for Hearts fans, it was the footballing equivalent of 'where were you when Kennedy was shot?' It was a moment that will be ceaselessly etched into my memory; up there with Andy Crane's national Willy Fog mass sing-along of '80 Days Around the World', or even Live Aid. I'll never forget it. When I got to The Diggers, the whole place was in stunned silence but for the TV blaring out the breaking news on Sky Sports. Not for the last time that season, Hearts would hold a UK wide audience captive. Just a few weeks earlier, I had stood and bantered with George Burley, slackening my own rules of speaking to football-types. It seemed so surreal now. Kevin then walked into the pub.

"Well that's that fucked then" he said; and his were the non-mincing words of prophesy. The atmosphere at Tynecastle was muted, but Hearts won the match 2-0. There was also a mid-week 1-0 win over Killie. Twelve games in, and we had won ten and drawn two.

It looked like we were holding our heads above water, but on October 29th 2005, Hearts lost 2-0 to Hibs and with it, pole position in the SPL. I watched the game in the Gorgie Suite with Les, Donald, 'Auld Jock' and Graham Anderson, and there were collective groans when the Hibs goals went in. In the Easter Road boardroom, Hearts' popular Chief Executive, 'Fireworks' Phil Anderton and Vladimir Romanov had an alleged shouting match. And a few days later, shortly before bonfire night, the 'Firework' was extinguished. His sacking sent sparks through the footballing world. It seemed as though Hearts were plotting to implode. As Anderton was fired, Chairman George Foulkes headed back to the Houses of Parliament and Romanov became the guy the press put over a barrel.

Hearts fans had to try and make their own sense of it all. Many became deeply suspicious of Romanov and his now exclusively Lithuanian board of directors. Others, like me, tried to stay calm and reasoned but the JambosKickback message board was often in meltdown and even 'Buffalo Bill' found it hard to stay positive. Whatever the rationale behind Burley's departure, all that was left was speculation and gossip; as confidentiality papers were signed all round. My own guess is that Vladimir didn't like George's self-rule and private court, and the Ayrshireman was probably the only person in the Romanov Empire that had any sort of autonomy. Some felt Romanov was meddling. Others reasoned that he just wanted explanations from Burley. Whatever the truth, it was such a huge pity that they couldn't have got their heads together and worked their problems out, and maybe even got to know each other a little bit better. Perhaps if they had agreed the ground rules at the start, their fall-out wouldn't have cost Hearts the championship. Rangers were pish and Celtic were, at best, average. It was all there for the taking. It just seemed so stupid.

Over this period, my peripatetic job had taken me to Liverpool, Glasgow and Bolton. The Bolton gig lasted for about six weeks in all. Every Monday morning at 6am, my company car would arrive and I'd drive down south. I'd stay at my crappy hotel, just yards from the shrilling drizzle of the M61. The work was dull and the days dragged. At night, my middle-aged colleague and I would head to some deserted Chinese or Italian restaurant, like the awkward setting of a single parent filling custody time; and I'd watch him spend his £25 food budget as accurately as he could. Then I'd go back to my room, and long to be at home with Lesley. I remember the cold, rundown hotel as if it was yesterday. By the sixth week, I was getting really down. One arctic November evening, after yet another mind-numbing day at work, I stood alone outside the hotel foyer. I lit my cigarette and held it up into the air, staring deep inside it. Then the bleak Lancashire distance faded and the screech of the M61 became quiet.

Looking over the edge of the cliff, the pink sun shone and the magnificent red mesas rose over a thousand feet above the white plateau. The Green River snaked its way through canyons and orange coloured rock formations. The warmth was still and the air, perfectly silent. And it was there that I remembered my vow: a vow to take stock of my career, my life, my happiness. The beauty and the serenity was magnificent. As a bird flew away in the distance, I threw the cigarette over the edge of the cliff and returned to my room with the broken radiator and no Channel Five.

As if I didn't have enough health problems to settle, I had one more hurdle to overcome on the Thursday evening on my final week in dreary old Bolton. It might've been the cold weather or possibly my chair at work, but something caused my back to hurt. And it hurt badly. As the evening wore on, it got to the point where I could barely move before a severe surge of pain came over me (which in turn set my heart off!) I could no longer stand, and could stand it no longer. I couldn't lie down either; which isn't a great situation to be in past midnight. What the hell was going on with me? It was so frustrating but there was nothing I could do to alleviate the pain. By 4am (my usual time for hospital visits in those days) I was dressed and ready to go – somewhere: but I didn't know where. I even contemplated going home, but I knew the bosses at work would go berserk at such a move. I thought about phoning Les but what was she to do? Call the A-Team? She had a big day at work ahead of her and although she would've wanted me to call her, I didn't. So I sat the night out on a chair, as miserable and as lonely as I'd ever been in my entire life. The chill of the room allowed my breath to appear with a clarity I'd never known before. When I eventually got home the next evening, Les had set me up with a doctor's appointment and I was given some tablets for my back. The tablets eased the immediate pain, but the only real cure for me would be that of my resignation.

Chapter 51
IvanIvanIvanIvanauskas
on the bench

Hearts replacement for George Burley was less than impressive. Not least because he took over when we were joint top of the league, and left us five months later trailing Celtic by over a dozen points. There was also the concern that he had spent time in prison in 1999 for a sex offence. This initially sparked protests from sections of the Hearts support and things didn't really improve for Graham Rix. But it wasn't just his past that was a problem. Rix's easy availability made him vulnerable to detractors on a wider scale. Speculation was rife that the former England striker was nothing but a puppet for Romanov, and that there was more than one person having an influence in team selection. This came to a head at Tannadice in January, when Rix informed his squad that he hadn't fully picked the team for that night's game. It sparked a furore, and Rix was gone by time we faced Hibs in the semi-final of the Scottish Cup. The Utd game was awful and the performance typified our away form over the winter. We also had to queue for an hour to get into one-horse-town Tannadice as there were only a couple of turnstiles open for over three thousand away fans. By the time we finally did get in (just before half-time), Utd scored and I would've happily queued to get back out again. Hearts fans weren't at all impressed with the controversial team selection and although we levelled late on, there was vehemence in the air as another two points were dropped.

It could be argued that Rix's demise occurred a few weeks before. When Hearts faced Celtic on January 1st 2006, we spurned a two goal lead to lose the game at the death. The difference between winning and losing was a gap of one point or seven behind Celtic. The Celtic fans went ballistic at the end, gaining ample revenge for Jose Quitongo's goal eight years previous. And it was as if they knew it would be a long time before they'd ever come to Tynecastle again and stroll to victory.

Either side of that game, I visited two of the world's greatest football stadiums, one of which fulfilled a long held ambition for me. Eadie and I, along with his brother Richard and his sister Clare, went to Old Trafford for Manchester Utd v Everton. Eadie happens to have the former Red

Devils and Scotland star, Arthur Albiston, as his uncle; and we sat chatting to him in his house, scoffing all the Hob Nobs. Arthur was a lovely guy and Utd's stadium is tremendous, but I had a mild panic attack during the game due to the deadly combination of hangover and height. But if I thought Old Trafford was good, it was nothing compared to the elation I felt when I finally visited the Estadio Santiago Bernabéu in Madrid. As 'Best Man' to Stuart, I took my opportunity to take the stag weekend there and make real my goal. And with Deportivo La Coruna providing the opposition, the game wasn't too bad either. What a jaw-dropping piece of architecture. I counted six tiers from pitch to stratosphere; a giant wedding cake of a stadium. Real Madrid won the game 4-0, with then Galácticos Zidane, Beckham and Ronaldo pulling all the strings. But the best bit was drinking beer and watching a game on a beautiful evening, all of seventy-two metres above the action. The day before, we had toured the stadium hungover, and my heart was racing again. But as I was more than a bypass away from the ERI, I just thought 'fuck it'. I had grown tired of constantly fearing over my ticker. And so with that, my heart calmed itself down and from then on, although I couldn't eradicate it, I could at least control it. Perhaps it was a case of mind over matter, and that my heart was fine but my head needed examining! They were amazing trips but I still can't look Eadie in the eye since being forced to share a double bed with him in Manchester.

Good news arrived: for as the league challenge vacillated after New Year, the Scottish Cup draw opened up tantalisingly for Hearts. Kilmarnock were negotiated in the third round, but the big news was Celtic's defeat at Clyde. And before Hearts had swept Aberdeen aside in the next round, Hibs had beaten Rangers 3-0 at Ibrox which left Hearts as the new *préférés de tournoi*. Partick Thistle was the opposition in the quarter-finals, and Hearts produced a quite shocking performance. I still feel slightly embarrassed about it now, but it was the only time I've ever booed a Hearts win, and I needed a good couple of lagers after it to cheer up. We won the game 2-1: but boy, only just.

The semi-final draw was eagerly awaited, and with fingers over eyes, it threw up the tie that all of Edinburgh and beyond was bracing itself for. Hearts immediately wanted the game played at Murrayfield and I agreed. With a Sunday lunchtime kick-off, why bother travelling to Glasgow when we have a bigger and better stadium on our own doorstep? Hibs contested the Hearts proposal. Their grim-faced manager, Tony Mowbrey felt it would hand Hearts an unfair advantage as we'd played our UEFA Cup games there the previous season (although barely a player remained from 2004/05). The SFA naturally backed Hibs and Mowbrey got his Hampden wish. Oh well, if you insist, Cheery Chops. My friend, Borthers, ran the bus from The Diggers and there was a huge mob of us going. I sat next to Tazio and despite the police warnings, we all found rather elaborate ways to disguise alcohol to get it onto the bus (though Taz never did carry out his plan for 'Russian' eggs). To add a bit of value to the day, I brought along my camcorder and in his piece to camera, Gigalo summed up the impending drama by mightily declaring that,

"It's just nice to get out from time to time, Man". The rest of us were chomping on our nerves.

As kick-off fast approached, something became rather apparent. The vociferous assertions from the Hibernian aficionados regarding their preferred location of this historic and imperative footballing occasion didn't appear to translate into them bothering to actually grace the event. Or simply put: there were huge gaps in the Hibs end! Whatever the reasons for their absence, the enormous aperture in the East Stand seemed to give us Jambos a massive boost and the Hearts end was bouncing before the game. The Hibs fans seemed much more muted, and it was as if those who weren't disguised as seats appeared a tad embarrassed at the lack of turnout. Of course it would only be fair to point out that Hearts didn't quite manage to completely sell out their South Stand allocation, but the sweeping terrace round our end was full and it gave us control off the pitch. My group were all strung out along the back row of Hampden's highest point. The view of the Hearts fans was mesmerising, and not least by contrasting the void of the other end. It was the biggest Edinburgh derby in one hundred and ten years and now it was time. During the week on JambosKickback, I had written a piece called 'Hibs fans you know and love'. I guess it was my attempt to find a humorous take on how relationships with certain friends and family would never be the same after the big game; all because they live out their lives supporting the other lot. Winning was the only option, but if we'd lost, I wrote that I'd be "heading to Fiji on a speedboat, with Ivan Sproule in my suitcase ready to begin my new life as 'Dr Linda Lovelorn'". The lipstick and wig were ready. All I needed was to win on Bullseye, and the speedboat would be mine.

And so the biggest derby game of our lives began. It was the tie we had to win. It was the match we dare not lose. Up for grabs was a place in the Scottish Cup Final against little Gretna. It was gripping, and I remember how my hands were shaking a little. Here we were, the two Edinburgh teams, but in Glasgow. The stakes were at an all-time high, but although the setting was different, one thing that never changes in an Edinburgh derby is the frantic pace. It was the usual one hundred and five miles per-hour stuff and fairly even, with both sides creating the odd chance here and there. Even though Hibs were missing a couple of players, every Hearts fan knew they were still a decent team and not to be taken lightly. But midway through the first half, Hearts got a break of the ball and went on a charging attack involving Skacel, Hartley and Jankauskas. When Janny slid the ball across the box, we held our breath as Hartley deftly connected with the outside of his foot. I was on my feet, and we watched as the ball went past the goalkeeper and in off the post for one-nil!

"YEEEEEEEEEEEEAAAAAAAHHHHHHHSSSSSSS!!!!!!!!"

"GET FUCKING IN THEEEEEERRRRRRRRREEEE!!!!!!!!!"

"AAAAAAAAAAAAAAAAAAAAAAAARRRRRRAAHH!!!!!!!"

There was a staggering celebration; a heap of bodies. We all piled in and grabbed a handful of whoever was there. The noise and hugging and the bouncing went on for ages; chaos. All the fret and burden of the occasion was liberated in that glorious moment. Half-time came and we were a goal up. We were happy, but not overly smug. It would need another goal for that. And when it arrived, we were not just smug towards our rivals, we were ridiculing them! Paul Hartley was weighing up a free kick out wide, when the unfortunate Hibs goalie, Zibi Malkowski, tried to steal too much territory towards the expected flight-zone of the ball. But Hartley, a wolf in sheep's clothes, spotted the Pole off his, er, pole. What should have been a cross ball, became a wicked and magnificent near post missile. The Hearts fans erupted again and we were in heaven. It was two-nil and the smell of victory was now upon us. The atmosphere was just incredible.

The maroon half of Hampden was rocking; the green quarter, silent. Hibs were losing their discipline, and after trying to perform a spinal tap on Miko, the impetuous Irishman, Ivan Sproule was sent off. I'm guessing he had his own speedboat waiting outside: and for what was about to happen next, I'm sure Hibs fans were wishing he'd taken Zibi the Hibby with him. The Leith team were now a disjointed shambles, and Rudi Skacel pinged a beautiful long pass that Malkowski read first. But the dithering goalie hesitated and allowed Jankauskas to nick the ball from his toe. We were all poised as the Lithuanian rolled the ball into the empty net; which sparked our 'that's us won it now' celebration and blissful chants of "EASY - EASY". It was my favourite goal of the day, and any Hibs fans that were still rattling around the East Stand quickly got the hell out of there and who could blame them? But the massacre wasn't over yet. In the last flickers of the one-sided contest, Gary Smith pulled down Mickey Pospisil and won himself a red card. He momentarily looked around but there was no one left to blame. And as he trudged off the park, Paul Hartley completed the rout and claimed his hat-trick. Now I have to say I enjoyed all of that.

When we poured out of Hampden, it was as if the trophy had been won there and then. If the cup win of 1998 was the high-point in my time as a

Hearts supporter, then that had to be a very close second. The significance of the game was incalculable. The Edinburgh derby isn't 'bigger' than its Glasgow counterpart, but such is the infrequency of success for either Hearts or Hibs, that a game of that magnitude will never be forgotten. Rangers and Celtic beat each other in cups all the time. So in one sense, that semi-final was a bigger game than any Old Firm match. We hang on to and treasure whatever glories come our way. Our great Edinburgh rivals, destroyed in Glasgow, humiliated in ticket sales and dumped out of a cup that we now seemed certain to win. What's more, Hibs hadn't won the cup since the days of Emmeline Pankhurst and Queen Victoria (ok, so Victoria was dead but her body was still warm!). And warm too, was the spring sunshine. The journey home was exquisite. We managed to play catch-up with a few Hibs' buses to which we all applauded them for remaining Europe's original 'flair team' in the face of such hoofballing rough-houses. Better still, we spotted a TV presenter who happens to be a well known Hibs fan, in his car on the M8. One of our lads, 'Therapist', sent him a kind message to pass on to his celebrity brother by carefully folding the name on the back of his Hearts shirt. Gorgie was ready for our heroic return, and the light nights and mild weather had Jambos spilling onto the streets for song-singing and cigarettes. Smoking had been banned in pubs, but thousands of revellers were more than willing to take to the pavements. I wish I could return to that night now. Everything about it was perfect. We knew less back then, but maybe that was a good thing. In my drunkenness, I decided to share with the world a little song that I had invented on the spot; a song that tried to capture the spirit of the 'Revolution':

Weeeeeeee'vvvvveee goooooooooottt
IvanIvanIvanIvan auskas on the bench, on the bench
We've got
IvanIvanIvanIvanauskas on the bench, on the bench
IVO Oh Ivanauskas, oh Ivanauskas on the bench
IVO Oh Ivanauskas, oh Ivanauskas on the bench

Now I know it all seems a bit bloody silly now, but it was a right good knees-up at the time and by the end of the night, all present in The Diggers were 'having it large'. Sometimes it is difficult to explain, and the words are more Eurovision than Joy Division, but for the lads, it became the soundtrack to our season's climax; and my dear friend Kevin would lead the masses in 'The Ivanauskas Song' with his Dick van Dyke cockney-sparrow dance. We swayed around, and drank lots of lager; possibly slurring our words a bit; hugging, kissing and the night went on…

It was now down to league business, and although the title was gone, if Hearts were able to finish second in the SPL, it would be the first time the Old Firm had been split in the league since 1995. However, much better still, there was still a place in the Champions League qualifiers up for grabs. Kilmarnock were taken care of, thanks again to Paul Hartley. Yet we inexplicably chose to field a weakened team and deservedly lost to Hibs at Easter Road. The home fans created a high-voltage atmosphere in their bid for revenge and not only did we lose, I was nearly electrocuted afterwards as some Hearts fans wrecked the stairwell lighting that collapsed right in front of me as I left. But Hearts recovered and Celtic were given a sound beating at Tynecastle, winning the match three-nil, with Ivanauskas (on the bench) proclaiming Hartley as one of Europe's best midfielders. We were keeping our nerve, but in order to avoid a last-day-of-the-season showdown with Rangers, we had to beat Aberdeen in our final home game. Tynecastle, our beloved and piercing residence, was finally awarded the setting for a momentous game.

It was a night laden with tension and Aberdeen were still in with a chance of making Europe themselves. Hearts never got going at all in the first half and I remember meeting my Uncle Ossie during the interval. We were both worried, and not without good reason. Hearts never played well when he was there (think of the number '7', and follow it with '0', and you catch my drift)! The second half kicked off, and Hearts started to get going, upping the pace and forcing The Dons back; looking for that priceless goal. "Come on the Hearts!" And as the match reached its fifty-third minute, our pressure paid off as gap-toothed Aberdeen defender, Zander Diamond punched the ball off the line. PENALTY! It took an age to come, but it was fitting that the magnificent Hartley took the kick and drilled the ball home to send Tynecastle and me into raptures. From my seat high up the Wheatfield Stand, I had the feeling that our stadium had never registered a noise like it. "Come on the Hearts!" The pressure was intense: but the goal we needed had now been scored. The Champions League dream was on, and all we had to do was see out the next forty minutes! Everyone in the stadium was fighting for the cause. Everyone had their part to play. It was Scottish Football at its best. I could barely sit down and all the nails on my fingers were gnawed to ribbons. A furious noise enveloped Tynecastle, and then I remembered...

It was May 3rd 2006. May 3rd? Now where did I know that date from? Exactly twenty years to the day, Albert Kidd's goals had destroyed my world and the world's of my friends and fellow Hearts supporters. Our substitute Lee Wallace hadn't even been born back then. And 1986 was long lost; lost to the distant past, slipping further away, never to be recovered. Yet I just couldn't forget about it, even in 2006. This night wasn't for the league championship, but it was for a crack at the Champions League. It was still a 'prize' worth winning and I was determined not to see Hearts blow it. As the game agonisingly inched into injury time, I stood from my seat and proceeded to clap and shout as loud as I could. It didn't matter what I looked like, because I soon became aware that not only were Les and Donald doing the same, but also Mozzer, Mark, Simon and Bob, just below me; and Bobby and Kevin way down in front of me and Tazio behind me. In fact as I looked around, the entire sixteen thousand-strong army of Hearts supporters were on their feet, creating a deafening and united roar, willing the team on to victory, and begging the referee to blow his whistle. We were there for the team, bound emotionally and unconditionally, doing it for them, just when they needed us most. It was one of the most powerful feelings I had ever felt, and then it became one of the greatest moments in the club's recent history, as the referee blew for full-time, and the roof just about came off Tynecastle!

Old friends embraced each other as Craig Gordon grabbed three of his colleagues to form an immediate bouncing, spinning huddle on the pitch. We stayed behind long after the final whistle, as Vladimir Romanov and the players took their bows. Then the celebrations kicked off in The Diggers, as 'The Ivanauskas Song' got a full-blooded airing. It was the great midweek Gorgie night, with laughter, singing and now dancing! And when the floodlights were switched off, it seemed that Tynecastle Stadium had hosted a historic and monumental occasion, and in return became the star of the show. I had a Billie Piper of a hangover at work the next day, but I cared not. The Old Firm had been split, and the season ended with Hearts travelling to Ibrox. I was gutted I couldn't get a ticket because our entire support went on the wind-up to pay back years of gloating from Rangers fans. As the game kicked off, the Blue legions were beside themselves, to see nearly every single happy Hearts fan – nonchalantly reading the Sunday papers, and with not a care in the world!

Chapter 52
Taking on Albert Kidd,
and it's going to penalties

Just as I had finally reached a stage in my career of white-collar respectability, I knew in my heart that I wasn't cut out for it. All the slogans, the appraisals, the huddles and the jargon-bingo left me disillusioned. I needed something real to me. My resolution took a huge weight off my shoulders. I remember walking in crunchy snow with Les, along the path that runs by the river, all the way to Leith. We had a deep and honest conversation about the future. Les had a great career. And now she was supporting me in my return to full-time education. Such a step felt frightening on one hand but very right on the other. The job I wanted to give up was safe and hardly anyone ever left. But I needed out, and I was determined to do it. All I had to do was sit tight at work until the next term started. All those years of being high on self-pity and low on self-esteem; my terrible job cleaning the sludge out of the car wash drain, sinking my van into a field; it no longer had to be my providence. And now, aged thirty-two, I didn't want to feel sorry for myself anymore. It was 2006, and wrongs needed putting right all over the place. And so I became a student, a mature student. Me: a student.

The week before the cup final, I threw a BBQ for some of my Hearts supporting friends. It was, according to Kevin, "the social event of the year, Baby", yet I could easily have been arrested the night before as I bought some accoutrements at Ikea. While there, I talked Les into buying a giant mirror and I convinced her that it would fit in the car. To be fair, the mirror did fit in the car, but only if it no longer required any humans to drive it. So instead of zipping round the bypass, we crawled the ten miles home with Les lying hostage underneath the mirror in the back and me driving with everything but my head inside the car! The police car I passed in third gear on Liberton Brae didn't seem to notice and somehow we made it back. At the party, there was a giant ice-bucket of alluringly cold beer and enough red meat on show to rewrite The Atkins Diet. I feel it's important to mention this party. Not for what it was but for when it was. It took place after the semi-final win and Champions League qualification: but it also happened before the cup final. Basically, we were all burning the candle big time, like some aging rock band that is forever on tour. And yet we didn't dare stop, because it's then that the hangover kicks in. The BBQ was a drunken link from the season's climax to its crescendo. It was a fantastic day, and there was just enough time for one last song…

As the cup final approached, I began to realise that if the date of May 3rd could be reclaimed and cleansed from twenty years of heartache, then by the same rule, something more tangible could also be repossessed from the pits of eternal suffering. The nightmare images of Dens Park 1986 were Albert Kidd gleefully scoring twice at the death to deny my beloved Heart of Midlothian the Championship, his goals leaving young Hearts players crying, with hands cusped over their streaked hair as tears stained shiny silver jerseys. Fans were lying crumpled and weeping on the pitch, many trying desperately to console each other. The silver jersey, such a powerful symbol from that day, and infamously paraded again the following Saturday in the cup final defeat; the epitome of glorious, yet shattering failure. Well now that I was on a career mission, I decided also that it was time to reclaim that silver jersey. I guess I wanted to at least try and associate it with some kind of success. By dredging up the past, maybe, just maybe, I could bury my ghost of 1986, once and for all. And so, like a phoenix from the flames, the silver jersey rose from the ashes of Dens Park; a man called 'Boof', who lives on Shetland, which is a thousand of miles north of Gorgie, sent me his silver top, after I made a plea on JambosKickback. Albert Kidd could get ready to kiss my ass. Of course, when I told Tazio that I'd be wearing the infamous jersey, he supportively responded by suggesting that,

"There's no fucking way you're sitting next to me wearing that". It seemed the curse had yet to wear off for some.

The day started off with a beer breakfast: three bottles of lager and a bacon roll for a fiver. I have to say I struggled, but it was only eight in the morning! Our friends, Will and Tom arrived with their dad. I'm always so amazed by that, just like when I see Mozzer and Bob. It seems like such a great thing, going to the cup final with yer old man. Nicer lads you couldn't wish to meet and Will's 'beat' lingo defies his air of Brideshead Revisited. All the guys: Gav, Cat, Cosa, Dougie, Keiran, Jonny, Big Ross, Borthers, Paul, Tazio, James, Andy, Pete, Scott, Simon, John, Gigalo and three lads called Kevin made being there worthwhile for me. But on that cup final trip, the bus was muted; perhaps a touch of nerves creeping in with this, the first cup final 'in colour' that Hearts had started as firm favourites. We reached our pre-match drinking destination at the Cardonald Bowling Club, allowing plenty of time to get those diaphragms loosened with the help of cold lager. But Kevin wasn't at all happy with the lads, and he demanded a better vocal performance en route to Hampden. By the time it came to leave, we were doing the 'The Ivanauskas Song' as old timers obliviously played on at bowls right beside us: a very avant-garde moment. Now we were ready for Hampden.

For this one, we sat in the West Stand. And what a sight it was, Hearts fans stretching majestically round three-quarters of The National Stadium. The atmosphere was cracking as the teams emerged onto the pitch and we got ourselves ready for cup glory. Our opponents were Gretna: the small team with the rich owner. Brooks Mileson, the loveable, chain-smoking, fish-supper scoffing, millionaire philanthropist, had taken his team from the northern English backwater leagues to the grand gala-day of Scottish football. But despite Gretna being a fine team of seasoned professionals, no one expected Hearts to slip up against the Second Division champions. Ironically, I had actually attended Gretna's First Round tie, as I watched Eadie's Preston Athletic take on The Black and Whites in 'The Pans'. Who'd have thought it but here they were again. I can't remember what my score prediction was for the final, but I doubt it was anything close to what I was about to witness. This was Hearts, remember?! The game kicked off at a fast pace and Hearts took an early grip on proceedings. To be fair to Gretna, they carved out a few chances of their own but six minutes before the break, just as things were becoming a little tense, Hearts scored through Rudi Skacel, and we celebrated as much in relief as we did in joy. Half-time arrived, and there were a few, long breaths and puffed-out cheeks, but the main thing here was that Hearts were on their way. However, the long dramatic season was beginning to take its toll on some. At 1-0, we were winning: but we weren't coasting, not by any means. In the seat immediately to my left, Les seemed a little anxious. In the seat immediately to my right, Kevin looked like he was about to explode; and as a former care worker, he knew all about apprehension, having once worked on the business end of a burst colostomy.

The second half got underway and it was becoming a fraught experience. At one point, Robbie Neilson had to pull off an absolutely miraculous last-ditch tackle to preserve our lead. This wasn't in the script. It wasn't supposed to be like this: being subjected to a now ominously torrid afternoon. Big Damien was trying to brighten things up, but Chewy had a face like thunder. And Gigalo's chain-smoking was a blatant flouting of the stadium rules! Les was adamant that I wouldn't be lighting up any ciggies. But for every time I leaned forward to exchange important and necessary opinion into Gig's ear, I somehow managed to come back with a lung-full of Benson and Hedges! Some of the lads became more and more animated as the game wore on, but it was Kevin who was causing me most concern;

not because I was particularly worried about his well-being or anything. It was just that I'd grown to be completely exasperated, having had to sit next to him as he spouted off all his woe!

"I'm telling you now, Andy they're going to fucking score and then we're totally fucked", he fizzed. And boil me an egg, he wasn't wrong. With just a quarter of an hour standing between Hearts and the cup, Gretna won a penalty, and scored it.

"Aw, fuck right off", protested Kevin. And as Hearts performance deteriorated further, so did Kevin's; as someone must have opened the stadium gates to let the Four Horsemen of the Apocalypse in to come galloping round the Hampden track. The following is a selection of the irascible griping that Kevin began to hiss into my ear:

"Shit."

"Fuck."

"Shit Fuck."

"We're fucking doomed now."

"I'll never live this down."

"That's us blown this big time."

"You'll never live this down."

"That's me finished with football, I'm going incommunicado."

"Imagine what those bastards are writing about us on Hibs.net."

"Your beers will be left out on the landing as I'm not coming out with you fucking losers."

"You're a bastard."

...and my personal favourite:

"It's all your fault for wearing that stupid fucking silver top."

Once again, Kevin was right. Borthers warned me, Tazio had forsaken me, and now Kevin was blaming me. As I sat there in my silver top, I felt the eyes of thirty-eight thousand Hearts fans cutting into me. What had made me pull a stunt like this? Just because we lost a cup final twenty years ago didn't mean to say I had to try and amend the past. What gave me the right to fix it? Why couldn't I just let it go, without the need for some conceited and futile gesture? I could sense Albert Kidd was close by, sniggering. As the ninety minutes ended in a draw, I decided to get head to the back of the stand to smoke a cigarette away from Les; but not after giving serious thought to ditching the jinxed silver top, and sitting out the rest of the final, wearing just a frown and my hairy chest.

Extra time began, and the game raged from end to end. Hearts had a surfeit of chances to kill the contest but at 1-1 we were also teetering close to a humiliating and unrecoverable disaster. Gretna just wouldn't cave in, and with our hearts in our mouths, they passed up a great chance to win it.

Les, Andy and Donald were still shouting encouragement on my left. Gav and Laura looked on worriedly in front of them. Tazio started to smoke along with Gig in front of me. Chewy looked irate. Paul was explaining to his little girl that things only get worse. Borthers and his guys were going through their own hell, and Eadie was staggering around the stadium drunk, broke and sporting a flat cap that belonged to some old codger from the bowling club. And then there was Kevin and me. He was ranting and raving, the contents of his bladder boiling. And me mortified and still; contemplating my inevitable mob lynching by hundreds of angry Hearts fans. I looked at Kevin momentarily and even his face and hair had changed. The match was tied and we lived on a knife-edge as my personal joust with the past was going tits-up. Skacel had the last chance from open play and should have sealed it, but the chance was lost as the game lurched towards deadlock. And then finally, Paul Hartley got himself sent off. Great: our expert penalty taker now banned from taking penalties. And penalties it was. With my silver top choking my neck, I sat in suppressed silence, completely withdrawn; my face, the same colour as my jersey. Les gave me a look of distress. Not only was she worried about me, but I think she'd been overhearing the Merchant of Tragedy on my right side for the past hour.

And yet it was again that at my lowest ebb, I found my salvation, just like I had done with the angelic voice at Celtic Park in 1998. I realised that if I was ever going to beat Albert Kidd, I was going to have to stop cowering and look him square in the eye. I had to show some fight and belief. So I stood up from my seat and joined my fellow supporters in a defiant and rousing version of 'The Hearts Song', which reverberated around Hampden. All throughout, Les had remained calm and hopeful on my left, with Kevin incensed and pessimistic, on my right. I was tired of being stuck in the middle, disengaged and without hope. Well if those stubborn little bastards from Gretna were going to ruin my day, then they were going to have to beat thirty-eight thousand Hearts fans as well as the team. "COME ON THE HEARTS!!" Come on the Hearts. And from that moment on, the Hearts fans seemed to accept their predicament, and redefined their expectations from 'comfortable win' onto 'WTF?' and now to 'let's just finish the bloody job and get home'. We did our job. It was now down to the players to do theirs.

From the Kill Bill soundtrack, the searing guitar of 'Battle without Honour or Humanity' confronted both team managers as they walked towards their players. But as one looked like a menacing mob-boss in a cool suit: the other looked like a Scottish guy heading for the buffet at a wedding. It proved to me that it was Hearts that meant business now. I grabbed Kevin and told him square on that we were going to do it, and that he wouldn't be going incommunicado; and that my beers won't be lying outside his front fucking door. This was the time for big men with big hearts. He got it, and I knew it.

"COME ON THE HEARTS!" Come on the Hearts, please.

Up stepped Steven Pressley. BANG, one nil but Grady crashed his penalty in to make it 1-1. And then we drew a collective gasp of disbelief. Kevin and I looked at each other in slow motion horror as the unlikely figure of Robbie Neilson made his way to take the next Hearts penalty. No one around me felt confident. But Neilson was way cooler than any of us and he slotted home his spot-kick to put Hearts 2-1 up. However, Mark Birch stepped forward, and made it level again. But I was steeled. There was no looking away now. I could feel Albert Kidd but I wanted this. At that moment, Hampden Park was my entire world. This game, was my life. And as Rudi Skacel made it three, I began to taste victory. Then the next player to walk forward was the lanky former Hibs player, Derek Townsley; and suddenly, the Hearts fans smelt blood. We created a furore, but much more so than with the other Gretna players, which seemed to leave Townsley shaking at the knees. I steadied myself as the Gretna man took only a few steps in his run-up. He hit the ball to his right, and Craig Gorgon saved it!

"YYYYYYYEEEEEEEEEEEEEEAAAAAAAASSSSSSSSSSSSSSSS!!!!"

Now we were close as silver-slate faces began to beam maroon. And for the first time, I felt that I was beating Albert Kidd in our tussle. Anxious and indolent men were now beating their chests and slapping the hands of their neighbours. Pospisil coolly walked up and drove his shot home to make it 4-2. I grabbed a hold of Kevin with my right arm and Les with my left. I was snarling now. "COME ON THE HEARTS!!!!!" Come on the Hearts. It could now be won on the next kick. Gavin Skelton was the next player to take. Unlike Townsley, Skelton's run-up was long, and I took in as big a breath as I possibly could.

"Miss it ya bastard", came the voice. This was the moment, and as Skelton smashed his penalty kick homewards, the ball clipped the top of the bar and mercy me, Hearts had won the cup.

Bedlam! At last the stands erupted into a massive roar, and I was jumping up and down, still holding on to Les and to Kevin, and still wearing my silver jersey! We screamed and we swayed, and we grabbed whoever was around us; Gigalo, Taz, Borthers; and still we bounced around the shallow steps of Hampden. Les hugged Donald and Andy. Paul threw his girl up into the air; Gavin and Borthers cried like Halle Berry and Gwyneth

Paltrow collecting Oscars; Tazio and Gig's ciggies were lost in the scrum; and Chewy still looked mightily unimpressed with the entire situation! And then as the roars of jubilation subsided maybe just a little, an incredible sound, like a massive, rumbling wave of relief overcame the stadium as each fan took stock of what they had just gone through. And it was just at that moment that I turned to Kevin. And I didn't have to say a fucking word. He knew exactly what I was thinking, and I knew exactly how he was feeling. But as we stood there, looking each other in the eye, we both burst out laughing as he picked me up and squeezed the last bit of air from my lungs. Kevin had put me through almighty living hell, and with tears in both our eyes, we did that sort of laugh/cry man thing as he said his many sorrys. But he needn't have. I didn't know it at the time, but Albert Kidd wasn't some old memory, lingering from my past. Albert Kidd had been sitting right next to me for the entire match; possessing poor Kevin's body as things went from bad to worse. He tried to kick my ass, drag me outside and set me on fire. But my silver jersey prevailed in the end and every Hearts fan won through; each with our own very personal demons to fight and defeat that day. It was a colossal battle, as much over ourselves as it was against Gretna; and it needed big hearts and strong minds to win through: because with my team, the drama always comes right at the end.

Every Jambo stood and sportingly applauded the outstanding efforts of Gretna, who afforded themselves a much deserved lap of honour. It was quite moving and most unusual. The little team may have lost out to the big boys in the end, but I guess it was a great sporting occasion, and watched the world over. Football though, is about winning, and although Gretna gave us one hell of a match, it was still a deserved victory for Hearts. We deserved it, because we won it. Yes, we played poorly, and yes we were lucky at times: but we still earned it because it was us, and not them, who finished the job when it mattered. And besides, I'd had enough of hard luck stories. This wasn't a victory like 1998, when we heroically out-wrestled the bigger team. This was a victory warranted by means of torture and calamity. We earned it, because we had to go through living hell to get it. We cheered as the cup was lifted, and we sang as loudly as our voices could carry as the team paraded the trophy around the stadium. The sun shined bright again, as it tends to do whenever things actually go right for The Jam Tarts. The silver strip was no longer a bad memory from 1986. But boy, it didn't half put me through the mill again in 2006, and had I not persevered enough to allow it to witness Heart of Midlothian winning the Scottish Cup at Hampden, it still would've been a most unpleasant spectre from my haunted youth. However, on May 13th 2006, I finally made my peace with the silver jersey, and with it, the past. And as I'd now seen my team win two Scottish Cups, and both at a good age, I felt relieved that Kevin had returned to repossess his own body, and that the ghost of Albert Kidd was gone; laid to rest forever.

Chapter 53
The mother of all

The race was on to be standing in Gorgie by the time Hearts' official coach got there. The slab of lager that Kevin had threatened to leave on his stairwell landing was now cradled in my arms, as we hurtled down Ardmillan towards McLeod Street. We pitched up just across from the Tynecastle Arms as it was the optimum place for us to congregate, get the beers out and start the party. Though slightly cooler than 1998, the weather was kind to us, warm enough for the streets to be teeming with celebrating, singing Hearts fans. The laboured performance at Hampden didn't count for anything here as there was only one truth: Hearts were bringing the cup home. It had taken forty miles, eight years and more than one major crisis to get back here. A massive rendition of 'The Ivanauskas Song' had passers-by amused and some joined in, like the 'Twist It' scene from The Blues Brothers. 'The Hearts Song' was belted out, and often with the wrong words by fans, neighbours, grannies and granddads; the whole Hearts community was out. It was our night.

A distant cheer could be heard from the direction of White Park. The furore spread, sparking a frenzy as everyone jostled for the best place for viewing. The victorious team coach was here, and once more, cup-winning heroes basked in the adulation of thousands of loyal fans, who stood to honour them. And like the legends of 1998, the players took to the roof of their transport as it slowly paraded between the narrow, grey tenements of Gorgie. I stood back a little, and watched as the crowd went wild. I was already in a great place. The goodwill gushing towards the team was incredible. The sun was setting, but the party was now in full swing, and fifty yards along the road at Robertson's Bar, a huge crowd congregated to begin a boisterous, spontaneous gathering. No one had planned it. No one was in charge. It was just a focal point, where thousands of carry-out carrying fans pitched-up and joined in the fun. The singing and revelry went on for a good couple of hours, but eventually, the police began to move us all on, so we headed up to The Diggers, but it was completely rammed, so we only stayed long enough to watch the highlights on Sportscene. As we couldn't get any space and seeing as I had a carry-out with me, I just cracked open a can in the pub. Borthers though, was a man with a plan; forever willing to host a group of drunken mates round at his for a piss up: so around thirty of us headed there to kick off another party. The night just got better and better. But some time much later on, and despite sitting upright with a can of lager in his hand, Kevin's eyes began to close, as I thought about heading home too. The Hearts were having a party, but by 4am, this fan needed his bed.

My silver Hearts away top was showing its age. When I awoke the next morning, it looked exactly how I felt: old, crumpled and stinking of booze! I might have been rougher than Jade Goody's mum but I knew that I had to pull myself together for another tough session of celebrations (it was hard work being a Hearts fan in those days). My friends gathered by the Gorgie Farm wall and I brought another carry-out of eight beers, two bottles of bubbly and a can of cider left over from the days when Strongbow was the club's main sponsor. I managed to get rid of the cider to someone needing a drink so there was no real loss to my stash. We exchanged stories from the night before which included my own three mile walk home witnessing a four man punch-up on Slateford Road and a five pie purchase from Malone's. The open top bus attracted a crowd of around a hundred thousand people and a near to full stadium awaited the winning team. Like everyone else, I was just another face in the crowd, savouring the brief passing moment. Vladimir Romanov was leading the celebrations, with the world in his hands. As happened in 1998, Hearts took over the whole of the city, and tourists looked on in awe. If it was up to me, Edinburgh city centre would be painted maroon, and Skip Wykowski from 'New Joy-sey' would be in no doubt as to who the big, local 'saccer' team were. The bus approached then passed me by, and I cheered as loudly as I could for those precious few seconds. 1985/86 had been exorcised; 1997/98 had been equalled; and now this, the third great adventure on my Hearts' supporting 'career' had come to pass. The season was over.

We broke up the day by heading to The Ettrick Hotel beer garden and I even managed a spot of lunch before we all headed back to reclaim The Diggers. There, we sang and we hugged and we danced and we drank beer, with similar scenes happening all over Edinburgh and beyond. The atmosphere was electric, even though we were now running on fumes; but there was always time for one more version of the classic 'Ivanauskas Song'. Something inside me knew that this was a day I had to treasure, and I squeezed as much from it as I could. It was amazing seeing everyone there; such a happy, ageless time and I could have stayed out all night as the love and goodwill I had for my fellow Jambos knew no bounds! But at 11pm, Kevin, who was heading off to Australia for a month, said his goodbyes. And when he left, I felt gutted. For all we'd been through, I felt as if I'd lost an arm. Eadie too was soon to leave for Australia, but for a year. It was a long time not to see friends I cherished. Outside, the weather that had been respectful to us all weekend, finally relented, and the heavens opened. It was time to go home, and I finished my pint. Besides, if I didn't leave soon, then the silver top I was still wearing would've jumped on the number one bus by itself!

The next morning, I was as ill as a rancid badger. The rain hadn't stopped, yet I had to wear sunglasses just to make it to the shop and back. For the second day running, I bought a pile of newspapers to keep as mementos, as football fans do. I looked at some of the pictures, like the one of the players strung across the half-way line, leaping in celebrating upon their first split-second as cup winners. But I couldn't really bring myself to read anything. Nor could I watch the cam-footage that I'd shot over the weekend. In truth, I was exhausted, and on something of a come-down. In those last few weeks, I had seen off one long party after another. But then I suppose I'd been going on like that for years. Just hours earlier, I was with my friends, bouncing around, celebrating and guzzling lager. Now I was looking down the straw of a raspberry and banana fruit smoothie. I was a bit emotional about it: not the smoothie, which was quite nice, but about my mates. Twelve hours after I had said my bear-hugging goodbyes, I was missing them all so much; and I then remembered my old friend Allan, and how he would've loved the festivities of 2006.

The summer was spent watching the World Cup, seeing out my job and waiting for my course to start. JambosKickback had given me the bug to write and people like Bobby and Kevin were urging me to do more with my hobby. So on a hot day in late June, I got home from work and grabbed a cold, icy beer out of the fridge, before opening up a new Word document on the PC. I sat there for a while, just staring at the blank screen and flashing cursor, wondering whether or not to start typing. Then I heard the front door open. Les was home from work just a bit sharper than usual. Minutes later, I discovered that I was soon to become a father for the first time. Les and I were so excited, and I was proud of her. The inspiration I was looking for had arrived, and right on cue I remembered the words of Joni Mitchell, when she sang so beautifully, "I really don't know life at all".

Chapter 54
All these things
that I've done

The future of Hearts lies with Vladimir Romanov. Many Hearts fans see him as a malevolent autocrat, who plans to destroy our treasured football club. I'm a little unsure now about his motives, yet sometimes I'm excited by his ambitions. I would question many of his decisions and his conduct but not his overall aspirations. Though I accept there is a huge risk, I think the world (Tynecastle) is (for now) a more interesting place with him around. We'll see. I just wish he'd communicate a bit more, and maybe play a more sensible game. I don't mind the current structure as such. I only care about the results it yields. That is, if the results are good, then great. If not, then sort it out Vlad! It's just a pity the football has been pretty dire since I started writing this. The season 2006/07 saw major controversy, like the removal of Steven Pressley and the temporary appointment of Edward Malofeev (help ma boab!). There was all of that, plus Vlad making bizarre rants through the club website and the fact that we were shit. I feel I've now gone full circle back to 1982. Yet the plans for Tynecastle are phenomenal (despite those bloody Lib-Dems) and the club seems to be building for the future, with the arrival of some highly sought youngsters. I'm not bothered about players anymore. I was lucky to have heroes as a kid, like John Robertson, Gary Mackay and Henry Smith. Nowadays, players come and go so fast and at the time of writing, I'd be delighted to just know some of their names. From my lofty position in the Wheatfield Stand, I just see ten maroon jerseys and a goalkeeper. Whoever fills those jerseys is of no interest to me anymore. They have my unflinching support: but not my love. If I was a kid now, Larry Kingston would be my hero. But how long will he be at Tynecastle for? Not long at all I bet. It's a shame, but hey, that's life Mama.

It's difficult to write about the present, when it could all go wrong again tomorrow and I've already put a jinx on the wretched early days of 2007/08. But the common theme for every Hearts crisis is that we always get through it. And besides: today's Miko-hating newspapers line tomorrow's fish and chips (or they did until it was banned). No matter what happens with Heart of Midlothian in the future, there will always be a

Heart of Midlothian. And there will always be room in my heart to support them. As I wrote earlier in the book: football to me is about laughter, and friends, and celebrating goals; singing and drinking lager. If I can still enjoy that, then I'll be there. I just grab what I can these days.

When I started writing this book, seeing images of the 2006 World Cup, with thousands of hysterical young South Koreans wearing identical replica strips, or glamorous Swedish ladies waving to TV cameras, I thought of Morrissey when he sang "it says nothing to me about my life". Gorgie is grey and cold: but not always. It's my world, and a footballing setting revered by thousands. The smoking ban means that the Robertson Bar now has a touch of The Riviera, as Big Bernie sips a mocha latte alfresco. In Gorgie, people hang in and out of the pubs that are true to them. Each has its own character, and all are choc full every other Saturday. I still love the whole match day experience. I try to get my inside info from Dexter, and I definitely get heart-on-sleeve opinion from Razamabaz and Nelly T. Big Ross Brown will mercilessly rip me to pieces in the pub, and I will berate the metro-sexual clothing that his wife bought for him at one of those 'taller man' shops. Gigalo and Kevin will invariably be there before their date with Lidl; Simon will have us all in stitches and the witty Borthers will turn up looking like a slightly hungover Willie Pettigrew. I love all the guys at the footy and I hope that never changes. If Romanov leads us to glory then I'll be there. If he leads us to ruin, then we'll just have to start again, back at The Meadows: and I'll be there too. The future is ours, but only if we want it. There are ambitions for Hearts, and the potential we have is frightening. All we need is a bit of communication, common sense and a decent football manager: not some fucking stooge. If he builds it, they will come. But build a winning team to go with it.

My father's health isn't great, and I don't see him much these days. I feel regretful that the past robbed me of a close relationship with him, but ultimately, I fully appreciate the old politics and I wish him health and contentment. I still see my mum fairly often, and my brother Bobby, his wife Denise and young Rebecca. Bobby is no longer the big brother from hell. He's now just a big brother, although I imagine he'll want to beat me up again after reading this book. But hey, I'm sorry and I'm not perfect. Not by a long shot. But I'm much better than I was and I'm looking forward to the future. My heart still races a bit too fast with a hangover and my PDC style of driving has never left me. When I look at the Scottish Parliament, rather than appreciating great architecture, I am reminded of the arse end of the Wester Hailes Shopping Centre; where I used to go to pay my mum's rent. The other day, I accidentally gave myself a haircut like Frank Ribery, and I'm still a little bit superstitious (well, I can't have the

TV volume at thirteen). If someone puts a neatly folded charity bag through my letter box, I use it for rubbish. When I took my little brother Ian to see Turner and Hooch at the cinema in 1989, he cried so much at the end I told him that the dog went 'on holiday'. It was a lie, and to this day, I think he still believes it. I should call him more often. Thinking of cinema, I'm sorry to Les for taking her to see Pearl Harbour, only for me to declare halfway through that I was "just going to get a drink". I think she thought I was going to get a Coke or something. Oh, and when I took the car into the garage after inexplicably pouring screenwash down the power-steering funnel, I told the mechanic, "it was the wife that did it" whilst shaking my head (though I always suspected he thought it was me anyway). When I get a cold, monks from the local abbey ring their bells to let everyone else know. And I'm still gullible: not least when three members of staff at HMV coaxed me into singing 'I Miss You' by Blink 182, after I couldn't remember the name of the band. Nobody is perfect. And I apologise now, for all the mistakes I have made in my life.

There are all these things that I still haven't done. I've never once swam under water, jumped or dived into a swimming pool; or bungee jumped, or had a tattoo, or ridden on a motorbike, or caught a fish, or even fished; or played rugby, or a round of golf, or squash. I've never been to Ireland or St Andrews or even Edinburgh Castle! I've never seen The Godfather or The Matrix, as I prefer films starring Hugh Grant as a bumbling Englishman. I'm still terrified of dental treatment, flying, heights and wasps; and I wish I could've learned to play music or get past the audition stage for a band. But all those things can happen tomorrow. Now I'm optimistic and happy (well come on, was I ever not?!). I like to remember the good times too, like the time when I asked Les out. I was with Allan and Sean in the pub that night. Both of those guys are now gone. But we had good times. Here's to the good times.

March 2007

I've not lived an astonishing life or a famous one, but this is the only one I've ever known. I'll continue to shop at Tesco, reluctantly cut my grass and pray the wheelie-bin doesn't end up somewhere over a rainbow during the next storm. My experiences have not always been amiable or appealing, but everything that I've gone through has been of benefit, should it have found its way into this book. I've just sat and watched Burt Landers keep up his unwavering fight in Get Over It, and I'll keep showing that fighting spirit. What has passed is prologue, and I'm now into my studying, as well as my writing. I've taken to both quite well. Once I get my degree, I'm thinking of using it to give a bit of help to those who might be going through the sort of trials that I once battled myself. Whether or not my plans pan out, I'll keep listening to what my heart tells me, and I'm under orders to keep writing. As ever, the job front continues to be the slowest mover of the 'Three Point Plan'. But there is a plan.

After two days of early labour, my daughter Jude-Lauren Bowie was born, weighing in at a whopping ten pounds three ounces. Words cannot describe the love that I have for my gorgeous little girl. I'm now a big, blubbering emotional wreck and I've already thought about my 'Father of the Bride' speech. My life has just turned upside down and I love it. Lesley did so well, despite the fact that we were left for hours in a waiting room and that little Jude was breached! But the good thing about such a swift C-section delivery is that I got to dress up as a surgeon and at one point, the anaesthetist actually fainted (maybe it was the sight of me in tight pants?). My baby girl is just beautiful, and I hope she likes the name that I've given her. I look at her in awe, and wonder what she'll be like; what adventures and mishaps she'll have, and what decisions and career paths she'll choose. But as Lennon said, "I guess we'll both just have to be patient". Whatever happens to Jude in the coming years, she'll have her mother and me to provide love and support, entertainment and advice. And when she is old enough, she can read the meandering reminiscences of her old man, and make up her own mind on just what sort of a person I am. As I look at Jude-Lauren, I just see a little, female reincarnation of me. And as I study the miracle of her hands and her feet, I am struck by the realisation that she's a real success already. Because in only nine months, she's achieved what it took me thirty-three years to attain: a clean slate.

Whatever path my girl chooses to walk, I will always love her unconditionally and totally. Les and I look forward to raising her, and she can do whatever she wants as an adult. But as a baby, now that I've found her I won't let her go. "Hey Jude, welcome to the world", wrote Dave McLaren on JambosKickback. Just don't grow up too soon. I can't wait to sing her songs from The White Album (though how I'll negotiate 'Revolution 9' is anyone's guess). And if the 2014 Commonwealth Games require kids from Edinburgh for the Opening Ceremony, I'll be teaching her how to avoid first round, first verse audition humiliation. I'm not sure if I'll ever be one of those 'Gillette' advert men, where they 'high-five' an office promotion as Chad goes fishing with Dad, but I'll do my best, Jude. Hopefully we'll have a house in the country, and another kid and two dogs: Fido and Rover. No one calls their dogs Fido and Rover anymore. I'm going to bring it back. Oh, and my garden will have a pitch 'n' putt course and a trampoline. In this dream house, sitting proudly above the fireplace, is a coffee mug that reads "Best Dad in the World". Now if I can have just that, then my life is complete. I'm not even that bothered about the trampoline.

November 2007

It's been nearly one and a half years since I started writing this book, and one and a half years since I found out about my new role as a father. In that time, as I've looked forward to my new life, I've been pondering and writing about the old one. To make sense of it all, I've taken one last drive around my old neighbourhood. 'Grazed Knees', by Snow Patrol plays on the iPod. It seems such a fitting song for the mood I'm in and I know The Killers will be up next. Saughton Mains Bank today, is all but changed from the place where I grew up. When I imagine it, I still see things as they were, back in the day when the long-haired scruffy kid kicked a ball about. His flesh and blood and grazed knees are pure-Saughton Mains housing scheme, but his heart belonged to an old football club just a little east of where he played. Now the red bricks of Carrick Vale have been replaced by housing, and the streets have been carved up to kerb traffic. In Saughton Mains Bank, the church grounds and their trees have been completely wiped out, as have the row of lock-up garages. And worst of all, the entire field where I played football with Bobby, Allan and our buddies has vanished. It too, has made way for new housing. Now the 'upgrading' of the area leaves me with little inherent value and almost nothing to show Jude-Lauren in years to come. 'You can have it all' is playing. I don't really like The Kaiser Chiefs all that much, but this song is damn good.

All that is left are the memories for all the things that I've done. And those recollections are slipping further and further away into the distant past. But no matter what tramples on top of the Saughton Mains Bank footprint, my old house and the place where I grew up, it will forever be just two miles from Tynecastle; and therefore just two miles to it; two miles to my beloved Hearts. I can still picture Bobby and me, crouching for a photo in terrible yellow tracksuits. Hurry up and take me to the game, Bobby! From a bird's eye view, we scurry like ants. Every Hearts fan has their own route that gets them to the game in time for kick-off. My own started here once, and that's what makes this place so special. I would close my eyes, and even though I've been gone for years, I'd still dream that I lived in Saughton Mains Bank. It took me a long time to let it go. But I had to: because if I didn't move on, then my memories would have haunted me and hindered me forever. It took a huge band of pursuing Romani travellers to tell me just that. And now, when I think back to that dream, as the last of them departed, taking with them their horses, their wagons and their carts; I too decide that now is the time for me to leave Saughton Mains Bank behind. I open my eyes, and see that the road leading out…is clear.